Escape from Pretoria

First published by Jacana Media in 2003
This new edition published in 2020

10 Orange Street
Sunnyside
Auckland Park 2092
South Africa
+2711 628 3200
www.jacana.co.za

This story was first published in 1987 by IDAF Kliptown

ISBN 978-1-4314-2986-8

Front cover photo courtesy of Momentum Pictures, LLC.
Editing by Nkhensani Manabe
Proofreading by Lara Jacob
Cover design by Trevor Paul
Layout by Aimèe Armstrong
Set in Sabon LT Std 10.5/14pt
Printed and bound by Tandym Print
Job no. 003681

Escape from Pretoria

Tim Jenkin

Contents

Preface

We stood staring at the final obstacle between us and freedom. How was it that this miserable little door would not yield to our persuasions? With minimal effort we had opened 14 other doors to get to it, most of them giant steel doors and grilles, yet this last one, an ordinary wooden door with an ordinary house lock, had decided to put a halt to 18 months of planning and preparation. We would have none of it. If our gentler persuasions would not open it, there was only one option – force!

Like a surgeon requesting a scalpel, Alex asked for the chisel. He was going to dig out the wood from behind the locking plate on the door frame and then when he'd removed enough, he would be able to bend it back so that the bolt could clear it when he pulled the door open. I was thinking that maybe we should make our way back to our cells and try again another day. If we did not get the door open before the sentry came on duty in the street outside, it would be the end of the road for us. We would not be able to make another attempt, as the damaged doorpost would be evidence that there had been an escape attempt and they would strengthen the prison's existing security to make it impossible to get out. But the others insisted there was only one direction we were going, and that was out!

I flinched as Alex dug the point of the chisel into the well-varnished wooden frame and a giant chip of wood fell onto the doormat. Now the prison authorities would know which way we had got out and our dream of having pulled off the perfect escape was no more. We had hoped to leave our captors completely baffled as to how three long-term, political prisoners had spirited themselves out of their cells and out of one of South Africa's reputedly most secure prisons.

Alex carried on chiselling furiously as we watched in terror. We knew that a sentry normally came on duty outside at six, and it was now approaching that time. It was more than an hour since lock-up at four thirty. The pile of wood chips on the floor looked greater than the hole out of which they came but the locking plate could still not be bent back far enough to allow the protruding bolt to pass it. Several times Alex tried to force it back with the large screwdriver we had brought along from the workshop but each time it just slipped and made a frightening noise. Each time it happened we were sure the night-warder, who was sitting less than 20 metres away and the guard on the catwalk just 5 metres above, had heard it. But nothing happened.

We prepared ourselves for departure. We pulled off our gloves and face masks and put on our running shoes: once outside we would have to get off the prison terrain, out of Pretoria and out of the country as quickly as possible. We knew they would treat us as dangerous, hunted fugitives and that there would be a nationwide search; we knew that if we got caught our already long sentences would be infinitely extended.

Eventually, Alex had removed sufficient wood to allow him to bend the locking plate back far enough. He grasped the door handle and gave it a sharp yank. With a loud grating sound, the bolt scraped past the plate and the door swung open. The sweet air of freedom wafted in.

Alex cautiously looked up towards the end of the catwalk above the door to see if the guard was in view. There was nobody – the guard had conveniently taken a walk down to the far end. Alex boldly stepped outside and signalled to us to follow him. I was the next out and then Stephen, who pulled the door closed behind him. It did not close properly on account of the still protruding bolt, but it didn't matter at that moment – we were out.

After making sure the coast was clear, we walked down the few steps leading from the door out of which we had just emerged and stepped into the warm summer sun in the street. We were free. We saw our hours, days, months, years of boredom, frustration and isolation behind us. And ahead, freedom...

Part One
Getting In

Chapter One

Recruitment

The question is frequently asked: how could white South Africans during the apartheid years abandon all the privileges that were theirs for the taking and choose instead to side with the oppressed?

For many, it seems an impossibility. Under apartheid, South Africa for white people was the land of milk and honey where they could expect a standard of living probably unmatched by any other country in the world. A beautiful country with such wealth that it literally oozes out of the ground and such an abundance of cheap labour that virtually every white family could afford a servant. It was a life of luxury, pleasure, holidays, travel, sunshine and sport.

At that time good jobs, good salaries, little prospect of unemployment, good homes, good education – you name it – were taken for granted. Why would anyone reject all this and choose instead a life of persecution: ostracism, banning, detention, prison and exile? Questioning the system of society under which they lived and rebelling against it were not natural responses for white South Africans. They were responses that had to be learned: from others, from unique personal experiences or from books. For most whites, breaking free of the web of privilege and racism and finding the route towards enlightenment was not easy. The apartheid system, through the rewards it bestowed on those who accepted it and through its insidious propaganda, did not breed many white dissidents. Despite all the forces ranged against them, some white South Africans did manage to break free and find their way into the camp of those who believed in a non-racial, democratic South Africa.

Some were fortunate to have had enlightened parents and so never became deeply ensnared in the barbs of racism. They broke free easily. Others may have met someone who had a deep influence on their lives or had personal experiences that helped them to break free. Most whites who did manage to see the light, however, reached that position via the intellectual route. It could not really be any other way, for whites were not usually at the receiving end of apartheid and hardly ever learned what it meant in any practical sense. For all who did find the way, however, the route was uphill and slippery all the way.

I was born and bred in South Africa and grew up a "normal", complacent, white South African. I unthinkingly accepted the system and for twenty-one years never questioned it. Why should I have done so? I knew nothing else and no one ever told me anything else. I never had any black friends, never spoke to any black person outside the master–servant relationship, never visited a black township or entered the home of a black person, and never worked with any black people. South Africans were white people – Europeans. Blacks just existed in the background – there to do the work and then disappear when we needed them no more.

I absorbed the normal white prejudices against blacks and bore a "healthy" hatred of them. The world view I imbibed put everything in its place: blacks could not rule as they had no understanding of democracy; they would just fight among themselves if granted power. They had to be kept separated from us as they had a different standard of living, a different – inferior – culture and a different set of moral values. Blacks were essentially lazy, dirty and uncivilised. All they wanted to do was steal the things we had acquired through hard work. We lived here; they lived there in their dirty slums. We had our buses and train compartments, our beaches, our restaurants, our cinemas, and they had theirs. It was all quite fair, all quite just. How else could things be ordered?

Occasionally the blacks would riot and some of them would get shot in the places where they lived. They would burn down the schools and bars that we whites had provided for them out of our taxes. How could they be so ungrateful for what we had given them? But what could you expect from people who were inherently violent and drunk most of the time?

They would never be allowed to come and make trouble in our areas so it was okay if they got themselves shot or killed in the areas where they lived. We whites would show them that we didn't really need them. They could go on strike or go away for good. We would manage. They needed us more than we needed them so they would be the ones to suffer the most.

I matriculated at the age of 17, leaving school totally ignorant of the world in which I lived. Not a single political thought had ever arisen in my head. Later, when my political understanding improved, I marvelled at the advanced level of political understanding of young black scholars, even at the primary school level. But then black people grew up in a totally different environment under apartheid. Their lives were a battle to survive, a battle against the system from the day they were born. The politics of struggle was infused into their veins at an early age. Whites, on the other hand, learned only the politics of preservation. The world was theirs and no one was going to take it from them.

I was fortunate – some would say unfortunate – in not having to go to the army after leaving school. At that time, not every white male was conscripted as there was a ballot system, and I was one of the lucky few not to be selected. If I had gone, my life would perhaps have followed an entirely different course. The army tended to amplify the worst racist tendencies inherent in white South Africans and turned most of those who experienced it into bigoted black-haters and ardent defenders of the white faith.

Instead, I went out to work and within two years had been through a number of jobs. I wasn't much interested in working, nor was I interested in studying. I didn't quite know what I wanted to do. All I was really interested in were my motorcycles and motorcycle racing. Jobs were easy to come by and the pay was good. Work a while, save a bit and then muck about for a few months – all quite normal, all part of growing up.

Wealthy parents kept me and my crazy hobby going. After three years I had reached the top of the league in the local bike-racing scene and wanted to go further. Lack of money prevented me doing so, and the only way I could see of making money in the quantities I needed was to set up my own business. I had some experience in glass-fibre work and to gain more experience in this field I decided to go overseas – which meant to Britain for white, English-speaking South Africans. I was also keen to acquire experience in the far more competitive and sophisticated British bike-racing scene.

In April 1970 I took a boat to Britain. At first, I was a model emissary for white South Africa. I tolerated no criticism of my country and defended it with naïve pride. South Africa was "not half as bad as shown in all those outrageous propaganda films on telly", I often responded. I could not understand why people said such harsh things about my country. Nobody at home complained, and they were there. Why should these people who had never been to South Africa be so critical? Why couldn't they wash their own dirty dishes first?

I soon learned that I was totally ignorant of the reality of my own country and that most people in Britain knew more about it than I did. They asked questions and made assertions I could not answer – they told me what was going on in my own country. From ten thousand kilometres away, I had within the space of a few months learned more about South Africa than I had in all the time I had lived there.

After spending a few weeks with relatives in London, I managed to get a job in a glass-fibre factory in Kent. The job that was offered to me was on the shop floor and at first I was a bit reluctant to accept it, as I had always considered factory work to be below my dignity. In South Africa, only blacks worked in factories. But I accepted the job because I wanted to gain experience with glass-fibre mouldings and there was no better way than to actually do the dirty work.

I could not believe the conditions under which we were required to work. The itching glass-fibre dust in that factory hung like a mist from the ceiling, and the air was infused with the pungent smell of polyester resin. The management had filtered air conditioners in their offices while the people who did the actual work had to breathe in the toxic vapours and that vicious dust. The resin stuck to your clothes like blobs of oil paint to a canvas, your hands got lacerated on hardened spikes of glass fibre, and dried and wrinkled from washing them in acetone.

The management periodically ventured out of their comfortable offices with white coats and clipboards to inspect your work. They poked their fingers into your layups looking for bubbles, and berated you for wasting so much resin. Why couldn't they do the work if they were so good? At the end of the week I'd take home £13, or £20 if I'd worked overtime, yet what I'd produced in that time could be sold for hundreds of pounds. It was obvious that the lazy sods who sat in their dust-free offices and drank coffee all day were creaming off the profits we, the workers, had made. They all had smart new Jaguars and we had to catch buses.

The unjustness of this set-up, as well as the sheer nastiness of factory work, forced me for the first time in my life to sit up and consider the manner in which the world worked. How was it that the workers who created such wealth got paid so little? How was it that the management cared so little about the conditions under which the workers had to work?

In an attempt to find answers to these sorts of questions and others, I began to read books. I didn't know where to start but began by reading books about self-improvement and human relationships. This led to an interest in sociology and psychology and ultimately politics. Before this I didn't even know what sociology was or the distinction between it and other social studies. Nor did I know the names of any famous sociological or political theorists.

I began to devour books by the ton and inevitably read some that I knew would not be allowed in South Africa. The fact that these were banned at home lent them a certain fascination. After a while I made a point of seeking out these books, not because I agreed more with the viewpoints expressed in them but because I felt that I had to broaden my horizons as much as possible while I had the opportunity. From them, however – especially the ones about South Africa – I learned that there was another way of looking at my country, and that the policies of its government were not altogether defensible.

My sudden awakening to the world led to a slight but short-lived religious revival. As I became aware of the complexities of the world and of the terrible things going on in it, I wanted to find immediate solutions to them. Not understanding the forces behind the events and appearances of things, and not knowing what I could do to change them, praying to God seemed to be a good way. While recognising that religion motivated some of the most progressive opponents of apartheid and is often the starting point for many people in the development of a social consciousness, for me it served only as a barrier to further development.

At first the turn to religion, combined with my growing awareness, made me feel fresh, – "born again" so to speak. In my reading, I had learned that "communists" were opposed to religion and I, therefore, became intensely anti-communist, in the most subjective sense. This was nothing more than the coming to the surface of the indoctrination to which I had been subjected all my life. As I understood it, communists were the devil incarnate. Their sole purpose of existence was to make trouble and take away our freedoms. Communists were always associated with evil and war; Christians with goodness and peace. I did not understand that our rulers used the word "communist" to label everyone they did not like – those who did not agree with their racist policies. By calling themselves Christians, they made us believe that they were acting in the name of God and that their motives were honest and sincere. Consequently, I found myself in the curious position of wanting to see change but of harbouring negative views of all those who advocated it.

At the end of 1970, still in Britain, I decided to continue in a formal way what I had been learning through the casual reading of books: I enrolled at the University of Cape Town to do a course in sociology. That is how it was if you were white and relatively well off – you could go overseas for a "gap year", expand your consciousness and then decide you'd like to further your education. For the vast majority of South Africans at that time, this style of living was unthinkable.

University turned my world upside down. It taught me how to be rational and critical, to question everything. Religion was the first casualty. It could not stand up to the questioning and exposed itself to me as no more than a set of superstitious answers to difficult questions. Science taught me that things should only be believed on the basis of the evidence that supports them; religion required that I just believe things without any evidence at all, that is, by faith alone. For me the inherited belief that there was a divine creator and a divine justice could no longer be upheld. It contradicted the belief that we could create a better world and that justice should be achieved here on earth.

In the sociology class I met Stephen Lee. Like me, he preferred to sit in the back row of the lecture room where students could talk and swap notes and books with each other. He had been at university for a year already, changing his course from business science to sociology. He found out in his first year that he did not want to become a "capitalist" and had developed, as a reaction to what he had been taught in the business classes, an interest in the Marxist conception of society. He had also been involved in student politics, which had contributed towards the leftward direction of his political evolution.

On one occasion I agreed to swap with him one of the banned books I had brought back to South Africa for an interesting book he was showing off. This led to regular exchanges of books and to combined searches for progressive articles and books in the university's exceptionally large library. There was not much literature of this kind as most books and magazines in that category had been banned by the state or "appropriated" by the students. However, between the two of us, we managed to ferret out a number of interesting titles in the most unlikely locations. These we photocopied from cover to cover and bound into books that we could then swap with other students who were also searching for "subversive" literature. Once we got into the right circles we were amazed by the huge quantity of banned literature in circulation. In a short while, we possessed trunk-loads of banned books and articles that we had photocopied. People went to extreme lengths to obtain the books that were supposed to be bad for them. We were thankful to the apartheid censors for the valuable service they provided by regularly printing their lists of prohibited publications in the *Government Gazette*. We knew that those were the ones worth reading!

The sociology course was a great disappointment. Economics, my second subject, was even more demoralising. Our textbooks were all American tomes that claimed to teach their subjects "scientifically" by looking at reality "as it is" and not "how it ought to be". It soon became obvious to us that we were being taught conservative politics disguised as sociology and economics. The world, we were taught, was essentially a static and harmonious entity and all social structures, such as classes, served equally important functions by holding society together. Human societies were characterised by consensus and harmony and everything that happened was the result of conscious decisions by people to make things happen, not the result of the working-out of intangible generalisations such as "social forces" and "class antagonisms". Change in society involved the authorities making small adjustments to relieve pressure points. There were no inherent antagonisms that could lead to conflict and, God forbid, revolution. Conflict was brought by outside forces impinging on this otherwise stable organism. You didn't have to be a genius to see that this was just a load of conservative nonsense.

It was particularly insulting to be taught this in a country like South Africa where social antagonisms were so blatant. By implication, our lecturers were telling us that the reactionary politics of the apartheid rulers was science. They, the apartheid politicians, were saying essentially the same thing as the sociologists every day: everyone in their station served a function; the whites had to rule as they had the skills and the tradition of ruling; the blacks provided the labour that society needed; South Africa's black citizens were happy with their lot and had no real grievances; all strains where they occurred would be relieved by slowly introducing reforms; conflict was brought from the outside by "communists" and "terrorists" who incited and intimidated people to rebel against the legitimate government for the political ends of foreign governments.

The claptrap that we were being taught contrasted sharply with the new perspective on things we were learning through the books we were reading on the side. These seemed to give a much more accurate portrayal of the society in which we lived, one torn apart by antagonism and conflict. Blacks did not need any "communists" to tell them that the society they lived in was oppressive and unjust or that the way to overcome it was to rebel against it. Apartheid meant conflict.

Our leftward political swing was also the best antidote for racism. It taught us that racial antagonism and conflict, far from being "natural" and "inevitable", were the products of colonialism and imperialism. Racism in South Africa began with colonial occupation and expansion and was fostered as part of the strategy of the settlers to win and maintain control over the local population. The racist policies of the apartheid regime were just the latter-day manifestation of continued colonial domination – the particular form of colonialism where the colonisers and colonised inhabited the same country.

My friendship with Stephen grew and after several months he invited me to join him and others who were planning to build a seaside shanty on a small, remote, rocky outcrop named Oudeschip, about fifteen kilometres down the coast from Cape Town. The plan was to build the hut out of driftwood found in the rocks along the coastline, and packing-case wood that would have to be carried some distance along a mountain track. We set to but the others dropped out after a short while when they realised how much work was involved. The hut was completed within six months and served as the perfect retreat for studying and discussing our changing world outlook. It was also the ideal place to invite female companions!

It was not long before we began to treat our university courses with disdain and cynicism, learning only so much as was necessary to satisfy supervisors and pass exams. We regularly skipped lectures and spent the time at Oudeschip instead. There we could read things more interesting and worthwhile. This reading did not remain within the ambit of the few subjects we were studying at university but broadened to the actual society we lived in, to history, to politics and to the struggle of the oppressed against racial domination.

The three years at university overturned all our beliefs, attitudes, prejudices and fears. The process was erratic, slow and traumatic. Deeply ingrained prejudices that we had not considered as such had to be eradicated. Beliefs we thought were our own turned out to be the product of years of racist and fascist indoctrination – notions of white superiority being the most persistent.

The great white myths had to be debunked. The first of these was the historical myth that white South Africans had a moral claim to the major portion of the country since most of the land was unoccupied when they moved into the interior. Those areas called the "homelands" were the only parts occupied by Africans and that was why they were being granted "independence". It came as a shock to find out that in fact all of the area labelled as South Africa had been occupied for hundreds if not thousands of years prior to the arrival of the Europeans and that the history of the settlers was a history of plunder, exploitation and death, a process that continued under apartheid.

The second myth, which flowed from the first, was that there were no majorities in South Africa – only a number of minorities. There were the whites, coloureds, Indians, Zulus, Xhosas, Sothos, Tswanas – 13 "ethnic groups" in all. Each of the African "tribes" was different to the next and all antagonistic to the others. No group could claim a right to South Africa – it was a "multinational" country.

Once the colonial principle of divide and rule was understood, this myth fell flat on its face. Why did Africans have to be subdivided into numerous linguistic or cultural groups while the whites were one homogeneous entity despite the fact that they were also divided linguistically and culturally? The identified "tribes" were, in any case, colonial designations and the indigenous peoples did not see themselves in the same way.

The next was the myth that South Africa's blacks had the best deal of all blacks on the continent and that the government was doing more for them than any black government in Africa was doing for its subjects. The total meaninglessness and irrelevance of this claim, which was brought up every time apartheid was criticised, was exposed when it was realised that this was no more than a ruse to deflect attention from apartheid onto some allegedly worse case somewhere else. Besides being untrue, it was an excuse for white privilege. The true injustice of apartheid was manifested when the comparison was made between the living conditions of white and black South Africans. Were blacks supposed to be grateful that they were living under apartheid and satisfied with their lot after being told that conditions were worse somewhere else?

Overcoming belief in the political myth that South Africa had a democratic, multi-party state gave a sharp boost to my political transformation. Realising that only 15 per cent of the population had the vote and that that vote was deliberately exercised to perpetuate a dictatorship of white rule over the black majority made the "government" as bad as any military dictatorship where no one had the vote at all.

The apartheid regime was a product of the illegal colonial creation that Britain set up when it brought the four colonies of Natal, the Orange Free State, Transvaal and Cape together to form the Union of South Africa in 1910. The wishes of the indigenous inhabitants of the country were ignored and only the white settler minority was consulted. Not once until 1994 had a South African government been democratically elected – by all the people, that is – and the regimes in power had only been "governments" in the sense that they had maintained control over the affairs of the area by force of arms.

The myth propagated with the most vigour was the one that claimed the omnipotence and invincibility of the regime. This had two sides: that white rule was complete and that the regime's "security forces" could meet any challenge; and that black opposition was insignificant and would never be powerful enough to overcome white rule.

Any undemocratic regime that has little popular support needs to perpetuate the myth that resistance is futile, since this achieved is half the battle won. Understanding this liberated us from the intimidating effect that the regime's *kragdadigheid* (show of force and toughness) had on those who wished to do something to undermine apartheid.

There were many other myths to be shaken off – so many that it is not possible to list them all. Life under apartheid was a life of lies. The system was so morally unjustifiable and indefensible that the only way most white people could live under it without suffering from the most debilitating guilt was by cloaking themselves in its lies and propaganda. As each lie was peeled off, so the truth – and horror – of apartheid became apparent.

Now the naked reality of apartheid stood before us: what had looked "normal" was a perversion; what we had always accepted was unacceptable. When you are faced with something that suddenly turns out to be the opposite of what you have always believed, your attitude towards it changes rapidly. A friend who deceives you can no longer be your friend; a lie revealed can no longer be believed. We were angry at having been deceived for so long. The system that had bestowed on us so many privileges had done so at the expense of others – at the expense of black people. It could no longer be defended, only challenged.

As everything grew clearer, we became fired with a burning desire to see the end of this monstrosity. Our desire was not motivated so much by guilt – a negative drive – but by the positive wish to see a new, more just and democratic society. To wish for the end of the society we had grown up in and which had given us so much – including the ability to see it for what it was – meant challenging everything. This was not easy for us, as we had always been taught to respect authority, to believe in the benevolence and justness of the government, and to believe that all change came out of the deliberations of politicians in parliament. Parliament was the ultimate political reality; everything outside of it the dark world of "treason" and "terrorism".

But how could a regime that enforced segregation, legitimised exploitation, tolerated abysmal poverty alongside great wealth, turned the majority of its people into semi-slaves, deliberately stunted their education, prevented their free movement, forcibly removed them from one part of the country to another and corralled them into reserves that it called their "homelands", jailed and tortured those who raised their voices in protest – how could a regime that did all this and worse expect loyalty and respect? It could only expect from the majority of its citizens "treasonable" behaviour. Only a truly democratic government that showed respect for its people, which responded fairly to its peoples' demands instead of eliminating those making them, could expect loyalty and respect.

As our perceptions changed, we were faced with the inevitable moral dilemma that confronted whites when they began to realise what apartheid was all about: what to do?

Students like ourselves tended to follow several distinct routes, most of which ended in abandonment and a return to the apartheid fold. Some became so incensed with what they saw that they became instant super-revolutionaries demanding that everyone immediately come out on the streets with their pitchforks. These ultra-leftists, commonly found on university campuses, formed themselves into little cliques that splintered over theoretical differences into various warring factions every few months. The world in which they wished to make revolution was a purely theoretical one, having little connection with reality. After a few years they had burned themselves out and invariably turned into cynics or vehement opponents of those still holding their former views.

Then there were those who were revolutionaries for as long as parents paid the university fees. As soon as they had to fend for themselves or landed well-paying jobs, there was no more time for playing revolution. They became taken up with their own lives. The pursuit of swimming pools and expensive cars became far more important.

14

There were also those who pretended that apartheid did not exist. They preferred to be seen with black people, to spend most of their time in the black townships and looked upon fellow whites as the enemy. Such behaviour was no more than a token protest and never led anywhere. The realities of life under apartheid soon "corrected" this "deviation".

We were determined not to follow any of these well-trodden paths but were not certain which way to go. We were treading new ground. There was no one to point the way and we had no examples to follow. It was easy to shout at apartheid from the comfort of our plush homes in the sanctity of our white suburbs, but to do something that was not patronising was another matter. Liberal-minded South Africans who reached this point found it difficult to take the next step.

The question of what to do was answered for me one day when a canvasser from the white opposition Progressive Party (which later became the Progressive Federal Party) came to the front door to sell the virtues of his party. When I expressed a lack of interest, he said that I should at least make up my mind about one thing. To make his point he held up a hand with outstretched fingers and said: "There are five choices open to every white person." Pointing with his other hand to his little finger he said: "One, you can join the Nationalist Party"; to the next finger he said, "Two, you can do nothing; three, you can leave the country; four, you can do something unconstitutional"; and finally to his thumb, "You can join the Progressive Party."

I thought about this and realised that he was absolutely right. The National Party, the party of apartheid, was obviously out of the question; doing nothing was the same as condoning the system even if you expressed rejection of it; emigrating was copping out; the Progressive Party, even if it claimed to be opposed to apartheid, was a totally irrelevant and ineffectual organisation that served no other purpose than to give credibility to the apartheid regime's claim that the "government" was democratically elected and that the Nationalists were the legitimate ruling party.

That left only the "unconstitutional" choice. From my re-reading of South African history, I had learned that constitutional opposition in South Africa did not mean opposition at all; it meant acceptance of white minority rule. Real opposition, namely, opposition that sought to end exclusive white rule and put in its place the democracy of one-person-one-vote, was by definition unconstitutional. Every oppressed people has faced these same choices: assimilation and absorption, flight or rebellion.

The constitution in force had been designed by whites to preserve their political hegemony. It completely denied blacks any constitutional rights whatsoever – they were the subjects of what whites decided was best for them. Denied constitutional avenues for bringing about meaningful change, what were the victims of apartheid supposed to do? Unflinchingly accept whatever dispensations were foisted upon them? Sit back and wait on the magnanimity of the whites to take pity on them? By declaring that the African National Congress and the Pan-Africanist Congress were "banned" in 1960, and the Communist Party before them in 1950, the regime had demonstrated that it would not tolerate any real opposition at all, constitutional or otherwise.

One could therefore not be afraid of this word "unconstitutional". It had none of the connotations that were associated with it in other parts of the world. What right, in any case, had an illegitimate regime to declare the bounds of constitutionality?

In the same way that it was more honourable to disobey the unjust laws created by an illegitimate parliament than obey them, it was more honourable to act outside the illegitimate constitution than inside it. Having accepted this, it was only natural that we should have sought a home for our views. All the legal political organisations or parties were part of the system in one way or another. In them all you could do was raise your voice in protest at the prevailing political set-up – a waste of time in a situation where the repressive forces had been given such draconian powers that they could physically remove or eliminate anyone who raised theirs too loudly. It seemed obvious to us that the only effective way of opposing this vicious regime was to confront it directly, but secretly and outside its framework of rules.

The only effective organisation that appeared to be doing this was one that had been declared "banned" by the regime – the African National Congress. It was the one organisation that stood for the complete eradication of apartheid and for the creation of a democratic South Africa not based on any racial premises. It was also the one organisation that made no distinction as to "race" when it came to membership.

The Freedom Charter to which the ANC subscribed was a particularly impressive document of intention. Its preamble started: "We the people of South Africa, declare for all our country and the world to know: that South Africa belongs to all who live in it, black and white, and that no government can justly claim authority unless it is based on the will of all our people." Its 10 clauses began:

The People Shall Govern!
All National Groups Shall Have Equal Rights!
The People Shall Share in the Country's Wealth!
The Land Shall Be Shared Among Those Who Work It!
All Shall Be Equal Before the Law!
All Shall Enjoy Equal Human Rights!
There Shall Be Work and Security!
The Doors of Learning and Culture Shall Be Opened!
There Shall Be Houses, Security, and Comfort!
There Shall Be Peace and Friendship!

If belief in such reasonable and universal principles amounted to terrorism and treason then so be it – we would be terrorists and traitors. These ideals were worth fighting for and worth any risk, even prison.

From this perspective our attitude towards the struggle against apartheid changed dramatically. The ANC had been forced by the regime to adopt a strategy of resistance that included armed struggle and this meant coming to terms with the question of the use of violence to achieve political ends.

The ANC's adoption of armed struggle was not a question of the end justifying the means. The history of South Africa quite clearly demonstrated to us the complete futility in opposing white minority rule by peaceful means alone. The ANC had for nearly fifty years striven by peaceful means to resist white domination, yet every manifestation of peaceful resistance, whether it took the form of protests, demonstrations, boycotts or strikes, whether it was passive or defiant, was put down by the authorities with the utmost brutality and bloodshed. Thousands had died in the attempt to advance their rights or protect the few they had. Each campaign of action against the white rulers had been answered with new and increasingly harsh "security laws", detentions, torture, imprisonment, bannings, banishments and death. How much more violent would the regime get when it saw that the demands of the oppressed went beyond demands for human rights and for the complete eradication of the system of white minority rule – for state power?

Peaceful resistance had led nowhere. Instead of halting or slowing down the implementation of the regime's apartheid laws, the apartheid rulers had enforced them with increasing vigour and barbarity. The laws were inherently violent in themselves: millions had been forcibly removed from their homes and dumped in the impoverished Bantustans where they died of starvation and disease; urban black populations had been herded into unsanitary townships on the outskirts of the white cities; millions had been arrested and imprisoned under the pass laws; families had been split up in the interests of "racial purity"; the black population had been denied proper education; patriots had been tortured and imprisoned or driven into exile...

The ANC, with its tradition of peaceful struggle, had not taken to armed struggle lightly or easily. Nor was the turn to arms an act of revenge or self-defence. A point had been reached where the only choice was to surrender to white minority rule or to fight on with whatever means were available. All peaceful and constitutional channels had been closed; the only alternative was to organise a people's army, Umkhonto we Sizwe – The Spear of the Nation – to defend the oppressed and fight for the kind of South Africa that the majority of people wanted. We had little difficulty in accepting that the ANC's turn to arms was justifiable and that the armed struggle against apartheid was a just and legitimate form of struggle.

Many people argued that there still remained peaceful avenues for bringing about change and that therefore all activity should be concentrated in this direction; that violent struggle should only be resorted to when there was absolutely no other choice. But we believed that such a point had long been reached and that peaceful methods alone would never be sufficient to wrest political power from the hands of the racists. Were the oppressed just supposed to stand and take bullets in the back and not return the fire? Were they to deny themselves a form of struggle simply because some people found it difficult to justify morally?

Those who pleaded that there were never moral grounds for

resorting to violence to achieve political ends were usually people who knew nothing of the violence of apartheid or of the history of the people's struggles against racist tyranny. Such people seldom made moral denunciations of the unceasing violence used by the regime to preserve and perpetuate white privilege and rule.

In our final year at university both Stephen and I, naturally, began to think about our future after we had completed our courses. Our political development had led us to a position where we could no longer live comfortably under apartheid. Our consciences would not allow us to find work and "settle down". If we identified with the oppressed, we could not live like the oppressor. The only way we could justify living in South Africa was if we were actively opposing the system. But if we were going to give ourselves to the struggle against apartheid it had to be through the medium of some organisation, and the only organisation we could consider joining – the ANC – could not be contacted inside South Africa. We knew that the ANC had missions in various African countries, but our South African passports prevented us from visiting them. The only choice was to go to Britain to make contact with the organisation there.

And that's what we did.

In February 1974, Stephen and I set off for Europe by ship – the cheapest way at the time. From Barcelona where we disembarked, we made our way directly to Holland to spend a few weeks seeing as much of that country as possible. Once we got to Britain we would immediately get down to business.

We arrived in London in the evening on 24 April and spent the first night at a youth hostel in Earls Court. There was no time to waste: first thing the next morning we would present ourselves at the ANC office.

Stephen had never been to London before so the next day we decided to take an underground train to Trafalgar Square to see a few sights before making our way to the office. When we surfaced at the Square, newspaper billboards greeted us with the portentous announcement: "Salazar overthrown in Portuguese coup". Immediately we realised the profound consequences this would have for apartheid South Africa. All the buffer zones it had relied on for so long would soon disappear and the armed struggle would rapidly be brought to its borders. The coincidence of this news with our plan to go to the ANC somehow seemed auspicious. We were entering a new era, both personally and politically speaking.

The ANC office was not quite what we had expected. First, we had trouble locating it and then when we did find the door number, there was no indication that it was the ANC's office. From the street door a steep, dark stairway led to another door through which we entered into a small, cluttered room. We introduced ourselves to someone at the entrance and said that we were from Cape Town and had come to find out more about the ANC. Someone else was beckoned from another office, who introduced himself as the chief representative (later we found out that his name was Reg September). He shook hands welcomingly and then immediately returned to his office, asking us to please wait. He typed something and then returned and handed us a note that read: "You should not come here like this. Please meet me at the café around the corner in half an hour." We nodded in understanding and left the office. Things looked promising!

When the chief representative came to the café he was with another person. We explained again that we had been studying at the University of Cape Town and had come to Britain to find out more about the ANC, and were keen to do something about the situation in South Africa when we returned.

Their first thoughts must have been that we were spies or police agents because it was hardly the usual thing for white South African tourists to walk in off the street and offer their services to the ANC. Nevertheless, we had a good chat and they were keen to hear our views on the current situation at home. A further meeting was arranged for the following day at a nearby pub.

At the next meeting, the chief representative arrived with a white comrade, who introduced himself as Ronnie (this was the legendary Ronnie Kasrils). This was reassuring to us, as we knew that in theory the ANC accepted whites into its ranks, but did not know if there were actually any white members. The Chief left us with Ronnie, who inquired more deeply into our political views than we had been required to express the previous day. There followed a number of similar meetings on subsequent days and at one of them, they asked us to write down our personal details, presumably so they could check on our *bona fides*.

Both of us were impatient in the extreme and wanted them to send us back to South Africa immediately so that we could carry out some tasks for the movement. We were prepared to do anything. Our naïvety would not allow us to give them the time to check up on our credentials. We knew that we were not police agents and somehow assumed they should too.

When it became clear that our incorporation was going to take somewhat longer than expected, we moved to another hostel with a longer-term tenancy. To pass the time we immersed ourselves in the literature of the liberation movement, attended political meetings and talks, and generally primed ourselves for our prospective role as revolutionaries.

At the new hostel I met Robin, to whom I was later to be married for a while. She and a friend had left South Africa on an impulse because they were fed up with life as typists in the offices of Johannesburg. Arriving penniless, Robin was forced to take up a job as a typist in the offices of London.

Robin and I struck up a close relationship and within a couple of months had moved out of the hostel and into cheap digs in the Fulham area of London. She was not politically minded when we first met, but was quick to shift her views on South Africa when encouraged to think about them politically. In no time she became embroiled in political activities with us and began to take an interest in exile politics.

Stephen grew impatient waiting for the ANC to decide if they were going to send us back to South Africa, so took off back to Holland where he got a job as a carpenter. Later he moved on to Spain where he earned a living teaching English to wealthy Spaniards.

I had sufficient funds to last a few months but was eventually forced to search for work. My South African passport acted to my detriment in this regard but I managed to find the occasional typing job through some less scrupulous employment agencies that did not ask for documents or National Insurance numbers. Through a friend of my parents, I was able, after much bureaucratic wrangling, to obtain a work permit for a social work job in a sort of glorified reformatory in Wiltshire. Robin and I parted company temporarily and she went back to the hostel.

Stephen returned to Britain around the end of the year (1974) and at his first meeting with the ANC they told him that it would be possible for us to go back to South Africa to do something for the movement. They must have found us acceptable.

He phoned me in Wiltshire to tell me the good news. At last things were moving. I immediately handed in my resignation even though I had gone through tremendous pains to obtain the work permit and had only worked for three months. I hated the job anyway and had felt totally cut off from the world there.

Stephen and I moved into a squat in Fulham with a number of other homeless people, to wait for the period of training the ANC had promised us before our return to South Africa. Stephen, on account of his having obtained a British passport, was able to take a job with London Transport as a bus conductor. I had no choice but to rely on my rapidly diminishing savings.

To pass the time both of us became involved, through friends we had met in the area, in the anti-Common Market campaign that was taking place at that time prior to the referendum. This involvement was foolish as we were associating with communist and left-wing Labour types while we should have been keeping our noses clean. Our political mentors in the ANC should have forbidden us from engaging in such activities, but we did learn a lot about how politics works!

The training that was given to us was designed to provide us with the practical and survival skills we would need to operate as a propaganda cell in underground conditions in South Africa. It was also to prepare us mentally for what could happen to us if we got caught.

The plan was that we would go back to South Africa as soon as possible after completing the training and then lie low for a few months to ensure that we were not being watched. During those first months we were to find ourselves jobs, settle down and become "respectable" citizens. Most importantly, we were in no way to expose our real political views but create the impression, especially among family and friends, that our trip overseas had "matured" us and that our former radical views had mellowed.

The training took place over a period of several months, but at a very leisurely pace. The lessons were conducted in various private homes – obviously ones considered "safe" – and, if only theoretical matters were being discussed, in pubs, parks, cars and restaurants. Over the period we were required to read a vast number of books, mostly about the detention and prison experiences of people who had been captured during the Second World War or in South Africa and other fascist countries. Although reading these felt somehow romantic at the time, they did prepare us for what was later to be our fate.

Since our major activity, at least for the first period of our operations in South Africa, was to be the production and distribution of propaganda material for and in the name of the liberation movement, the training concentrated on preparing us for this sort of activity. We were instructed in the art of writing political propaganda and how to reproduce it using simple methods such as stencil duplicating machines. Instruction was given on the use of the postal system for mass distribution and a number of mechanical methods of distributing revolutionary literature were demonstrated.

One of these methods was the leaflet bomb. These were hardly bombs in the real sense of the word but simple, timed explosive devices designed to throw bundles of leaflets high into the air in order to spread them over a large area where a target crowd was gathered. They had been used with spectacular effect many times before in South Africa and had become one of the hallmarks of the liberation movement's internal propaganda activities. Peculiarly, there is little evidence that this method of propaganda distribution was used in other situations throughout the world where there was severe suppression of revolutionary viewpoints.

The last part of our training involved setting up communication structures and working out financial arrangements. We swapped false names and safe addresses and adopted a set of code words for open communications. These included a set of signals that we could relay to each other if we suspected the enemy was on to us. We were also introduced to more formal encryption and concealment methods. These included various book codes, invisible inks and other ways of disguising and hiding messages.

This done, our instructors gave us a pep talk about the value of the work we were about to undertake. We would be letting the people and the enemy know that the ANC was alive and working hard for liberation; we would be participating in the historic task of removing from the face of the earth one of the most abominable scourges to be visited upon humankind. Finally, they wished us luck and said, jokingly, that they would write to us in prison. They never kept their word!

Chapter Two

Underground

The two "trained terrorists" arrived back in South Africa in July 1975. For me departure from Britain was not easy as I was leaving Robin behind. At first, I had to remind myself that the job we'd been entrusted to do was more important than any personal suffering I would have to put up with. Apartheid caused suffering on such a scale that feeling sorry for myself was pathetic and selfish. But private sorrows were closer to the bone and no amount of virtuous thought was able to stop the pain and loneliness of separation; only time would heal that.

Robin and I had exchanged false names and safe addresses so that we could keep in contact, but neither of us knew when or if we would ever see each other again. We had agreed that we could not maintain a proper relationship from such a distance and in any case, I had been instructed to lead as "normal" a life as possible – and that included trying not to be celibate.

Everything looked different when we got back; it also looked so much the same. While we had been away changing our lives so that we could help bring an end to apartheid, people we had known were carrying on with their lives in much the same way as before. They were doing the same old things in the same old places and bore the same old attitudes, and had kept their heads firmly buried in the ground.

People who had been close to us, our relatives and friends, were now in the enemy camp, and we found ourselves living in their midst as "traitors". Our own parents, sisters, brothers were on the side that stood against everything we were fighting for and for everything we were fighting against.

The full horror of apartheid was clearer than ever. It angered us intensely and made us even more determined to do something about it. But no longer was there any question of feeling guilty about having to live the lives of white South Africans in apartheid South Africa; we would be doing so in order to end doing so.

Our first task was to sort out our mundane aboveground affairs, such as finding jobs and places to live. Within a few weeks I found work at the segregated University of the Western Cape, for those whom the regime had classified as "coloured". The job was in a sociological research institute attached to the university, with the pretentious name of Institute for Social Development (ISD). My job was to enquire into various matters affecting the coloured community – with what purpose I never really found out.

The job proved to be an ideal cover for me because any whites who worked at such places – known as "bush colleges" or "tribal colleges" – were usually regarded as supporters of the regime. The facilities at ISD were immensely useful for our purposes. It received and kept vast quantities of information on all subjects, including a newspaper clippings library. After a while it became my responsibility to organise the marking, cutting, pasting and filing of the clippings and it does not require too much imagination to guess how the library was adapted to provide us with the information we needed for our work!

Not only were the facilities useful but the research I did there took me right into the townships and into black people's homes, where I was able to feel their mood and begin to understand what it was like to live on the dark side of apartheid. I got to know every township in the Cape Town area inside out. This was important as I was still living the life of a white person and the whole exercise could have become academic if I had been confined to my secure little white suburb.

As they were only interested in results, there were no strict hours of work at ISD and I could even "work at home" if I wished. The freedom to come and go as I pleased was the most valuable aspect of the job, without which participating in an underground cell would have been much more difficult.

Stephen was not so lucky in finding work but as ISD had just been set up and was looking for more staff I suggested he apply for a job there as well. He was given employment but could not see eye to eye with the boss and resigned after a few months. This was a great pity as he was not able to find another job after that and eventually had to leave Cape Town to earn a living.

At ISD I met Daphne, who was also working as a researcher. Correctly I shouldn't have developed a relationship with her as she was "coloured" and therefore unsuitable as a girlfriend for someone who was meant to be working underground and attempting to appear normal while doing so. But what could I do? I felt attracted to her. Was I supposed to reject friendships with people with whom I worked every day because of their colour? That would have appeared even less normal.

Daphne and I got on well but she couldn't help thinking that I was a very secretive person. I'm certain she thought I was having an affair with another woman because I kept disappearing for long periods with only feeble explanations. Whenever our conversations got onto political matters I would attempt to steer away from the subject, leading her to think that I was totally apathetic and cynical. At times my lack of concern about the awkward situations that our "mixed" relationship created drove her to desperation and she walked out on me several times. I found it extremely difficult to maintain a close relationship without being able to talk about the most important things in my life. Personal ethics crumble on a relationship of lies.

After a couple of months Stephen and I began to grow restless. There had been no signs of police surveillance and any further delay in getting on with the job of setting up our cell seemed to be over-cautious. Both of us began to collect newspaper clippings of current events and carefully pasted them into scrapbooks for use when we got going. I went to a number of estate agents to see what sorts of premises we could hire to set up shop. There were three possibilities: small flats, offices and garages. Most agents advertised all three but only garages were within our meagre budget at that time. I noted the addresses of a few and went to see if they would be suitable. Most weren't as they were just fenced off parking bays at the bottom of blocks of flats, but some had bricked partition walls so looked suitable.

Towards the end of the year we found a garage in a huge block of flats in Green Point, a suburb of Cape Town, and took out a lease for six months. The garage appeared to be suitable as it had thick walls and a strong door to contain the sounds of printing. Its position allowed us to reach it in such a way that we could tell if we were being followed.

We bought a second-hand typewriter and duplicator, as well as the stationery needed to print and post pamphlets. Our first purchases were made with obsessive attention to the rules of conspiracy that we had been taught: only small quantities at a time so as not to attract attention, no names given and appearances changed so that salespeople would not remember us.

We produced our first pamphlet in early December 1975 – about the South African invasion of Angola. It was not a long run as we had only managed to collect about a hundred names of people to whom we could send it. The ANC had promised to send us a list of names as soon as we got going, but I suppose they wanted us first to prove that we were going to use the training and money they had given us for the agreed purpose before taking the risk of sending a mailing list through the post.

The garage proved to be completely unsuitable for the job. It had no light and ventilation when the door was shut. To provide light we had to use a gas lamp, but coupled with the mid-summer heat it became unbearably hot. Unfamiliarity with the duplicator meant that there were more dud than good copies and there was nowhere to dispose of the rejects. There was also nowhere to wash our hands, which got covered in black ink. The surplus leaflets we later took up the side of the mountain and burnt in a sacrificial bonfire but the wind, of course, blew bits of charred but still readable leaflets all over the place. We were learning.

That one experience convinced us that we would have to find a more suitable place from which to operate, so it was back to the estate agents. A few weeks later I found a small room in an annexe to a block of flats in the Gardens area of Cape Town. It was not ideal but all we could afford and far better than the garage. It was a small, sparsely-furnished room but with a window for ventilation, a light for working at night and a hand basin for washing ink off our hands. There was also a bathroom and toilet, but it was down the passage and we had to share it with other tenants in the block. The main drawback with the place was the other tenants: they were too friendly and kept knocking on the door for a chat or to invite us around to their rooms for a drink. They must have found us very unfriendly and thought it strange that we were hardly ever there and even more strange that two young blokes should occasionally spend time together in a small room!

Stephen was still without work and getting desperate. The two of us were sharing a flat with his sister in the respectable suburb of Rondebosch and this was costing a lot of money. He was beginning to think of going to Johannesburg to look for work. This was tragic as it meant that our two-man cell would be split just as it was getting going, and that in effect I would be working alone. The ANC wanted us to work together and would not finance two sets of equipment. But he had to live.

In February we produced our second pamphlet and our first in the new place. Like the first, it was about the South African invasion of Angola, but we produced it in far greater numbers as the ANC had sent us a list of five hundred names and addresses. As we had no addressing machine at that stage, we had to laboriously type these onto the envelopes.

The room proved to be much more suitable than the garage. We could type the stencils and envelopes there rather than at home and do the printing at leisure with genuine tea breaks. The spoilt copies, of which there were far fewer, were disposed of down the toilet after first soaking them in water and tearing them into fine shreds. Best of all we could wash and emerge from the room with clean hands.

There was one problem we had not considered before: how to post six or seven hundred envelopes without exposing ourselves. The dilemma was whether to post them all at once or over a period of time, a problem we were never to resolve satisfactorily. If we posted them all at once, the post collectors or sorters would notice the sudden flood of letters in the post and intercept them for inspection. If we posted them over time in small batches the post collectors and sorters would not notice anything unusual but we would increase our chances of being seen posting the envelopes, especially if the police were watching particular post boxes after intercepting some of the envelopes. Obviously, whichever method we chose, it was important to vary the appearance of the items as much as possible by using different sorts of envelopes, addressing systems and stamps. Uniformity and pattern is what cops look for.

In March, Stephen decided to move to Johannesburg to look for work. Conveniently the ANC had sent us a draft for a leaflet that they wanted to be dispersed by leaflet bomb in Johannesburg on or around 21 March – the anniversary of the Sharpeville massacre in 1960. So we decided to kill two birds with one stone by combining his search for work with our first leaflet-bomb mission.

I had been experimenting with some new-style leaflet bombs and had developed a much more compact version of what had been demonstrated to us in London. The ones we had been shown, and which had previously been used by other operatives, were of a very complicated design. They had been used camouflaged in buckets and had thus become labelled by the media as "bucket bombs". This seemed a peculiar way of disguising them, for nothing would appear more abnormal than someone walking around town with a covered bucket. The new design fitted inside a cardboard box and could be placed inside an ordinary plastic shopping bag. This alteration was essential as the bombs had to be transported inside our suitcases to Johannesburg by air. Thank goodness they had no x-ray inspections of luggage in those days!

Stephen left for Johannesburg a few days before me and booked into a hotel. He went to a few places to look for work and while doing so sought out the best locations to place the bombs, such as railway and bus stations around the centre of Johannesburg. I took a plane to Johannesburg the day before we were due to place the devices, having left word at work that I would be working at home for the next two days.

Stephen had taken three leaflet bombs with him and I brought another three. He met me at the airport bus terminus and took me to his hotel. Fortunately, he had been given a double room so there was a bed for me too. Under normal circumstances I would never have thought of staying in a hotel without paying, but under those extraordinary circumstances normal ethics had to be put aside.

Both of us were absolutely terrified at having to carry out the mission. We had never done anything like it before and were only too aware of the consequences of being caught. Neither of us slept a wink that night, lying awake wondering how we would muster the courage to do it.

The next morning Stephen took me on a tour of the centre of Johannesburg to point out the places he had chosen for the bombs: the black entrance to the main Johannesburg railway station, a bus station, a narrow market street, the *Rand Daily Mail* newspaper office building and Faraday Station – a station from where many blacks caught trains back to Soweto.

I booked into another hotel and then we divided the targets between ourselves, planned routes to get to them and worked out a plan of action. We would each first take one bomb from our respective hotels, set them off, and then return for the other two if the first ones were a success. The time chosen was the afternoon rush hour.

At midday we bought a large bottle of wine in the hope that the alcohol would give us Dutch courage, but the stuff was totally ineffective against the torrents of adrenaline in our bloodstreams. At about four we separated and went to our respective hotels to prepare the bombs. We had agreed to meet after it was all over at the observation floor at the top of the Carlton Tower – Johannesburg's tallest building.

I took one bomb out of my suitcase and placed it on the dresser to make sure everything was in order. The device consisted of a wooden base about the size of an average book. Mounted vertically on the base was a short piece of aluminium tubing. Sitting on top of the tube, and fixed to a plunger made from a piece of broomstick that fitted inside it, was a platform the same size as the base. On this I placed five hundred of the leaflets we had brought with us. An ordinary kitchen timer gave the time delay and a battery fired the homemade detonator inside the tube. The whole device was placed in a topless cardboard box, put inside a plastic shopping bag and then covered with newspaper to disguise it.

I walked out of the hotel as nonchalantly as possible but couldn't help thinking that I was transparent and that the people sitting in the lobby knew what I was carrying. They were all laughing inside because I was soon about to be caught. "Terrorists" had no chance!

I had been allocated the black entrance to the Johannesburg railway station. First, I went into the station toilet – a whites-only toilet of course – to prime the bomb. In a cubicle I removed the leaflets and lifted off the platform so that I could pour the ready-mixed explosive powder down the tube. Then I set the timer for twenty minutes, enough time I thought to get around to the other side of the station and away. My heart was pounding so violently that I was certain people could hear it. I felt faint, sick with fear.

With my shopping bag ticking away, I emerged from that toilet feeling quite ridiculous. Surely everyone could hear the ticking? Surely, they could all see the guilty look on my face? I just knew I would bump into some long-lost friend who would want to stop for a chat and then the bomb would go off in my hand.

I walked around to the rear-side of the station where the black entrance was located. For the life of me I couldn't see a suitable place to deposit the bomb. Some distance from the entrance I spotted a rubbish bin – it would have to do. Fortunately, it was nearly empty, so I dropped my bundle in it and made off as quickly as I could. There were hundreds of black people walking by, so even if it was not as close as it could have been it was a good place. I continued walking past the black entrance and disappeared into the bustling crowd of homeward-bound commuters heading for the station.

I rushed back to my hotel without waiting to hear if the bomb had gone off. Back in my room I primed the other two, set the timers for half an hour and placed them next to each other in a very large shopping bag. This time I was feeling more confident. Some of the fear had subsided and I was beginning to feel defiant instead of feeling that I was just doing my duty.

It took longer than anticipated to reach the bus terminus where I was to place my second bomb. As soon as I reached it I took one of the bombs out of the bag and deposited it next to some rubbish bags on the pavement. It was in its own bag so did not look out of place; I just hoped some curious person would not come and peek into it.

There was less than 10 minutes left to get to the next place, a narrow, busy shopping and market street. The ticking of the timer seemed to be in unison with my heart; both would explode simultaneously if I did not get to the place in time. With what I thought was about a minute to spare I reached the place, dropped the bag and ran. As I turned the corner, I heard a loud bang – it had been less than a minute. I raced from that place as fast as I could without breaking into a sprint, and headed for the Carlton Centre, top floor.

Stephen was already there and looking through one of the telescopes on the observation deck. He could see the flashing lights of police cars outside the offices of the *Rand Daily Mail* where he had placed one of his bombs. Multitudes of cops were milling around investigating the remains of the bomb and picking up the remaining leaflets that were still blowing about in the street. We turned the telescope to Faraday Station where he had placed his other two. There we could see hundreds of leaflets in the street but no sign of cops or of the bombs. Someone must have scooped them up and made off with them.

We congratulated ourselves on our success and felt a sort of defiant pride at having pulled off our first leaflet-bomb operation and for bringing out the police. We treated ourselves to a lavish meal in downtown Joburg that night and felt no guilt for using our ANC money to pay the bill – the perks of the job!

The next day it was headlines in all the papers. That was the time when a small thing like a leaflet bomb made big news.

ANC flyer distributed by 'leaflet bomb', 19 March 1976, to commemorate the anniversary of 1960 Sharpeville massacre

PEOPLE OF SOUTH AFRICA – SONS AND DAUGHTERS OF THE SOIL – THE AFRICAN NATIONAL CONGRESS BRINGS YOU THIS MESSAGE

The conditions for developing our liberation struggle, smashing the Apartheid monster and winning our freedom, are greater than ever before. Nothing can hide the fact that White South Africa is in irreversible crisis from which it cannot escape. The opportunities for developing the armed struggle right inside South Africa are becoming more possible. Through armed force, with Umkhonto We Sizwe – the ANC's military wing – as the armed spearhead, we will smash the brute force of the oppressors. But do not wait for that day. It cannot come unless the masses are involved in all forms of struggle. The time to act – to hit back – is NOW!!

Rally to the ANC – the tried and trusted organisation of all our people that Vorster and his police can never crush!

EVERYONE MUST BE A FREEDOM FIGHTER! Our men, our women, our youth – the toilers in the town and countryside – the scholars and the professional groups. The MPLA and FRELIMO are victorious because the entire people supported them.

OUR ORGANISED STRENGTH, UNITY AND MILITANT ACTIONS ARE THE KEY TO FREEDOM! Organise wherever you are. In the factories, townships, mines, farms, schools, countryside – mobilise the power of our people and of all genuine democrats. Intensify the freedom struggle in every possible way. We, African, Indian and Coloured people must resist Vorster's policy of divide and rule. Reject tribal politics, Bantustans, Indian Councils and all dummy institutions! Smash the stooges and traitors! Fight the unjust laws and fight for a new life!

PEOPLE OF SOUTH AFRICA – DEMONSTRATE OUR SUPPORT FOR THOSE VORSTER SEEKS TO CRUSH! It is within our power to prevent his aggression against our brothers and sisters in Angola, Namibia or anywhere else. We must not permit subversive activities against the people and state of Angola! By intensifying our struggle we will tie Vorster's army down and make it impossible for him to launch his war machine across the borders. The struggle in Angola, Zimbabwe, Namibia is our struggle – a struggle against a common enemy – racism and imperialism. Together we will win!

THE ANC SAYS: AMANDLA NGAWETHU! MAATLA KE ARONA! POWER TO THE PEOPLE!

THE ANC SAYS TO VORSTER AND HIS RACIST REGIME: ALL POWER TO THE MPLA – LIBERATORS OF ANGOLA! ALL POWER TO THE PEOPLE!

VORSTER – GET OUT OF ANGOLA! GET OUT OF NAMIBIA!

NO INTERFERENCE IN ZIMBABWE! HANDS OFF AFRICA!

PEOPLE OF SOUTH AFRICA! *The MPLA have scored an outstanding victory over the forces of racism and imperialism. Vorster's defeat in Angola is of outstanding significance to our struggle.*

VORSTER TRIED TO SWALLOW ANGOLA BUT NOW HE IS CHOKING TO DEATH! THE MPLA *have taught him the lesson of his life. He thought he could send his army into Angola and place his stooges in power, but the MPLA thrashed him in battle and sent his White soldiers and stooges fleeing in terror. The MPLA proved that his racist arrogance is hollow, that White South Africa is not invincible, that the forces of freedom are growing in strength and will soon be powerful enough to completely destroy him.*

VORSTER DOES NOT HAVE THE GUTS TO TELL HIS FOLLOWERS THE TRUTH! *He does not want to admit that Africans defeated him. There is no 'Russian' or 'Cuban' plot' to dominate Africa.*

The Soviet Union and Cuba, together with progressive African states, gave legitimate aid to the MPLA in face of the plot by Vorster and his imperialist backers – particularly in the USA – to sabotage Angola's independence. Vorster's lies cannot hide who Africa's true friends really are. The Soviet Union and Cuba always supported the MPLA in its long struggle against Portuguese colonialism; whilst South Africa, the USA and West European countries supported Portugal's barbarous oppression of Africans. It is Vorster and his Western allies who have been caught out trying to recolonise Africa. It is they who are the imperialists!

THE LESSON OF ANGOLA IS CLEAR: *Nothing can prevent the flames of freedom sweeping through the whole of Southern Africa.*

Portuguese colonialism is dead. Smith is doomed. Vorster's turn has come. The days of baasskap are over!

WE, THE ANC, WARN VORSTER – IZAK'UNYATHELI AFRIKA!

AFRICA WILL SMASH YOU VORSTER!

That first round of leaflet bombs was successful in that all went off and the message got spread. It also taught us a number of valuable lessons. The most important was that we needed to devise some form of triggering mechanism so that we did not have to walk through the streets with a live device in our hands. Anything could go wrong: you might not be able to deposit your device at a chosen place (a cop at the spot, perhaps), you might meet someone you knew, there might not be the anticipated crowd, there might not be a suitable dropping place, and so on.

The solution was very simple: a triggering pin that held the timer at the desired timing until released. On location, the pin could be pulled out to set the timer in motion. I tested this innovation two months later on Cape Town's Grand Parade, which became a market area every Saturday. The triggering mechanism gave me such confidence that I was able to walk around with the bomb for a long time in search of the ideal dropping place. I pulled the pin, dropped the package and casually walked away. I didn't wait to see if it had gone off but reports in the papers later in the day confirmed that it had.

Stephen had by this time secured a job as a career adviser at the University of the Witwatersrand in Johannesburg. His period of job seeking had given him a unique qualification. His departure left me in control of the cell and finances – if you can call a one-person operation a cell. As there were insufficient funds to set up another cell in Johannesburg, Stephen was effectively prevented from taking part in most of our underground activities.

Running the cell on my own was the most desperately lonely experience in the world. Everything took twice as long to do and there was nobody to discuss things with. While friends were going camping, to movies, parties and the beach, I was buried in that dark little room like a hermit mole.

Many people have the impression that underground work is

romantic and exciting. This is far from the truth. It is laborious, lonely, monotonous work with no immediately observable rewards. My average day, after work, consisted of reading through three or four newspapers in fine detail, dating the important articles, cutting out and pasting them, and then writing articles for the next pamphlet. I had to do these time-consuming tasks out of sight of friends and on top of all the other daily tasks, such as making small purchases of stamps and stationery. I spent most weekends at the room preparing leaflet bombs, typing stencils, duplicating leaflets, shoving them into envelopes and licking stamps. Postings usually took me the whole night, as I had to drive at least 200 kilometres to spread the load as thinly as possible in the post boxes of Cape Town and its environs.

There was so much to do and it had to be done with such meticulous care that the distinction between underground life and normal life became increasingly blurred. Yet life had to be lived and people convinced that I was not involved in anything suspicious. Living became a complete lie – a double-sided existence in which I was often unsure which side I was living on. Such a schizophrenic existence was hard to maintain and at times I thought I was going mad. What normal person spent hours cutting up newspapers, rushing around buying fifty stamps here, a packet of envelopes there, or hiding themselves in dingy, secret rooms on sunny weekends to duplicate leaflets? What normal person had to tell lies constantly to explain periods of disappearance from the real world?

In May a letter arrived from the ANC instructing one of us to come to Britain to receive some special training. As Stephen was in no position to take leave from his newly acquired job, the duty fell on me. I flew up to Johannesburg on the way to London early in July, with a suitcase full of leaflet bombs. It was barely two weeks after the start of the Soweto uprising and the police were shooting school kids like rabbits. No better time to set off a few leaflet bombs, we thought.

I told no one, apart from Stephen, that I was going to Europe. To friends, family and employer alike I said that I was taking a holiday with friends in the Northern Transvaal. To back up my story I left a batch of postcards, dated a few days apart, for Stephen to post to Daphne and my parents telling them what a wonderful time I was having.

While in London I read in the papers that a number of leaflet bombs had gone off in central Johannesburg early in July. Later Stephen told me that he had found the triggering mechanism a vast improvement. By the time he had placed the fourth leaflet bomb that day he had become so blasé that he simply put the bomb down, stood back a distance and watched it go off. He experienced none of the terror that accompanied us during our first operation in March.

The overseas visit was not all work and I was able to see Robin again. My sudden appearance came as a complete surprise to her as she had not been told that I was coming. In the year that I had been away she had become fully involved in ANC work in London, to the extent that she felt it would not be wise for her to return to South Africa. I did not get much time to see her but promised that if I could save up enough money, I would make a special trip the next year to come and see her.

I was not told the purpose of my visit to Europe before leaving South Africa so I was surprised when I was sent off to East Germany for "special training", which turned out to be training in the art of creating and using improvised explosive devices. On returning to London I was told that my mission, when I got back to South Africa, was to blow up the coloured "Parliament" located next to the University of the Western Cape where I worked! The idea that I would be a latter-day Guy Fawkes was an exciting one, but I was told to wait for further instructions before doing anything.

At the end of July, shortly before I was due to return to South Africa, four ANC operatives were arrested in Cape Town for engaging in more or less the same kind of work that Steve and I had been doing. Their names were David and Sue Rabkin, Jeremy Cronin and Anthony Holiday. Steve and I were not to know it then but we were to meet Dave, Jeremy and Tony in prison two years later. Their arrests came as a shock to the comrades in London as they had been involved in the training of the four and had considered them a proficient and valuable team. The arrests altered the plans the ANC had in store for us – the sabotage of the coloured "Parliament" in Cape Town. Steve and I were now to take over from the four arrested and become the main propaganda cell in the Cape.

Back in Johannesburg I found that Stephen had only sent off one or two of the postcards I had left with him, and people all over were wondering what had happened to me. Normally I was a good letter-writer so it was understandable that my parents were growing frantic, especially after Stephen had told them some cock-and-bull story that I had been sick or was in hospital or something. Daphne was phoning for news every day and my boss at the university was also under the impression that I had been overcome by some dire misfortune.

I was instructed by the ANC to do nothing until further instruction when I got back to Cape Town. No word came for months and I grew increasingly frustrated and frantic. Something had to be done: the townships were in flames, the people were demonstrating in Cape Town's central business area, the whites were smelling teargas for the first time and seeing with their own eyes the brutality of the apartheid police. I wanted to break discipline, to do something, anything. I was a revolutionary after all. I couldn't sit around like everyone else and just watch events going by. To contain my impatience, I churned out leaflet bombs for the moment the signal was given.

During September the trial of David and Sue Rabkin and Jeremy Cronin took place in Cape Town. I followed the proceedings with close interest but could not take the risk of attending the court sessions. It was clear from the newspaper reports that the three were exemplary operatives and had done a good job in spreading the movement's literature during their three-year period of operation. They were charged with producing and posting 14 different pamphlets. What they had done was certainly inspirational and spurred us on to even greater efforts. But it made us angry that some of our comrades had been captured and that the enemy was using their trial as an opportunity to demonstrate to the public that "seditious" activity achieves nothing.

After being convicted, the prosecution called on the judge to consider the death penalty because of the seriousness of the case. There would have been a massive outcry had he resorted to it as whites were only sentenced to death in the most extreme circumstances. David Rabkin was sentenced to 10 years' imprisonment and Jeremy Cronin to seven. Sue Rabkin was sentenced to 12 months with 11 months suspended: she was pregnant and gave birth while in prison. The judge explicitly stated that he was imposing such harsh sentences because he wanted them, above all, to act as a deterrent to others. It had exactly the opposite effect on us.

Tony Holiday's trial took place separately in Pretoria in November and had the same effect upon us as the earlier trial. He was charged with producing and distributing 12 different leaflets and pamphlets, of recruiting people and receiving financial assistance from the ANC. He was sentenced to six years' imprisonment.

Now we knew the price of commitment.

Instruction finally came from the ANC in the form of a draft for a leaflet to be disseminated by means of leaflet bombs on or around Heroes' Day – 16 December. Stephen, fortunately, was going to be in Cape Town at that time as his university was closed over the Christmas period. As the 16th was a public holiday – a day celebrated by the whites as the day of a major victory over the forces of black resistance the previous century – we chose to do the job on the 15th.

Stephen placed two bombs in central Cape Town at around midday and I did two after work at a railway station and bus station in the suburbs. The incidents made headlines again.

The message on the leaflets, important as it was, was not as important as the fact that it was coming from the ANC. The newspapers, by reporting the incidents, spread the message that the ANC was alive and active. This had a far greater impact than the actual leaflets. It is because of the propaganda effect that these actions had, that restrictions were later placed on giving prominence to them.

At the end of 1976 I abandoned the secret room for a new place. I had found the perfect premises: a small flat in a quiet area of Cape Town on the side of Table Mountain. The flat was around the back of a block of flats and had originally been used by a caretaker, but for some reason was no longer used for that purpose. It was separate from the other flats in the block and did not use the same entrance. It had a bedroom, kitchen and small bathroom. Our finances had improved somewhat so I fitted it out to look like a normal habitation. I brought in furniture, a small cooker, a fridge and other paraphernalia. While most of these luxuries were superfluous to the job in hand, they made the work more bearable as I could carry on late into the night, prepare meals, have a shower, stay overnight and then go to work the next morning.

Not only did I change our premises but I changed our equipment too. I bought an addressing machine and a new typewriter, and buried the old one in a deep hole in the dense bush of the Cape Flats. We had been taught that it was essential to make regular changes of equipment – typewriters especially – as the police could only prove that you had produced a particular pamphlet or leaflet if they could link it to specific items of equipment in your possession.

Changing premises, purchasing equipment and just doing what we were doing made us realise how advantageous it was to have white skin while running an underground cell in apartheid South Africa. No one suspected a white person of being engaged in subversive activities against the state – whites were never "terrorists". A white skin was a passport to places where blacks would automatically be under suspicion. A black person could not, for instance, walk into a shop and buy a duplicator without questions being asked; go to an estate agent and rent a flat to set up a printing factory or hide arms. In the overcrowded housing in the townships, where could a black person hide to produce revolutionary literature or make weapons for the armed struggle?

It struck us as a great pity that so few whites were prepared to participate in the struggle for a free and democratic South Africa.

In January 1977 I carried out the first major job in our new role. It was to produce and distribute *Vukani! – Awake!* – the underground journal of the "ANC Support Group". Pamphlets under this title had been produced and distributed by several groups before us – Dave Rabkin's and Jeremy Cronin's being the last. Our mailing list had grown very long by this stage so the job took me many days to complete. How I wished Stephen was there to help me.

In February a draft arrived for *Inkululeko – Freedom*, No.20, the underground journal of the South African Communist Party. It was pages and pages in length and it took so long to produce that I developed muscular cramps while sitting on an upended bucket turning that duplicator handle.

In early June, Stephen rang to tell me that some right-wing outfit at his university was organising a sociology conference at the university and were so desperate for delegates that they were dishing out free air tickets. I understood him to mean that I should take advantage of the offer to bring him some leaflet bombs to be set off on the anniversary of the start of the Soweto uprising on 16 June. I felt no compunction in doing so as the organisation in question had clearly demonstrated its antipathy towards the liberation struggle, and the ANC had said that we should try to set off some leaflet bombs around that date.

So off I flew to Johannesburg, free of charge, with a suitcase full of leaflet bombs for Stephen. I attended one token session of the conference and then returned to Cape Town. Stephen did a marvellous job with the bombs on 15 and 16 June, the incidents receiving wide coverage in the press.

Leaflet "bombings" had become our stock in trade and we no longer regarded placing them as any big deal. In fact, we looked at them as routine operations and enjoyed watching their effects. From the half hour that we had set the timers on the first occasion, we had reduced the timing to three minutes. That gave us plenty of time to get out of the immediate vicinity of the blast and to a suitable vantage point. The packaging of the bombs was such that they never aroused suspicion and no one ever took any notice if you dumped one next to a pile of rubbish or in a bin. We could not help thinking how easy it would have been to carry out acts of sabotage in the same way, for the puny leaflet bombs were, technically speaking, the same as real bombs. This, probably, was why the cops took them so seriously.

In June 1977 I went to Britain again but this time openly and at my own expense. The objective was to see Robin and spend some time with her. But, as I should have expected, my holiday turned into a work session for the ANC. This was largely because the ANC was reluctant to let me return after I reported a number of suspicious incidents that had occurred shortly before leaving for Britain. Several letters written in invisible ink that I had received had not developed properly, leading them to suspect that they had been "pressed" by the security police to make a copy of the cryptic message before being sent on; a card containing a list of names on microfilm appeared to have come apart, revealing the film. In addition, on the day of my departure for Britain there had been a strange phone call allegedly from South Africa to one of my secret postal contacts in London. On checking with the telephone exchange, the comrades found that there had not been any long-distance calls to the number – meaning that it must have been made locally.

I had only meant to stay for two weeks but ended up staying

six. At the end of that time I was given clearance to return, but only because of the pressure I had exerted. Prison, I insisted, was preferable to spending the rest of my life in exile in London. However, I agreed that if there were any more signs that could be interpreted as police surveillance, both Stephen and I would leave immediately.

On return to South Africa everything appeared normal. To make sure, I did nothing for a month. There were no signs that I was being watched and no more strange happenings. Either the police were playing a game or their investigative skills were better than I had given them credit for. The episode made me angry: The cops can go to hell, I thought. If we allow ourselves to be intimidated by our own imaginings then we'll get nothing done. Let's get on with the job. If they're going to pounce then let them do so, but only after we've done something spectacular.

This line of thinking prompted our next action, the one of which we felt the proudest at the time. To coincide with a visit by Stephen to Cape Town in September, I made two leaflet bombs and a large banner to hang from a tall building in the centre of Cape Town. The banner was huge: about ten metres long by one metre wide with the words "ANC LIVES" painted on it, and at the bottom the black, green and gold colours of the ANC flag.

It was rolled up with hundreds of leaflets inside and fitted with an exploding release-device set to go off after five minutes of being hung up. With a loud report it would unfurl and drop the leaflets into the street below.

At lunchtime on the chosen day, I fixed the banner to a railing on the outside of the top floor of a parking garage in the centre of Cape Town by means of a steel chain and a large padlock. To prevent the cops simply cutting the chain to remove it, I threaded an electrical wire through the links to make it appear as if the device was booby-trapped. On the box containing the timer and battery I stuck a label with the words: "*Danger!/Gevaar!* Do not remove. Explosives inside." The timer controlling the explosive release-device was started in the same way as the leaflet bombs, by pulling out a triggering pin.

At the same time as I fixed the banner, Stephen placed the two leaflet bombs in the street below. All went off more or less simultaneously, creating a tremendous effect with leaflets cascading to the ground from the banner above and rising to the sky from the blasts below. Leaflets were blowing around in the air for a long time afterwards. We stood around to watch the effects. People ran from all directions to snatch up the leaflets, others in the opposite direction to escape the scene.

Some civic-minded citizens (white of course) gathered up as many leaflets as they could to hand to the police. But there were so many leaflets in the street that there were enough for everyone. People stood in bewilderment at the spectacle. One pedestrian even asked Stephen what was going on: "Some bloody terrorists have put a bomb in the street," he replied agitatedly.

In no time police vehicles with sirens blaring and lights flashing arrived on the scene. Even an ambulance arrived – to create an effect no doubt. The banner remained in position for at least half an hour as the police struggled to remove the padlock. Clearly the fake wires had acted as the deterrent they were intended to be. A cop told us after our detention six months later that they went through half a dozen hacksaw blades trying to cut the hardened steel hasp of the padlock.

While Stephen was in Cape Town, he indicated that he couldn't tolerate Johannesburg any longer; that he was thinking of chucking in his job at the university and returning to Cape Town. He realised that he would be out of work again but had decided that unemployment was preferable to not being involved in underground work. To survive, he could get a grant to do a master's degree in sociology at the University of Cape Town. This would have to be paid back at a later date but the imperatives of our underground work were more important than any future financial problems he would have to face. He could only return to Cape Town at the end of the university term in December, however.

After the exploding banner we produced a *Vukani! – Awake!* every month until February 1978. The October, November and December issues I produced on my own but the two 1978 issues were produced together with Stephen. Producing the pamphlets – you could call them newspapers – was a mammoth task as each consisted of about six typed, foolscap-sized pages. The articles were thoroughly researched and carefully written and covered a range of topical subjects. We bought vast quantities of paper, envelopes and stamps; our mailing list had become as long as we could handle.

Several amusing but frightening incidents happened while out posting the *Vukanis*. On one occasion when I got out of my car to post a bundle of letters across the road, the door slammed shut and I was locked out with the engine still running. I had no choice but to smash a fanlight window. The street was busy and I'm sure a passing pedestrian took my registration number. On another occasion I was stopped for speeding. On the back seat were two suitcases full of unposted *Vukanis*. When the cop jumped out in the road to flag me down I did not know it was for speeding and thought it might be a roadblock. When he did not search my car or arrest me for subversion, and only presented me with a speeding ticket, I actually thanked him gratefully. He thought I was weird.

The most frightening incident happened, of all places, about a hundred metres from the headquarters of the security police in Cape Town. As I pulled away from a set of traffic lights I smelt something burning. Suddenly a cloud of smoke poured through the dashboard. The car was on fire, and on the back seat were thousands of leaflets in suitcases. I quickly stopped at the side of the road, opened the bonnet and saw that the battery lead was shorting against the bodywork – the sparks had set alight the oily residue on the side of the engine compartment. Fortunately I had some old rags in the boot and quickly smothered the flames. If the car had burned out at that spot, I would undoubtedly have been in hiding that night.

At the end of the year Stephen handed in his resignation and moved back to Cape Town. As my two flatmates, Heri Hirt and Klaus Hartmuth – German students at the University of Cape Town – were away on holiday, Stephen temporarily came to stay with me. When he started his course, he would move to his parents'.

It was good to have comradeship again, to be able to work together and plan our operations collectively. I tended to become a bit disorganised when working alone. There was no one to observe if I stuck to my programmes or even had any. Hardest of all was maintaining discipline. I tended to work too much as there was more certainty in my underground life than in my aboveground one. This resulted in endless personal problems and family complications. Daphne broke up with me a number of times but I could never tell her the reasons for the tensions in our relationship; my family thought I was the most uncommunicative person in the world.

Our first action as a reconstituted cell was also our last leafletbombing action. We planned it for 16 December, Heroes' Day, again. But acting on a premonition, we decided at the last moment to postpone it for a week. Since we had carried out most of our actions around commemorative days, we reckoned it would be safer to avoid them for a while. And we can thank our lucky stars that we did, for the security police, as we later found out, had sent one of their big-shots from Pretoria to Cape Town to witness the expected "bombings". This particular cop later told us that he was "damn annoyed" that he had to come all the way to Cape Town for nothing and then as soon as he got back to Pretoria he saw on television that a spate of leaflet bombs had gone off in Cape Town.

Over a period of two days we set off ten leaflet bombs. They were targeted at crowds of Christmas shoppers in the centre of Cape Town and other suburban shopping areas. In order to watch the fireworks, we set the timers for a mere two and a half minutes. They certainly were spectacular. The leaflets shot up into the air about fifteen metres but if there was any wind, they were lifted much higher. A cop later told us that they found leaflets on the tops of buildings 75 metres high and up to half a kilometre away.

During January and February 1978 there were a number of strange occurrences that worried us greatly. Every few days there were odd phone calls. The same voice always asked for "John" and we repetitiously replied that there was no "John" at the number. After a while we started to keep a diary of the phone calls. Then one day there was a suspicious-looking character sitting on the balcony railing directly outside our front door. Another day there was someone standing on the pavement directly opposite our flat. The person looked like the stereotypical security cop: short hair, obligatory moustache, clashing outfit, mean appearance.

From all this it might seem obvious that we were being watched. But after you have being working underground for two and a half years you begin to think everybody is watching you – paranoia easily gets the better of you. The trouble is that you're never quite sure. You can't flee the country every time someone appears to be staring at you or every time you get a wrong number. In the end, when you do see someone who appears to be watching you, you tell yourself that you're just getting paranoid and that you shouldn't worry about it.

But, as it so happened, these were real cops doing real surveillance and not our imaginations playing games with us. The police told us after our arrest of some of the things we had done while they had us under surveillance, which indicated how long they had been watching us. On one occasion we had lost them by driving down a one-way street. On another they had placed someone disguised as a drunkard in the graveyard opposite our flat, who was able to relate how I had removed and replaced my diving equipment from the built-in cupboard in my bedroom.

How the cops got on to us we will probably never know. I doubt if it was the result of one particular mistake on our part; more likely the result of careful police work over a long period of time. The security police were meticulous in their investigations and followed up the minutest details. For instance, I always bought the wood we used for the bases of the leaflet bombs from the same hardware dealer who sold it as off-cuts. The cops measured the wood and found it to be a non-standard gauge, leftovers from a commercial job. They were able to trace the manufacturer of the wood, who had originally ordered the wood and created the off-cuts, and ultimately where the off-cuts ended up – the hardware store from which I bought them.

Naturally we did make mistakes – that was inevitable. But I don't believe any of them were major, mostly just the result of not being thorough enough. It was easy to take short cuts, to not take enough care; you never knew how careful you needed to be. For example, to spread the word about ANC Radio Freedom broadcasts, I made up a rubber stamp giving the frequencies and times it could be received. I used it to stamp the details in telephone directories and on railway timetables but was not careful enough to do this far enough away from where we lived. It would thus have been reasonable for the police to conclude that the mystery stamper lived in the vicinity of the stampings. If the cops had investigated where most of our envelopes had been posted they would have found the heaviest concentrations nearest to where we lived.

Piecing together hundreds of unrelated scraps of evidence the cops were probably able to narrow down their suspicions to a very small number of people. Without doubt they had files on us from long before we began our work for the ANC. At university neither of us had been very circumspect about hiding our political leanings. From that starting point they would at a certain stage have been able to connect some of the evidence with us. Then it was only a matter of time if they decided to watch either of us.

Our own manner of operation and living was not beyond criticism. After a while it was easy to become blasé and let your guard slip: you stopped taking the necessary precautionary measures; you stopped looking over your shoulder and in your rear-view mirror; you stopped being disciplined in the way you were taught. I was going out with Daphne, a coloured woman, and Stephen was going out with an Indian woman, Feroza. This was bound to attract attention as only people with left-wing views were prepared to show open contempt for racist laws. While in Johannesburg, Stephen had made friends with "banned" people, some of whom regularly flouted their banning orders and visited him at his flat. Many of his other friends were politically involved types. Through my job I too had made a number of "undesirable" friends – i.e. blacks – who invited me to their homes in the townships, some of which places were out of bounds for white folks.

Our last action was one that the cops must have gloated about and which they used to time the moment of our arrest. We had decided to move our operating premises again and at the end of February foolishly brought all our equipment together for the move. We did this because the new place was due to become available a week after the old one had to be vacated. To span the gap, we hired a garage near our (residential) flat and moved everything from the old premises into it. We also moved several trunks of equipment to it, as well as banned books that we had hidden in other places, so that they too could be moved to new places.

The cops observed the move, which we carelessly made in broad daylight. From that moment a permanent watch was placed on us, which, if we had been alert enough, we would undoubtedly have noticed. In fact, we were so blind to what was happening that the cops started to play games with us. On the last Sunday before our arrest, Steve and I, together with Heri, Klaus, Daphne, Feroza and several other friends, held a braai (barbecue) at the side of the road running along the base of Table Mountain. While cooking our meat and swigging our wine, the cops drove up in their car and started their own braai just 30 metres away. As we were a "multi-racial" gathering someone from our group jokingly suggested that they were cops spying on us. To find out, Stephen in his drunken state went over and invited them to join us. Needless to say, they declined the offer!

Probably thinking that the moving of the equipment signalled that we were about to cease production or scarper, they decided to close in. Convinced that we were unaware of their surveillance, the cops planned their moves carefully, choosing the worst possible moment for us.

In the early hours of the morning of Thursday 2 March 1978 they moved in. Talk about being caught red handed!

Chapter Three

Detention

They came at three in the morning. The bell rang in an aggressive way and there was a loud banging on the front door. Instinctively we knew who it was. Stephen said to Feroza, who was sleeping with him that night, that he thought it must be the police – but he was thinking of a different sort of police to the sort she was thinking of. She leapt out of his bed and made herself a separate bed of blankets on the floor – she was thinking that she was about to be done for "immorality".

I sombrely climbed out of bed and made my way to the front door. What about all those contingency plans you've made for the day they come? Leap out the window, barricade yourself in your room and shoot at the bastards through the door! It all seemed a bit unrealistic at that moment and I found myself moving lemming-like towards my doom. Stephen parted the curtains above his bed and peered out into the street. The place was surrounded with police and police cars.

I could see torches waving about through the glass-panelled front door. I loosened the latch and immediately the door was pushed open. A bright beam of light shone into my face and someone asked if I was Timothy Jenkin. I replied in the affirmative, thinking fleetingly that maybe I should have said, "No, he's out!" A crowd of nasty faces leered at me. One of them formally pronounced: "We have reason to believe that you've been engaged in terrorist activities. We're coming in to search." Whereupon six or seven brutes barged in and began to tear the place apart. Whatever happened to search warrants?

The one who had spoken to me was dressed in clothes that were covered in blood. If this was meant to intimidate us, it did. When I saw it I thought, "Oh God! That must be the blood of some poor bastard he's been torturing. Soon mine'll be on there too." Later we found out that this blood-bespattered security policeman, who seemed to be heading the investigation, was the notorious "Spyker" ("Nails") van Wyk. His name cropped up in practically every major political case and especially whenever allegations of torture were heard. A self-confessed admirer of Hitler, he sported a little moustache like the Führer's but parted his dark, greasy hair down the centre instead of to the side. He was widely regarded by those who had the misfortune to find themselves in his company as a pathological sadist, the ideal-type interrogator of a totalitarian regime. The blood on his clothes could have come from a torture victim but it would not have surprised me if he had bought a pound of prime beef and squeezed the blood onto his trousers and shirt before knocking on our front door. His name definitely sits near the top of the list of the most notorious apartheid criminals.

I sat cross-legged on my bed and watched dejectedly as two or three of them emptied my drawers and wardrobe. The bookshelf was a source of considerable fascination and all "suspect" books were put to one side. I had always been careful to have only the most innocuous titles on my shelves but different people have different ideas of what constitutes innocuous.

Two policewomen walked past my bedroom door accompanying Feroza. They took her outside, presumably to an awaiting car. Then Klaus was taken outside, with a rather bewildered look on his face. "Lucky thing that Heri moved out last week", I thought. "He wouldn't have liked getting tangled up in something like this."

The chest at the end of my bed was locked so they demanded the key. I picked up from my bedside table the bunch of house and car keys that contained the key for the padlock on the chest, and tossed it to the cop. He opened the chest and pocketed the bunch of keys. As he did so a vision still lingering on my retina made me look back at the bedside table. On it lay the bunch of keys for our secret flat, the garage where all our equipment was stored and for all the trunks and toolboxes in it. It was a personal rule that those keys were never to be brought into the flat; they were always meant to be hidden in the springs under the front seat of my car. And never before had I brought them into the flat, except on that fatal night. Life is cussed.

Inside the chest were about fifteen volumes of carefully pasted and bound newspaper clippings, the main source of our articles for *Vukani – Awake!* Between the volumes the cop retrieved what at that moment seemed like a big find – my 9mm Star pistol.

I had bought the pistol on the instructions of the ANC and with ANC money at the height of the Soweto uprisings in 1976. The day I went to the gun shop to buy it there were so many scared whites clamouring for firearms that there were three rows of people against the counter. When I finally made it to the front, they presented the Star and said that it was all they had left. It looked suitable to my untrained eye so I paid R300 for it and forced my way out of the shop.

I had been instructed to take a gun on leaflet-bomb missions and to use it if accosted. I took it along once – on the time we did the banner – but never again because it was so bulky under my jacket it would have prevented me making a quick getaway. I probably couldn't have fired it in defence anyway – not for a leaflet bomb.

The cop who found the gun asked what I intended to use it for, but wasn't interested enough to wait for a reply. They must have known that I had a licence because no issue was made of it, and the gun was even handed back to my parents after our trial. The clippings seemed to be of more interest. The volumes were tied together and carted away, most of them never to be seen again.

After about half an hour they told me to get dressed and then accompanied me outside to an awaiting car, in which Stephen was already sitting. In a convoy we set off for Caledon Square Police Station, the head office of the Security Branch in Cape Town.

Up till then nothing too bad had happened but when we arrived at Caledon Square the weight of what was happening suddenly descended upon me: I was in the hands of South Africa's security police, a gang of thugs with a notorious reputation. What we had always thought about was now really happening and the reality of it was far more frightening than I had ever imagined.

Events began to connect: all those strange phone calls, the dark characters lurking about outside our flat. Why the hell hadn't we trusted our suspicions? If they've arrested us then they must have been watching us for the past several days or weeks. They must have seen us moving all the equipment, seen where our secret flat was. They must know everything!

At Caledon Square, Stephen and I were separated. I was taken into a room that was bare, save for a couple of tables and chairs. They handcuffed my right arm to the backrest of one of the chairs and told me to sit down. The cops vacated the room except for a tall, lanky, thick-looking one. He sat on the other chair and began to read his newspaper, as if what was happening was quite normal in his day's work. Stephen was being processed in another room.

I was left in the room like this for about half an hour before they came back. Some of them I recognised as members of the party that had invaded our flat, the others were new. One of them seated himself next to me while the others crowded around behind. Without saying anything, the sitting cop dropped the offending bunch of keys (the ones I had forgotten to hide) on the table in front of me. The clever bastards! How are you going to get out of this one? In front of me lay not just a bunch of keys for doors and padlocks, but the keys to unlock us – the keys to our entire case.

I sat staring at the keys for a long time not believing my rotten luck. I admonished myself: If only you'd been more disciplined and made sure the keys were put in their place under the front seat of your car. But you've always put them there. How did they know to come on the one night you forgot?

Eventually the sitting cop asked what the keys were for. To make sure I gave the right answer he whisked my bunch of flat and car keys out of his coat pocket, jingled them in front of my nose and said that the keys on the table were neither for my flat nor my car – they had tested them. I looked at his mean face and swallowed, but said nothing. I stared at the keys again.

The silence was terrible. I wanted to speak, just to hear a friendly voice, but couldn't. Everything I had read and been told about interrogation suddenly came back to me: hold out as long as you can so that your comrades can get away. But there are no comrades to get away; we've both been captured. Be strong, never admit anything and deny everything. But it's obvious they know what the keys are for, otherwise why would they use them for their opening move? Well just for your own self-respect don't speak to the fascist bastards.

I sat staring at the keys for what must have been the best part of half an hour. They seemed to be in no immediate hurry. The interrogator did not become vicious, and remained remarkably patient. He pointed to a particular key on the bunch and asked what it was used for. "What about this one? And these ones here?" I refused to respond.

Some of the spectators could not contain their curiosity and began to egg on the interrogator. "Perhaps his tongue needs a little loosening? Should we bring some oil? We'll make your tongue start wagging. Soon you won't be able to stop talking."

In response, the interrogator appeared to become a bit impatient and started to raise his voice, which cut at the nerves in my stomach. The others joined in, in chorus. Then the name-calling and racist taunts started – the usual fare of South African interrogation sessions. "This little *kaffir*-lover must speak to us now. He's been *naai*-ing (from the Afrikaans to "sew", meaning to have sex with) coloured girls again. Can't find a nice white *meisie* (girl) so he's got to screw *kaffir meide* (black maids). This one likes to *naai* with the *dame* on top; the other one likes to do it standing. You piece of communist filth, you shouldn't be allowed to live. You're just wasting air. Let's muck him up."

They didn't muck me up. The mob went away and I was left in peace again. It was obvious that their strategy, apart from trying to frighten the hell out of me, was to make me feel like a piece of worthless rubbish – a well-known interrogation tactic. Make them hate themselves; make them lose their self-esteem; then they talk.

A short while later a second shift came in. At the head of the team was the ubiquitous Spyker van Wyk. This time he was washed, shaved, combed and dressed in a fresh safari suit. No sign of any blood. A clean canvas, I thought. With him was a particularly nasty specimen of a security cop by the name of Van Aggenbach. Torturer's lines were deeply ingrained into his prematurely wrinkled face and his drooping mouth uttered suitably vicious threats of the actions he would soon be carrying out.

Spyker sat down beside me and grasped the bunch of keys. "You're going to tell us what these keys are for. I don't care if you won't tell us now. We've got plenty of time. We've got ways of making you talk." "Ve haf our vays!" So, fascists really do say these things: I had thought they were only said in caricatures of evil Nazi interrogators.

Spyker was the heavy. He was the nasty, coarse, rough interrogator who frightened the life out of you but to whom you were determined to say nothing. The previous one was the pleasant, civilised, friendly interrogator who pretended almost to be sympathetic with you, in whom you almost felt you could confide after the rough one had done you over. This was the "hot and cold treatment" we had read about – another well-known interrogation technique.

Spyker wanted an answer – quickly. The threats increased. He alluded to the previous interrogator by saying that it didn't pay to have patience with the likes of us. Van Aggenbach in particular wanted action. He wanted Spyker to hand me over to him; he would soon get me singing like a canary.

Their next moves were totally stereotypical: "We know everything so you may as well speak. Your comrade has told us everything. He's not being stubborn like you. This will soon be over if you just cooperate." Spyker then accompanied me to an adjacent room where piles of intercepted *Vukanis* were being sorted and processed by a team of typists.

"See how you've been wasting your time. We pick up every pamphlet you send. We've got them all, every single one you've ever sent. We've been watching you since the day you put your foot back in South Africa. The ANC just used you people to do their dirty work. Those bastards in London are the ones we'd really like to get our hands on. They're the ones who cause all the trouble, from the comfort of their big mansions. The ANC has forgotten you now. You're all on your own. Nobody cares..."

Then up to the photographic department. A balaclava was pulled over my head and a dozen pictures of different profiles were taken with blinding flood lights shining in my eyes. "That's him. We've got him now. He's the one who's been causing all the trouble. You're in for big shit my friend." After about two hours with Spyker and his team I was beginning to feel that there was no longer any reason for not saying what the keys were for.

It was obvious that they knew, otherwise why would they be so interested in them. Spyker did not want to listen to answers that I didn't know what they were for or that they belonged to someone who had left them in my flat by mistake. I could sense that Van Aggenbach was dying to get started on his tongue-loosening techniques, and so to prevent Spyker getting any more blood on his clothes I said I would take them to see.

This seemed to please them but it made me hate myself. I felt like a collaborator. But I had no stomach for the sort of violence that would surely have followed. A protected upbringing had not prepared me well for the interrogation room. I had always been one of the smallest at school and soon learned to avoid playground fights. Later I abhorred body sports such as rugby that were compulsory at high school. And quiet suburban life meant that there were no street brawls and scenes of violence to immunise me. It made me realise that in a perverse sort of way black people had an advantage here. Forced to live under the poverty of apartheid, life in the townships was characterised by street life, crime and violence of the worst kind. Knife battles, shootings, murders, rapes and gang fights were so common that the unfortunate residents of those places become immune to violence and bloodletting. On top of this, they regularly experienced police violence and the heavy-handedness of the apartheid authorities.

They handcuffed me to another cop and marched me out to an awaiting car in the street. Without me giving any directions, they set off for Mowbray where the garage was located. When the car turned into the narrow cul-de-sac where the garage was situated, there was a grand reception waiting for us. There was Steve, Klaus and – oh no! – Heri too, all waiting with their escorts to whom they were handcuffed, plus a large contingent of police spectators. I felt like the star arriving at the gala opening of the opera.

Despite the reception ceremony directly in front of the suspect garage, the charade was kept up. I was handed the bunch of keys and asked to open whatever it was I had brought them along to see. I unlocked the padlock on garage number 50 and swung up the door. There it all stood. All the evidence any prosecutor could ever want. I don't know what they had told Heri and Klaus but I'm sure the two of them were thinking that they'd got themselves tied up in a big-time robbery investigation. A garage full of furniture, metal trunks, toolboxes and household goods. What else could it be?

The detectives moved in. They opened the trunks but did not

touch the contents until everything had been well photographed. One trunk contained all the banned books we had accumulated over the years. Goodbye to those. The other trunk contained all our addressing machine stencils – thousands of names – and bits and pieces of partly-made leaflet bombs. The toolboxes contained the specialised collection of tools we had managed to build up. Goodbye to all that.

One of the cops dug out of the trunk with the books a Russian dictionary I had bought seven years previously with the intention of learning the language one day. "Aha!" he exclaimed in seriousness, "I suppose youßre working for the KGB too." Vaunting his investigative skills, Spyker asked if we had not seen his ten-year-old son watching us the previous Sunday while we were unloading the equipment into the garage. Maybe we had, but who would suspect a little kid of spying on you?

On the way back to Caledon Square I wondered what more they could possibly want from us. They already had enough evidence to put us away for life. In our carelessness we had certainly made things easy for them. I felt embarrassed in a way. In one of our leaflets we had advised activists how to run an underground cell: "Don't keep all your equipment in one place; keep revolutionary literature and secret documents hidden..." We had broken all the most obvious and basic rules. We hoped our comrades would never find out.

Back in the office they threw a pad and pen on the table in front of me and told me to write: about everything, from the first day till the last. So I started to write. I wrote four pages and handed it to them. Spyker took one look, smiled, and tore it up. He repeated threateningly that he wanted everything, not just the obvious. He wanted to know how we had got involved with the ANC, what sort of training we had received, what we had done in South Africa. Everything, and lots of names. He especially wanted names.

The next pad I filled completely. They took it away for scrutiny and I was presented with another and told that I would be filling many, many such pads before I was finished. I felt as if I was writing an examination. So, I continued to write. I didn't mind writing. So long as I was writing I wasn't being beaten up. I reasoned that if there was going to be any violence it would surely be at this early stage soon after capture. If I wrote about things they seemed to know then it would be possible to write without giving much away. The things they didn't know about needn't be mentioned, provided that what I wrote was within the realms of the possible. I invented many names, James Bond situations and fantastic "terrorist" plots to satisfy their insatiable interrogators' appetites.

As soon as I completed each pad it was whisked away for examination and a new one was placed on the table. By the end of the day I had written so much that I was suffering from severe writer's cramp. What I wrote was loosely based on the truth but was mostly fiction: how we had gone abroad to join the ANC, how the organisation had given us months of specialised training in secret hideouts deep in the countryside, how we had been "indoctrinated" and taught to write "subversive" literature, how we planned to set up nationwide underground networks and anything else I thought would excite them. I was able to avoid giving away any names by saying that the people who trained us had used *noms de guerre*.

By late afternoon the cops who had been up all night decided they'd had enough. I was handed over to three fresher looking specimens and driven to the Milnerton Police Station about ten kilometres away to be stored for the night. In the charge office they removed my spectacles, watch, belt and shoelaces. They didn't want a suicide on their hands, they hinted.

Then to the cells. I had never seen a cell before. First a heavy, solid steel door. Then a sort of cage with a barred gate. Through this and into what appeared to be an exercise yard: a small concrete rectangle with smooth, high walls and more bars across the top. No helicopter is going to lift you out of here, matey! Then into the cell proper: first another solid steel door, then another cage and grille, and then the cold concrete darkness of the cell itself.

The clang of the doors closing on me and the sound of the keys turning suddenly drove home to me the gravity of my situation. I stood for a long time staring disbelievingly at the back of the closed door. Was it really me in this situation? The cell was cold, dank and stark; the two windows so heavily barred and meshed that very little light penetrated from the outside and the cell's lamp so weak that it lit no more than an orange ring around itself.

I thought of those books we had read while receiving our training. Yes, they were accurate. I felt as if I'd been here before. What did the prisoners do to overcome the nothingness of such situations? They paced up and down. But there was no space to walk in this cage. Two paces and I was up against the wall. I wasn't going to be like them so I lay down on the bed and stared at the ceiling. Spider webs hung from the corners and the paint was grey and peeling. As I looked at it I saw the face of Spyker in the dust and flaking paint. Terror filled my body and I burst into tears.

At no stage of our detention were Stephen and I informed that we had been detained under Section 6 of the notorious Terrorism Act. Although we guessed that this was the case, no mention was made of any rights that we might have had, of the nature of our detention or even of why we were being detained. Both of us knew that under Section 6 we had no rights at all. No outsiders, not even lawyers, family or friends were allowed access to us or any information about or from us. No court was allowed to "pronounce upon the validity of any action taken under the section". In other words we were being held incommunicado and at the mercy of the security police in a totally closed system. What happened to the rule of law?

Section 6 was created explicitly for interrogation purposes. This meant that detainees were held indefinitely without charge until they had "satisfactorily replied to all questions" or until "no useful purpose (was) served by... further detention". "No useful purpose" usually meant that the detainee was dead. From June 1967 to July 1982, the period the Act was in force, no less than sixty people died in detention while being held under Section 6. Naturally, the police denied on all occasions being responsible for the deaths and always explained them away as "suicides" or due to "natural causes". Even if this was the case, it was never explained why so many detainees found the need to commit suicide while being held under Section 6.

The Terrorism Act came under such intense criticism that it was replaced by the Internal Security Act in July 1982. The new Act was a more refined piece of legislation but Section 29 of the Act, which was the equivalent of Section 6, differed very little from the latter as far as detainees were concerned. To mollify public opinion about mistreatment and torture, certain "safeguards" were added to give the impression that detainees were held under the watchful eye of "inspectors", doctors and magistrates, and thus protected from harm. But in a totally closed system there was no one to check that the "inspectors" had carried out their duty, and even if they had, no one could know what the outcome of the "inspections" were or whether any action was taken if it was necessary to do so. In theory there was a maximum detention period of six months built into the Section but this could be overstepped if the police provided reasons to the Minister of Law and Order (euphemism for police) why the detainee should not be released. Many people were held for well over the six-month period and deaths in detention continued.

These so-called security laws were in fact not laws at all. They were merely a disguise used by the regime to give a legal appearance to arbitrary actions it took against its opponents. They were the direct antithesis of law, a cover for barbarism, a means to bypass the law altogether.

The interrogation continued the next day. While waiting for them to begin, Stephen was brought into the room. Spyker pointed to Stephen's knee that was swollen and told him to tell me how it had happened. He'd tried to escape! I felt very proud of Stephen at that moment, although the object of the demonstration was to try to show me how silly it was to try to get away. Although I was not allowed to know it then, Stephen had very nearly broken free of their clutches. The previous day he had complained of a serious stomach ache and was taken to a doctor who happened to have his rooms on the first floor of a building. In the doctor's surgery, Stephen's minders had carelessly not placed themselves between him and the window. Stephen, seeing his chance, leapt out of the window, onto a ledge outside and then onto a lower building next door. As he made the final leap his knee caved in and he crouched for a moment in agony. This gave the cops their chance. One of them ran to the window and pointed his pistol at Stephen and ordered him to freeze. The cop was so shocked at this brazen escape attempt that his hand was shaking violently, but Stephen reckoned it wisest not to take another chance and raised his hands in submission. He would have got clean away had he landed properly because the next leap to the ground was a short distance and the cops would have had to run from the first floor and a long way around the building to get to the place where he would have reached ground.

Stephen set a fine example that first day, which set the tone for the future. He planted in our minds the seed that grew into an obsession: to find a way of eluding our captors. I wasn't to see him again after that until much later. His interrogation, I found out later, followed much the same pattern as my own.

Meanwhile, I was required to continue writing and each completed pad was followed by an interrogation session. After a while they appeared to lose interest in what I was writing. I was making it too easy for them. They appeared also to lose "respect" for me because I did not resist their demands sufficiently. I was accused of being "not properly trained" and the names of certain people, who had alleged torture while in detention, were mentioned as examples of people who had been "well-trained". Plainly I had denied them the opportunity to engage in some wholesome torturing and this had led to their declining interest in me.

What they were most interested in was in laying their hands on the different typewriters we had used in our work since the beginning of our activities. Only if they could connect the different typewriters to us could they positively identify a particular leaflet or address label as being produced by our cell. If there was no typewriter, they could not claim in court that we were responsible for producing a particular leaflet or for posting it, even if we admitted to it.

By studying the typefaces of the leaflets and addresses they had identified five different typewriters. One was already in their possession, found in the garage with all the other equipment. It could only be connected to the leaflets and pamphlets produced during the previous year – in other words, our current typewriter. They wanted to know where all the others were.

One I admitted belonged to my parents, so that was immediately fetched. Another was one at the university where I had worked, which had only been used to type some address labels. So it was into the cars and off in a convoy to the university. At the university the rector, Dr Richard van der Ross, an obdurate stooge, received the delegation. He insisted my handcuffs be removed and then proudly led the way to the outbuilding where I had worked. As we trooped down the corridor of the Institute, sympathetic (to me) heads peeked out of doorways, but no one said a word. The secretary was busy typing on the offending typewriter and was unceremoniously forced to end her duties when the typewriter was unplugged in front of her and carried off.

The cops wanted the other two typewriters, one of which they knew had been used to type all our leaflets of 1975 and 1976. The one they had in mind was the one that I had buried, but I was damned if they were going to get it. The fifth one I wasn't sure about: it could have been one of many but probably another one at the university. Because of their eagerness to get the typewriters I told them that the one that we had used for the leaflets (the buried one) I had thrown into the sea and the other probably belonged to my brother who was then living in Johannesburg. Being so far away I thought they would just write that one off as it had been used very little. But no, not only did they get the Johannesburg police to "arrest" the suspect typewriter, they arrested my brother as well.

The typewriter that I said I had thrown into the sea they wanted too. Some quick thinking was needed. The Cape Peninsula consists of many kilometres of coastline, much of it sandy beaches. It was these parts that I knew best but I couldn't say I threw it into the waves on a flat beach. I had to think of a specific precipitous and rocky place where the water was deep. There was only one such spot that I knew well, a place where I had frequently been to poach crayfish, so I thought I would try it on. The place was a rocky headland a few kilometres south of the coastal suburb of Camps Bay, along the scenic coastal road to Llandudno. At that point, the rocks rose steeply, about fifty metres out of the sea to the road. A short distance down from the road was an ideal place from where it would have been possible to discard a typewriter. The pools below were deep and surrounded by rocks. Invariably the water was rough.

One afternoon they took me to point out the spot. It certainly was splendid to see the sun and waves again after days and nights in dark interrogation rooms and police cells. Having pointed out the supposed location and been photographed doing so, I imagined that was the end of the story. Not a chance. Two days later I was driven back to the same spot and there, waiting eagerly for us, was a team of reserve police divers kitted out with wetsuits and aqualungs and raring to go.

The divers donned their equipment and each chose an area of the seabed to cover. The search went on for a good two hours, but I didn't mind: I was getting a nice tan and knew that I wouldn't be seeing that beautiful place again for a long time. Eventually the divers emerged from the water, cold, tired and without the typewriter. The leader of the group wagged an angry finger at me and accused me of misleading them – the nerve. He demanded to know exactly where I had dropped the machine, but I apologised that I could be no more helpful. Maybe it had corroded away or some recreational divers had found it, I suggested.

This he would not accept, claiming that his team had found wedding rings in muddy dams. Security policemen mumbling terrible retribution hurriedly took me away from the place. I expected the worst but nothing more was said about the typewriter. I suppose they had enough evidence without it.

The next stage of the investigation involved our being taken out, separately and without the other knowing, to the places where we had placed leaflet bombs. These "pointing out" sessions were common in the investigation of political cases in South Africa. They involved the accused being forced to point out the places where they were supposed to have committed their alleged crimes.

In our case they told us to direct them to the places where we had planted the leaflet bombs, even though they knew exactly where most of them were. At the places, they told us to stand and point to the exact spot so that they could take a photograph. While this gave the police evidence for their case against us, it also gave us evidence of how effective their efforts had been in tracing the places where we had placed leaflet bombs. On a number of occasions both of us pointed out spots about which the police knew nothing. This made them really mad because they thought we were having them on. As it turned out, the police only knew of 26 leaflet bombs while we had planted at least 10 more. Never had any failed to go off, so technical failure was not an explanation for this disparity. Excited witnesses of the explosions on the undiscovered occasions must have scooped up all the leaflets as well as the remains of the bombs.

Under normal circumstances, we would of course never have allowed ourselves to be used by our legal opponents to collect their evidence against us. Lawyers would definitely have advised against it – if we had been allowed to receive legal advice while being held in detention. But what could we do when we were in the clutches of the security police and entirely cut off from the outside world? Under their "security laws" they were "entitled" to keep us in detention for as long as it took them to amass all the evidence they needed. They were not at all concerned about our defence or with the niceties of regular law.

After pointing out the scenes of our "crimes" in Cape Town, Stephen and I were taken separately in two cars to Johannesburg to point out the places where we had placed leaflet bombs there. Arriving on a Friday evening, our minders deposited us at the notorious John Vorster Square police cells, where we were lodged for the weekend while they had a restful two days at a comfortable police residence.

The local cops, after issuing us with straw mats, ordered us to undress and hand in our clothes. But when we protested strongly at the prospect of being kept naked for two days, our security police mentors for some reason supported our pleas and we were allowed to remain clothed.

Our cells were dreadful – large, dirty and barren. There was no water apart from what you could get from your toilet when you flushed it, and they refused to supply any toilet paper. Since I was not accustomed to using my hand to clean myself, I was compelled to rip out and use pages of the tatty Bible they provided. Forgive me God for it was all I could do!

John Vorster Square (now Johannesburg Central Police Station) was also a police station and the headquarters of the Johannesburg District and Witwatersrand Division of the South African Police. It contained one of the main offices of the security police and from this building, many floors up, a number of detainees had been thrown out of windows to meet their deaths on the pavement below. Both of us were taken up to these offices for further interrogation and, in Stephen's case, for an identification parade. In passing, the distance to the pavement below was pointed out to us.

Stephen's identification parade was a complete farce. The other members of the parade were all well-groomed and well-dressed security policemen while Stephen was haggard and unshaven after spending two days in the cells. It did not take the witness long to put her hand on his shoulder. It was alleged that the witness was a fruit seller who had seen Stephen place a leaflet bomb near the black entrance of Johannesburg station, nine months earlier.

After returning to Cape Town there were no more interrogation sessions – they had all the evidence they needed. I was dumped again in the Milnerton police cells to rot, while Stephen was kept in the less salubrious cells at Caledon Square. The only reading matter they allowed us was the Bible. Stephen managed to read quite far into his but I found it so boring that I gave up after a few pages and preferred to lie against the wall with only my thoughts to comfort me. I dreamed of escaping – I was not going to allow these bastards the privilege of seeing me put away for years. I studied my cell and exercise yard, looking for cracks. But without my glasses I couldn't find any. The time would come though; I could wait.

Our interrogation had been relatively uneventful compared to what the average detainee had to go through. We were fully aware that it was our white skins that had saved us from the usual mistreatment and torture. It was not that the security police never tortured white detainees – they were just more reluctant to do so. Coming from "respectable" backgrounds also helped us. My father was an eminent Cape Town anaesthetist and it would not have looked too good for the security police if it had come out in our trial that they had tortured the son of a well-known doctor.

Another factor that helped us, we found out later, was that the security police knew we were the last propaganda cell operating in the Cape. They knew what we had done and that there were no more cells to round up. David Rabkin and Jeremy Cronin before us had had a much rougher passage, as the cops knew that there was another group operating at the same time as theirs and wanted to know what they knew about the other group(s) (i.e. us).

The period of detention ended abruptly on the morning of 31 March, four weeks after our arrest, when I was unexpectedly released from my cell and told there was a surprise for me. I was taken into the charge office and there waiting for me was my sister and mother, tearful and looking burdened by the month's traumas. They brought the news that Stephen and I were to appear later that day in the Cape Town Magistrates' Court to face charges and that an attorney had been appointed by my father to look after my affairs. My mother muttered something about whether it was true that I had been held for planting bombs. As it was too complicated to explain there and then, I could only reply that it was the function of the court to find out.

By prevailing standards, our period in detention was almost a record because it was so short. We put this down to the same factors that applied to our length of interrogation, but also because we had handed them all the evidence they could have wanted on a platter. The worst aspects of detention, apart from worrying about what could happen to us while under interrogation, were not knowing what was going to happen next and how long they would hold us in solitary confinement. We always expected the worst but hoped for the best. We waited for them to come in and tell us it was all a terrible mistake, that they didn't think what we had done was very serious and that if we promised to be good, we could go home. It was the solitary confinement that messed things up. Left with our disturbed thoughts, we are unable to think about things rationally. When they locked us up after a day's interrogation, we were happy to be left on our own but if they didn't turn up the next day we couldn't help wondering where they were, when they were coming and what they had in store for us that day.

Solitary is very disorienting, a torture in itself. A week without seeing anyone feels like an eternity, but knowing that you might lie there for six months or longer is enough to weaken even the strongest. Certainties give hope; indeterminacy breeds despair. It was a very unpleasant experience but our period was too short and uneventful for me to be able to comment on its long-term effects.

As I have mentioned, ours were not the only detentions on 2 March. Our girlfriends Daphne and Feroza, our flatmate Klaus and ex-flatmate Heri were detained under Section 6 for between four and seven days. Klaus was the first to be released, after four days – probably because the German embassy kicked up a stink. Daphne and Feroza were released after six days and Heri after a week. All were held in solitary confinement in separate police cells around Cape Town. They were all thoroughly grilled for information on us but were unable to provide anything the police did not already know. Heri's room in the house he had been sharing with several other students was turned over, but was found to be devoid of any clues about our activities.

My brother Michael was also detained for several days; his typewriter for longer. The reason he was held, apparently, was to find out what he knew of Stephen's acquaintances while Stephen had been living in Johannesburg. The two of them had shared a flat and knew many of the same people. He also provided the police with information about my personal life. I did not hold this against him, as he was not a political person and probably did not know why we had been detained. He probably thought he was pleading in mitigation for me.

Meanwhile, Robin in London had not taken our detentions sitting down. By this stage she was working full time in the ANC office and so was in a good position to muster forces. Together with an uncle of Stephen's who was incensed by his nephew's predicament, friends who knew us while we were in London in 1974/75 and the Anti-Apartheid Movement, she organised a Stephen Lee and Tim Jenkin Defence Committee. Hundreds of postcards protesting our detentions were printed for sympathisers to send to Prime Minister BJ Vorster. The committee also, amongst other things, commissioned articles about our plight in trade union, left-wing and Catholic newspapers – the latter through the uncle. A demonstration was held outside the South African embassy in London at the start of our trial, calling for our release and the release of all South African political prisoners.

Chapter Four

Awaiting Trial

The court appearance on 31 March served no other purpose than to convert us from detainees into awaiting-trial prisoners. The security police had finished with us and were now placing us in the custody of the Prisons Service. Their preparations for indicting us were not complete but, as the real trial was set for 1 June, two months away, they had plenty of time to complete their work.

In a sense our appearance in court was a relief. It meant the re-establishment of links with the world and an end to uncertainty. Although our period of detention had been short compared to the average time detainees were held at that time, it had been wearing enough. In fact it was hard to imagine how people managed to put up with the strains of detention for six months or more.

The best part was being able to see some familiar and friendly faces again. In the courtroom were members of our respective families, friends from work and Heri, Klaus and Daphne. The appearance only took a few minutes. The Magistrate announced that we were to be charged under Article 2(1) of the Terrorism Act of 1967 and Article 11(e) of the Internal Security Act of 1950 (formerly called the Suppression of Communism Act).

We were not asked to plead to the charges and a state representative handed the Magistrate an order from the Attorney General stating that we were to be remanded in custody until we appeared for trial in the Cape Town Supreme Court. Bail was seldom granted in political cases, especially when the charges were considered to be serious.

The security police delivered us personally to Pollsmoor Prison – Cape Town's main prison – not trusting the courts or Prisons Service to do it. The new section of Pollsmoor to which we were taken had only been completed two years earlier and looked like a huge square fortress. Several floors of tiny slatted windows pockmarked the red exterior wall and at each of the four corners of the block was a tall guard-tower with armed guards.

Spyker and Van Aggenbach accompanied us into the reception room and then left without any human remark, not even a rude one. Hundreds of black prisoners were sitting in rows on the floor waiting for their turn to be fingerprinted and signed in. Those who had had their fingerprints done ritually wiped their inky thumbs in their hair and were hustled out of the room by impatient warders. There was much shouting and racist cursing, an ugly apartheid scene being repeated in one of the hundreds of prisons across the country.

We felt like queue jumpers when they told us to go to the head of the queue. But then we were whites and in apartheid South Africa it was not dignified for white people to stand in the same queue as blacks. Not only were we treated more speedily, but a pair of subdued warders personally accompanied us through the reception process and the maze of corridors to our new quarters.

Unlike most black South Africans, we had never seen the inside of a prison before. We had certain preconceived ideas about prisons from seeing American cop movies, but this was something different: very long corridors stretching into the distance with highly polished floors and along both walls, every two metres or so, large flush-fitting steel doors looking like giant safes in some vast underground bullion vault. The clinical, almost sterile, atmosphere was frightening. It was impossible to imagine how human beings could live in such a place.

This was the awaiting-trial prisoners' section, where not-yet-sentenced prisoners who had not been granted bail or who could not afford bail were held. At that time there were at least 20,000 such prisoners in custody in South Africa each day, most of them black.

Stephen and I were placed in two completely isolated cells in the section. They were extremely small, even smaller than the police cells we had been held in while in detention: about 2 metres by 1.5 metres.

The cells were bare, save for a tiny stainless steel basin on the one wall, a toilet bowl, and a small metal locker fixed to the opposite wall. High on the outer wall was a sealed, vertically slatted window with frosted glass, and looking into a short corridor was another, smaller, slatted window.

Two prisoners brought us thin rope mats – our beds they informed us – and our bedding. They later also brought us a meal and asked why we had been placed in "the bomb". At first, we thought this meant that we had been placed in special cells set aside for "bombers" like us. They gave us our first lesson in "prisonese": the "bomb" was an isolation section consisting of three cells used for the punishment of prisoners who had infringed prison regulations. Through the door of the "bomb" section we could hear the movements of other prisoners. They did not appear to be confined to their cells like us. So, our punishment was to start here, before we had been sentenced.

Although Steve and I could talk to each other through the locked, barred grilles (inner doors) of our cells (the outer steel panelled doors were left open during the day), both of us wondered how we were going to last two months being cooped up in those tiny cells with only half an hour of exercise each day. Admittedly, things were not as bad as in detention as we were permitted visits from relatives, reading matter and food parcels, and could write letters. On the other hand, the food was worse and the cells more cramped. In fact, the food was so awful that it made us vomit after two or three spoonfuls. Everything was boiled in fat and it was as though all the various ingredients had been slung into a giant boiler and cooked for at least six hours. The only way you could distinguish chicken from pork, say, was by the shape of the pieces of bone on which you choked. There was no way of identifying what vegetables, if any, had been thrown into the slop. After eating this swill for a few days both of us refused to eat it any longer and persuaded our parents to bring us salad vegetables and tinned meats that we could turn into relatively respectable meals.

It was hard to believe that black prisoners were much worse off than we were, as far as food was concerned. At that time, diets were graded according to your racial group. The Prisons Service later claimed that differential diets were eliminated and that everyone received the same diet "prescribed by professional dieticians... and based on modern requirements for the maintenance of health".

Africans received the worst and least food while coloureds and Indians received intermediary diets below the Grade I white man's diet that we received. Later we were to see black prisoners being made to squat in the exercise yard while they ate their meals. Their diet appeared to consist mainly of *mielie pap* (maize-meal porridge) with occasionally what could have been a piece of meat floating on top.

At Stephen's first visit, his father brought him, amongst other things, the book *Papillon* by Henri Charrière. This is the story of Charrière's multiple escapes from the French prison colonies on Devil's Island and in Guiana. Although reputed to be a true story, much of it is too fantastic to be believed. Nonetheless, it was one of the most fascinating books I had ever read and without a doubt one that profoundly affected our lives.

Both of us, naturally, had thought about escaping, but only in the most reflexive way. *Papillon* set us on the course of seriously considering the prospect. It taught us a number of valuable lessons that guided our thinking and actions in the months ahead. The first and most important of these was that if you want to escape from prison you have to approach the task with single-minded determination. Every moment of every day has to be devoted to observing, planning and preparation. No escape will be successful if it is approached in a half-hearted manner or if you place it below other objectives.

The second lesson was that while lucky breaks do occur, you can't depend on them and should avoid them. You have to plan your way out with obsessive thoroughness, taking into account every conceivable factor. At every point where something may not go according to plan you have to have a contingency plan, including one that allows you to reverse the action should it fail. While your plan has to take into account every possible detail, it has to be flexible enough to adapt to changes in routine or security that take place.

The third and most practical lesson was that an escape does not end once you are beyond the physical confines of your prison. This point boiled down to the fact that if you want to get away from the immediate vicinity of your prison quickly you must have money.

Papillon warned us to expect to find prisoners who would not be interested in escaping: such people could not contemplate the risks involved and were more interested in making their immediate circumstances as comfortable and bearable as possible. This was difficult for us to understand as we had always imagined that prisoners thought of nothing else but escaping. On top of this, our fellow prisoners would all be political prisoners who had a duty to escape. It was inconceivable that the struggle should cease while behind bars.

The overall message of the book, as we read it, was that there are two basic philosophies a prisoner can adopt while serving a sentence: a "getting out" philosophy or a "making out" philosophy. The former involves thinking of nothing else but how to get out of prison – to the extent that everything else is of little consequence, while the latter is the philosophy of acquiescence and resignation.

For us, *Papillon* was truly a manual of escape and came with many other valuable tips, chief of which are that an escape consists of two phases: (1) getting out and (2) getting away. Once out of your prison you should get away as far and fast as possible. Recapture activities will always be the most intense closest to the prison. Obviously, you need to have civilian attire when escaping as your prison uniform is a clear giveaway. After your escape, don't go to the nearest pub to whoop it up or anywhere that the prison authorities might expect you to go, such as your girlfriend, family or friends. Also, try as far as possible not to leave any clues about how you got out. This includes not using violence or accosting your captors. The use of violence will rebound on you heavily should you be recaptured, and if you damage the prison on your way out you can't abort the attempt to try another day.

Four days in the isolation cells were as much as we could stand. When the officer-in-charge came around to hear our "complaints and requests" we asked him why we were being kept apart from the other prisoners and subjected to the punishment of segregation before we had been sentenced.

His reply surprised us as we had thought that our separate confinement was something that had been prescribed by the security police or because they feared that we would contaminate the other prisoners with our radical ideas. He said that he had thought he was doing us a favour by keeping us apart from the "scum", as he could see that we were "decent" people. No, we assured him, we would rather be placed among the other prisoners because we did not wish to be treated differently. He shook his head and went away.

Within an hour we were moved out of the "bomb" and relocated in cells alongside the "scum", although next door to the warders' office in the section. Life was more bearable after that. Most of our fellow awaiting-trial prisoners were harmless down-and-outs who in most cases were in prison because they could not afford the bail that had been granted them. One poor fellow had been inside for four months because he could not muster the R2 bail he'd been granted after being accused of stealing a blanket from a train.

Some of the other prisoners were out-and-out criminals but certainly interesting characters. There was a bloke who had shot his wife with a crossbow, several drug smugglers – one of whom proudly went about displaying the hole between his nostrils caused by sniffing cocaine – some pimps and others who could not explain why they were in prison.

One talkative crook, who tried to cultivate our company in order to get at our food, told us of the many ingenious methods he had devised to smuggle money out of the country for rich businessmen. On one occasion he hollowed out a pair of cricket pads and re-stuffed them with rolled up banknotes. He flew out of the country with his cricket togs to the accompaniment of well-wishes from the passport controller. On another occasion he cut up the frame of a scrambler motorcycle, stuffed the tubes with notes and then welded it together again. He crated the bike and had it lifted aboard the ship on which he was travelling to Britain. He explained to customs that he was a member of the team of motorcyclists who were "going to show the Brits how to ride". Again, he was sent off with the blessings of the authorities. His philosophy was that if you were into smuggling you always had to have a reason for travelling that met with the approval of the authorities. That way there would be no problems.

He was also into fraud. He would hang about in the lobbies of large blocks of flats where the mailboxes were situated. After the postman had made a delivery, he would put his hand into the boxes and feel for credit cards. When he found one, he would do a pre-planned lightning tour of all the banks in the area where the card was valid and withdraw R50 from each. If he "hit" 30 banks he could take home R1,500 in a day. He could also buy himself a new wardrobe of clothes and much else besides.

There were many other crooked types who were only too eager

to boast about their misdemeanours. Most of them were sordid characters, who were incapable of separating fact from fantasy. They could all sense that we were not "ordinary criminals" and at times they were queuing up to clean our cells in return for favours of tobacco and food.

Prisoners were allowed to have visitors twice a week for half an hour at a time. There was no physical contact, and speech was through a telephone intercom. The panes through which prisoner and visitor viewed each other were of thick bulletproof glass. To demonstrate the strength of the panes, the warders were wont to point out the marks on one of the windows caused by a bullet fired by them at point blank range.

Usually there was a warder in attendance on the visitors' side but as each prisoner/visitor pair sat in a sort of cubicle it was impossible for him to see all the windows at the same time. When he was not looking directly in your cubicle it was possible to quickly flash up a message written on the palm of your hand or a piece of paper for your visitor to see. If you wanted to pass an important or confidential message to your visitor, this is what you had to do because conversations through the telephones were recorded. We found this out after my father had read a letter to me during a session when no warder was in attendance. When he left the visiting room, he was severely reprimanded and told that he would be prohibited from visiting me if he did it again. All letters had to be censored first, he was warned.

Daphne applied for permission to visit me but it was not granted on the grounds that she was a "coloured" and so could not use the whites' visiting room. When I then asked to be able to see her in the coloureds' visiting room I was told that that too was out of the question because white prisoners could not use the coloureds' visiting room. They were not being vindictive – just being good order followers!

Awaiting-trial prisoners were not only entitled to receive food, books, newspapers and magazines from outside but could send out their dirty clothes for washing and receive clean clothes in return. This twice-weekly exchange afforded an excellent opportunity to smuggle in all manner of contraband and to send out screeds of uncensored written material.

Theoretically, you were allowed to write and receive as many letters as you wished, but in practice, the censorship was so rigid that very few letters got through in either direction. When they did get through, they were so cut to pieces or blanked out that alternative methods of communication were inevitably sought. Many of the other prisoners sent out their letters with prisoners going to court but this had its dangers, as some of them would report the "felony" to a warder in order to ingratiate themselves. Stephen and I, after first using the official channel and finding it unsatisfactory, wrote our letters on sheets of toilet paper and then folded and sewed these into the hems of our trousers being sent out for washing. Our parents did likewise in the opposite direction. Flashing a message during a visit set up the system. Thereafter a thumbs-up sign meant there was something being sent in or out in the agreed way.

In this manner we were able to send out letters to many people, expressing our true feelings and opinions. I was able to communicate with Robin regularly and thereby pass on to the ANC some of our thoughts about the events leading up to our arrest. My mother or sister copied out the messages and sent them on to her using the false names and addresses I supplied. They did the reverse with letters from her.

Food parcels, too, permitted a ceaseless flow of contraband, although in one direction only. The first illicit substance we arranged to have sent in was booze. In one of my toilet paper letters I explained to my parents how to remove the plastic cap of a bottle of orange squash without breaking the seal, by holding it in steam. Once it was removed, half the squash could be emptied out and replaced with a clear spirit such as gin, vodka or cane. With the cap replaced the same way, no one could tell the difference. Twice a week Stephen and I shared our bottle of "orange juice" and got totally smashed. The feeling of being inebriated in front of the warders was exhilarating, to say the least, and also helped us to get through the day.

Most important of all, the food parcels enabled us to smuggle in money. Stephen managed to persuade his parents to send in a large sum – R360 in total. The money was concealed inside boxes of powdered milk that had been carefully opened and resealed. In *Papillon* the convicts hid their money up their anuses in what they called "chargers". These were metal tubes with screw-on lids in which the money was rolled and inserted. Borrowing this idea, we "ordered" a couple of cigars of the sort that come sealed in aluminium tubes.

Neither of us smoked but our parents never questioned our requests. The tubes, about twelve centimetres long, had plastic pop-fit lids that on test under water were prone to leak slightly. To overcome this problem, we "ordered" two rubber sheaths, which were sent concealed in a packet of sugar.

The money was divided two ways, rolled up, sealed in the sheaths and put into the tubes. These we then shoved up our rectums *à la Papillon*. The first time was the scariest, but with the help of a little Vaseline it went up with ease. In fact, it went up so easily that I thought it was going to shoot up into my bowels and get stuck somewhere right inside my guts. I immediately went to the toilet to try to expel it. I expected it to be a hard push and when my bowels worked with such ease, I thought the tube had not come out at all. I started to panic, thinking that I would have to call a warder to explain what had happened. But then I spotted a glint in the bowl and realised that it had come out after all. The handling of the object was a bit off-putting at first but we soon overcame our squeamishness. The money remained in place for over three months, until we reached our ultimate destination.

The "chargers" were the first practical step that we took towards our escape, a step not taken on the off-chance that we might be able to escape – we were definitely going to escape. From the moment we were brought together as awaiting-trial prisoners we made a solemn pledge to each other that we would be out within six months of being sentenced. Our overriding direction of thought after installing the "chargers" was not towards our defence but towards breaking out.

We did not hide the fact that we intended to escape, but neither did any of the other prisoners. Prisoners, especially when facing long prison terms, talked of escaping as if it was an inherent part of imprisonment. Turning that talk into reality, into freedom, was another matter. Many of our fellow prisoners were people who had already done time and so could relate many stories of escapes, most of them unsuccessful.

Two that I recall resulted in the quick recapture of those involved. Both of them were daring attempts but seemed to be no more than the exploitation of minor cracks in security. Neither contained planning that extended beyond the initial breaking-out phase and were consequently doomed to failure.

One of them took place at Pollsmoor. Two prisoners managed to find a way onto the roof of the prison, a flat walled area used as an exercise yard, and made a rope of sheets to get over the wall and down the side. The rope must have been very long as the height they had to drop was equivalent to the height of a five-storey building. The two must have realised that they would be seen by the guards in the watchtowers and banked on being able to get away before any recapturing forces could be mustered.

They managed to get over the wall and to the ground before the alarm went off. As the prison building is in the centre of a large complex comprising a number of other prison buildings, warders' houses and facilities, they had nowhere suitable to hide; they were also still dressed in their prison clothing. The two fugitives took refuge in the rafters of a garage belonging to a warder but were soon tracked down by sniffer dogs.

The other escape was more ingenious. Two prisoners in charge of packing dirty laundry to be sent out for washing, hid themselves in the baskets and were driven out of the prison to freedom. I do not remember how they were recaptured but their freedom was short-lived. It appears that the attempt was more of an impromptu act than a well-planned escape.

The lessons gleaned from listening to these escape stories confirmed exactly what we had read in *Papillon*: you should not rely on lucky breaks or even contemplate escaping without a realistic getaway plan; you can't escape looking like an escaped convict; once out, get away from the immediate vicinity of your prison as quickly as possible; don't go into hiding near your prison – get as far away as possible in the time that you imagine you have before your escape is discovered; don't celebrate freedom too soon and; don't go where the search party might expect you to go!

The authorities did not take kindly to escapes. Those who were recaptured not only had their sentences dramatically extended but had their legs chained together for several months. In true mediaeval style, iron shackles were riveted around the escapees' ankles. The shackles were joined together by a long chain that the recaptured prisoners had to carry in their hands. Because ordinary trousers could not slide over the chains, such prisoners were issued special ones that consisted of front and rear panels that buttoned together on the sides.

* * *

Awaiting-trial prisoners could consult with their lawyers in a number of bare rooms just off the section where they were held. Curiously, our first consultations did not take place in these rooms but in an office belonging to the commanding officer of the prison. Why this happened we never found out, but for some reason the warders at Pollsmoor treated us quite differently to the other prisoners, according us more respect. Perhaps they were acting under instructions to show how well political prisoners were treated in South Africa, or perhaps they really did not see us as "normal" prisoners.

The office had no barred or frosted windows, affording us sight of the beautiful mountains of the Cape Peninsula. We had only been cut off from such views for a month and a half, yet we already found ourselves deprived of visual relief. How would we feel after being cut off from the sights of nature for years on end?

Our consultations took place separately, as Stephen's parents had appointed a separate advocate to deal with his affairs. It would have made more sense to have had a single legal representative but his parents refused to have anything to do with mine as they believed at the time that I was responsible for their son's plight.

I was bitterly disappointed with my first consultation. The lawyer in charge of my defence appeared to have been well briefed by the security police because he had a good knowledge of the details of our case and could not have got it from anywhere else. This horrified me as I was expecting him to find out about the case from the person he was supposed to be defending rather than from the side of the prosecution. He appeared to know so much that he was not bothered to ask me any questions relating to the alleged offences for which I was being charged. The feeling he gave me right from the start was that he believed I was guilty of the charges and that he could not really defend me in the sense that he would try to refute the allegations or prove my innocence. All he could do was prevent an outrageous sentence being imposed.

This attitude, to say the least, did not inspire confidence. Later consultations, which were held in the normal consultation rooms, were equally disappointing as he continued to display little interest in the specific acts that constituted the "offences" with which I was being charged. My suspicion that he had very little sympathy for our cause was confirmed when he announced at one session that he thought the best approach would be for me to plead guilty and that he would attempt to play down the significance of the acts.

Foolishly, I did not argue the point and even went to great lengths to provide him with information about the leaflet bombs so that he could use it to prove that they were not "real" bombs. I went along with him because he was the legal expert; I was merely being guided by my prejudices and emotions. I was made to feel "guilty" because in their terms I was, but couldn't help feeling that I should plead not guilty in order to force the damn police to provide the full, raw, details in order to prove their rotten case and reveal to all what we had done and how we had achieved it.

Stephen was having much the same problems with his legal "help". The family lawyer had dug up some decrepit old dog of an advocate who, let alone not being able to speak coherently, had not the faintest clue what a political trial was about. Stephen came back from his consultations each time in a terribly bad mood, swearing that he had to find a better advocate. But his family would have none of it. They wanted no "political" lawyers near their son and felt insulted that he was rejecting their best efforts to ensure that he was not going to spend the rest of his life in prison.

In retrospect, however, most of the blame for the appalling advocates that we ended up with can be put down to our general attitude towards our trial. We did not take it seriously and viewed it simply as a hurdle we had to jump between our state of being awaiting-trial prisoners and our future state as full-blown prisoners – a state we would soon relieve ourselves of by escaping. Both of us were of the opinion that the trial was going to be a farce, a big show trial – in fact not a trial at all but an occasion for the security police to swagger and boast that another threat to the "security of the state" (i.e. to white minority rule and privilege) had been tracked down and was soon to be eliminated. We wanted nothing to do with it. They could have their trial, they could score their points, they could lavish massive sentences, but we would show them in the end.

Politically speaking it was wrong to adopt such an attitude as the battle had to be continued at every point of contact, even when it appeared futile or pointless. This error was not due to a lack of understanding about the nature of the political trials in South Africa: we knew that the courts were used to hide the fact that the security laws actually by-passed normal law; we knew that the courts were used to give legitimacy to state action against its political opponents. Our determination to escape sapped our motivation to make the most of our trial. We also did not wish to offend our parents who believed that they were doing their best for us.

If we had decided to take our trial seriously there were two ways we could have approached it: participating actively or rejecting it completely. It was important to adopt one of these two tactical options because a political trial, at that time, was not a trial in a purely legalistic sense – it was a battle between two opposing political forces.

As defendants in a political trial, we should have seen the courtroom as a battleground where we were obliged to defend ourselves and fight back, even though we found ourselves severely disadvantaged because our opponent had defined the conditions and rules of the battle. A political trial is akin to an ambush, where your enemy chooses the best circumstances to favour themselves and disadvantage you the most. But even in an ambush, if you want to avoid a massacre, you have to fight your way through as best you can. Sometimes, if you are skilful enough, you can get through without too disastrous results and on the rare occasion even turn the tables.

There is, however, one fundamental difference between an ambush and a political trial. The first usually takes place without spectators while the latter is watched by many people. It is imperative to make the correct impression in such a trial because the public does not see you so much as an individual but as representing an organisation or cause. Although our indictment said "State versus Jenkin and Lee", it should really have read "State versus ANC". We should not have given them the opportunity to score any victories over the organisation we represented.

For us, participating actively would have meant, firstly, expelling our lawyers and taking on a single advocate with a reputation for defending accused activists in political trials. Secondly, we should have demanded that we be allowed to plead not guilty so that the police would have to bring all their evidence before the court. This would have meant, most importantly, that we could have been brought before the court to present evidence in our defence. Evidence from our mouths would have been in the form of political statements explaining our motivations for engaging in activities that challenged the racist state and our contempt for apartheid "justice".

The previous year (1977), the apartheid legislators had decided that they could no longer tolerate political trialists using the dock to make political statements against them and had amended the law (Criminal Procedure Act) to prevent this happening. In the past, newly convicted trialists had used the dock to make brilliant statements against the regime and these had been reported in many history books. Now that this could no longer happen, we should have taken the opportunity to use the witness stand instead.

Participating in the court processes defiantly, we well knew, had never got any trialists anywhere in terms of reduced sentences. There was no evidence, however, that participating submissively had ever had the opposite effect – of leading to shorter sentences. Most terms were worked out on the basis of precedent and not on the court behaviour of the accused. For this reason we should have seen it as our duty to confront the court defiantly.

To reject our trial completely would also have involved expelling our advocates, but not taking on new ones. It would also have involved making a statement in the court, but before the proceedings started. The statement would have been to the effect that we did not recognise the court, that we were not prepared to participate in the proceedings and that we would be prepared to face the consequences, however bitter they were.

This approach was more in line with our way of thinking. We regarded the apartheid regime as illegitimate and illegal and therefore believed that its courts had no right to try us. Additionally, by employing lawyers we were in a sense collaborating with and giving legitimacy to the court that was about to try us. To participate in the proceedings was a betrayal to everything we believed in, to the oppressed in whose name we had carried out our activities and to the international community that had declared apartheid a crime against humanity. Apartheid's courts were not courts at all, just forums used by the regime to shout defiance at its opponents and the world.

However, ANC trialists had studiously avoided this option because it had been shown to be ineffective in producing any useful outcomes.

Some Pan-Africanist Congress members refused to participate in their trials in the early 1960s, with the result that their trials became non-trials and the accused simply vanished into prisons. So, for us there were no precedents to follow and instead we looked to those who had made the most of being brought before the courts. After our time, a number of political trialists did refuse to participate in their trials and made powerful statements condemning the apartheid courts and justice. These made a strong impact on people who were inspired by the actions of those brought before the courts for engaging in "illegal" political activity.

The two months before our trial went by quickly. The jail routine was monotonous but not intolerable. The day began when a warder released his frustrations on a large gong at half past five in the morning. The cells were opened at about seven thirty, followed by an inspection and count of prisoners before breakfast. The warders had great difficulty in performing this count because if they counted each individual prisoner it took too long and they lost count. To speed up the process we were required to stand in twos – then they only had to count half the number. Clever blighters! The only problem with this trick was that they were not too good at division and often detected a shortage of prisoners if there was an odd number. This would lead to an alert and a frenzied search for the "missing" prisoner(s). When they could not be found, a more senior warder would suggest a recount. Any prisoner who laughed was in trouble.

Most days, breakfast consisted of *mielie pap* (maize meal), so-called coffee and a few slices of bread. Stephen and I were never allowed out of the section to fetch our meals but had them brought to us – if we wanted them. The rationale for this, as far as we could work out, was that the kitchens were considered a prime area for smuggling. Outsiders brought in food and other supplies on a daily basis and perhaps they thought we were so devious that we would be able to open a channel there. If only they knew that we had already opened such a channel!

The mornings were set aside for cleaning cells, passages and ourselves. At about eleven everyone was taken out to one of the prison's internal courtyards for an hour of exercise. Some people played soccer but most just lay against a wall and soaked up the fading autumn sunshine. Stephen and I did not accept the midday meal and instead put together our own meals from the food brought to us by our parents. After the midday meal we were locked up for the afternoon, alone or with more than two people per cell: two people might get up to something "unsavoury". Most of the time we spent reading, playing chess or just chatting. At about four the cells were opened and the prisoners let out to fetch their evening meal. This normally consisted of a sort of thickened liquid that they said was soup, a brown liquid alleged to be coffee and bread smeared with a disgusting pink jelly.

At four thirty the prisoners were locked in their individual cells for the night and after eight they were supposed to keep quiet. The long evening hours gave us the most wonderful opportunity to read those books we'd always wanted to read but for which we'd never found the time – such as Tolstoy's *War and Peace*. To overcome the boredom, Steve and I would sometimes remove the water from our toilet bowls so that we could talk to each other through the pipes. The sound carried remarkably well and we were able, after we had each acquired a chess set, to play the game late into the night. The lights were never switched off so you could go to sleep whenever you wished, although official bedtime was 11 pm.

The straw mats that were our beds were rolled out on the floor. They were required to be immaculately made in the morning and not slept on during the day. As with most things over which you have no choice, you soon got used to your bed despite it being extremely hard and cold on the concrete floor.

The cells were almost completely inhospitable. The tiny hand basin was practically useless except as something on which to stand to look out of the window. The tap operated by pushing a knob, but as there was no plug in the basin it was almost impossible to wash as one hand had to keep the knob depressed. And whenever you pressed it, the plumbing throughout the prison juddered and made a most frightful noise. For this reason, hardly anyone used their taps at night and instead drew their water from their toilets. These were flushed by pressing a button on the floor with your foot, sending endless torrents of water into the bowl. Everything, including plates and bodies, was washed in toilet bowls and after you had overcome your squeamishness, they also became the main source of drinking water. It seemed a shame to have to use them for other purposes.

We were sustained through the two months before our trial by the visits, bottles of laced orange squash, illicit letters, newspapers and the determination not to stay in prison longer than was absolutely necessary. Our morale sagged a little at times but a sudden flood of solidarity letters that arrived in our last days cheered us no end. The letters came from Britain – the result of our defence committee's good work. They proved to us that we were not forgotten, as had been alleged by the security police, and that people far away were concerned about our plight. The authorities must have realised this too, for after a few days the flood dried up as suddenly as it had begun. No matter how much we pleaded, they insisted that there were no more letters and took offence at our suggestions that they were deliberately withholding them. We were not yet used to our powerlessness.

Chapter Five

Trial

Our appearance in the Cape Town Supreme Court on 1 June was a bit of an anti-climax. We'd had our best clothes sent in, geared ourselves mentally for the start of the trial ... and then nothing happened. No charges were read out, we were not asked to plead and the case was postponed to 6 June. Why, we never found out. The judge mumbled something, our advocates acknowledged him in some kind of bookies' code and we were led off to the cells below the court and then driven back to Pollsmoor. Quite clearly, we were still remanded in custody.

On 6 June the same thing happened, but this time the court had an altogether different appearance. The spectator gallery was packed with people, many of them friends. At least 15 senior security police were present and at the front of the court a mountain of exhibits: the recovered leaflet bombs, the banner, piles of leaflets and envelopes all neatly tied together with string, steel trunks, toolboxes, banned literature, cardboard boxes, typewriters, the duplicator, and sundry items of furniture, bedding and kitchenware. A toaster took pride of place on top of the trunks.

Our parents were allowed to sit on the benches immediately in front of the dock, enabling us to chat to them before the trial started. My mother eyed the piles of exhibits and said: "What's my bedspread doing there? And my kitchen chair? And my...? So that's where my other toaster got to." She had forgotten that she had lent me the items or thought I had been using them in my "above-ground" flat.

A fat charge sheet with two detailed schedules was made available. It listed the activities that comprised the offences we had allegedly committed as well as each incidence of dissemination of leaflets – by post and leaflet bomb. Ten different leaflets distributed by post and seven spread by leaflet bomb were mentioned. Twenty-six leaflet bombs were listed as well as one banner.

Again, the charges were not put and we were not asked to plead. The state prosecutor, Tielman Louw, applied for a postponement to the next day because, he said, there were matters to be "straightened out" between the state and the defence. The defence agreed to the postponement. We were never told what these "matters" were but the easy agreement between the two sides made us feel uneasy, as if they were colluding in our prosecution. The court was dismissed after a few minutes and we were taken back to Pollsmoor.

In London meanwhile – although not to our knowledge at the time – a picket organised by our defence committee was being held outside the South African embassy to demand our release and the release of all South African political prisoners. Hundreds of leaflets were handed out to passersby giving details of our case.

Such actions were hugely appreciated by political trialists and prisoners. When they got to hear of them, morale was raised to a high level as they were reminded that they were not forgotten and that people far away were concerned with their plight and fighting for them.

After breakfast on 7 June, as happened the previous times, they marched us out of the awaiting-trial section to a sort of internal garage in the prison where several armoured prison vans were parked ready to take the prisoners to court. The two of us were locked in a special compartment towards the front of a van and separately from the other prisoners – we were not to be allowed to contaminate the black prisoners.

At the court the procedure was the reverse. The van passed through a set of very solid gates into a yard at the side of the court. First the black prisoners were removed and then we were briskly led through a couple of sets of heavily barred grilles and into a small cell below the courtrooms.

The cell was without windows and a weak yellow light lit the room that was empty save for a slop bucket and a narrow bench along one wall. The walls reminded us of the interior of an Egyptian tomb, covered from floor to ceiling in graffiti, drawings, verse and nonsense. Since there was nothing else to do, we scanned the walls: "Fifteen years for rape – Mogamoet" ... "I was here for shit" ... "Sweet Lord have mercy" ... "I love you Mary, I didn't mean it" ... As we read this pitiful record left behind by countless victims of the racist legal system, we spotted in a hole in the wall a tiny stub of a pencil. A trap, we thought. They must want us to write revolutionary slogans on the walls so they can charge us with more offences – we're not falling for that one, oh no! But what the hell! If they want to charge us further, that's okay. We're going to escape so it doesn't matter! Stephen extracted the pencil and with much delight we boldly wrote and drew, wherever there were gaps, revolutionary slogans and insignia.

After an hour in the dungeon we were driven upstairs and seated in the dock. When the judge entered, an orderly shouted "*Staan in die hof!*" – "Stand up in court!" But we had decided that there would be no standing for us: standing meant recognising the legitimacy of the court. Our tardy arousal was met with agitated prods in the back and angry shouts from another orderly: "*Staan op! Staan op!*" – "Stand up! Stand up!" Slowly we lifted ourselves, realising that it would not be productive to refuse to stand each time.

Along with the judge, Acting Justice Nel, entered two assessors – the South African equivalent of a jury. There was – and still is – no trial by jury in South Africa and in most cases only a judge is present. Assessors were obliged to be present when the death sentence might be imposed. In our case this was a possibility and provided for under the Terrorism Act. At that time, when assessors were present, they were not allowed to decide on any questions of law but final judgments were based on a majority decision. In later years this changed slightly. The reason given for not holding jury trials was that in South Africa the bias of the jurors were so clear-cut that the system would not ensure justice. In cases involving a black accused, white jurors would most likely judge against the person irrespective of the evidence, and if the jurors were black, they would always judge the accused not guilty. There is probably some truth in this explanation, as blacks knew that the judicial system was loaded against them and was part of the machinery of their oppression.

We looked at these honourable gentlemen as they occupied their positions on the bench and could not help wondering where South African courts had got their reputation for being impartial and independent. Here were three so-called legal experts about to interpret what we had done in terms of a law that was so obviously political and partisan and that overturned the normal legal principle that you are innocent until proven guilty. The onus was going to be on us to prove that our actions were not intended to have any of the effects of "terrorism" (i.e. virtually any anti-state activity) – we were presumed guilty and had to prove that we were innocent. By willingly sitting there these gentlemen were saying that they agreed with the law they were about to apply, that they believed they were about to dispense justice.

The prosecution read out the charges and we were asked to plead. Before either of us could respond to the judge's call our defence leapt to their respective feet and declared that they would be doing the pleading for us. This seemed out of order to us, but how were we to know? My advocate managed to get the first word in, telling the court that the defence was "purely technical" in that there had been an improper duplication of charges etc., and that therefore I was guilty on count one, namely, of "taking part in terrorist activities", but not guilty on count two, which alleged contravention of the Internal Security Act. Stephen's advocate pleaded for him in much the same way. So that was it: we had no say. We looked at each other in disbelief but not knowing what we could do just shrugged our shoulders.

State Prosecutor Louw handed in a list of exhibits to the judge – "because there were a rather large number of them" – and announced that he would be calling five policemen and a "Mr X" for the state. Mr X was a person whose name should not be published – "for security reasons".

Spyker van Wyk was the first state witness to be called. He told the court that his investigations began on 10 December 1975, being on that first occasion an investigation into the distribution of subversive pamphlets through the post. He went on to detail each pamphlet intercepted and each leaflet bomb his team had to investigate. He gave the number of pamphlets intercepted in the mail each time, and the number of leaflets recovered after each leaflet bomb.

This was of great interest to us as it gave some indication of the effectiveness of our distributions and of their counter-actions. Of the first three mailings, only a handful of pamphlets ended up in their hands – in one case no more than two. Most of these were probably ones they had intercepted on the way to several banned people who were on our mailing list; others were handed in by people who had received them. Admittedly our mailing list held only a few hundred names on those first mailings but it showed that the police had no regular methods of detecting or intercepting the posted matter. After the first three mailings the number that they intercepted increased more and more rapidly until the last one, of which they intercepted about eighty per cent. Our conclusion was that our failure to regularly change our addressing system had made it easy for them to identify the envelopes and our failure to post from other centres permitted them to keep a small number of sorting offices in one area permanently on the alert.

The details also belied police claims that they had recovered most of the leaflets after leaflet bombings. The most that were ever recovered was 272; on average they only found about eighty. An "expert" who later appeared told the court that a leaflet bomb – or "ideological bombs" as they called them – could only lift 300 leaflets. Sorry to disappoint, but the number was always 500 – one ream.

Spyker claimed that the police had kept us under observation from 22 February 1978, the date of our last posting. This was highly unlikely as it would have been too much of a coincidence that they just happened to start watching us on the day we decided to do a posting. Our suspicion was that they had been watching us for much longer (what about all the strange phone calls and suspicious characters?) and knew when we were about to do the posting. How otherwise could they have intercepted practically all the pamphlets of that posting?

Our defence responded to Spyker's testimony with some pathetic cross-questioning about the nature of "real terrorists". The point they were trying to get across to the court was that we were not "terrorists" in the normal sense of the word and that our cell did not have the usual aim of "terrorist cells", which is sabotage. Spyker responded that our activities during a period of unrest would, in his opinion, have had "a helluva effect".

The next day a police "explosives expert", a Major J.G. van Tonder of the police bomb disposal unit, gave details of the components, construction and workings of the leaflet bombs. The 26 "ideological bombs" were "neatly built, the work of a perfectionist" and made by someone "obviously proud of his work". In a cool and informed manner, he held up one of the "bombs" and described to the court how the parts fitted together, how the timing mechanism worked and how the platform shot the leaflets into the air when the explosive powder was detonated. Anyone in the spectator gallery would have been sufficiently informed to go home and make their own. Van Tonder spoke about the books on explosives that had been found in our trunks. He was convinced, he said, that our knowledge of explosives and detonators had been obtained from these books. Why, then, had they interrogated us about our training, we wondered?

In characteristic manner our defence attempted to get the court to view the leaflet bombs not as "real bombs" but rather as harmless little "leaflet launchers" – kind of like jack-in-the-boxes. Under cross-examination Van Tonder had to concede that the "bombs" would not have damaged property or harmed anyone. One of the assessors awoke from his slumber at this point and commented with raised finger that as far as he could see the leaflet bombs were not much more dangerous than a large firecracker. My advocate thought he had scored a major victory; we were not impressed.

And so it went on for several days. One state witness, a Lieutenant Deon Greyling of the police bomb disposal unit, told how one of the "bombs" had gone off in his hands while he was attempting to defuse it. Unfortunately, the point he was trying to make – that the leaflet bombs were dangerous and unpredictable devices – backfired on him as he was forced to admit to the judge that he had not been harmed.

The monster Van Aggenbach displayed to the court the mailing lists and addressing equipment that we had used. The police had printed out all the names using our addressing machine to confirm that they corresponded to the envelopes they had intercepted in the post. Sure enough they did. He proudly demonstrated the piles of letters that had been intercepted, intimating that he personally was responsible for stopping the material from spreading to its unsuspecting victims and thereby preventing a revolutionary situation from developing.

On one of the mornings my parents brought my prison food parcel to the court and it was handed to me in the cell below the court before the day's proceedings started. The bottle of laced orange squash was there as usual so we thought we would have a little swig before being called up. Of course, the swig turned into a drinking party and in no time the entire bottle was polished off. Everyone must have wondered why we sat in court that day with contented smiles on our faces!

As the morning dragged on, nature had its revenge, pressurising us to ask one of the court orderlies standing behind us for permission to visit the toilet. He reminded us that the accused had to be present in court all the time and that if we wanted to leave the room the trial would have to be adjourned. Being too embarrassed to expose our simultaneous need before all those people, there was nothing we could do but cross our legs and hope the proceedings would not carry on for too long.

A big shot from security police headquarters in Pretoria, a Colonel Broodryk, testified on publications of the ANC and the South African Communist Party (SACP). He was the "expert" on "communism" and banned organisations such as the ANC and SACP, one of whom always appeared in South African political trials. The racists were of the opinion, at least at the propaganda level, that every manifestation of resistance against apartheid was the result of a communist plot. Basically, they believed, blacks were happy with their lot and if they raised their voices against apartheid it was only because the Kremlin had sent its dupes to incite them for extraneous political purposes. Colonel Broodryk went to pains to stress the point that we were either witting or unwitting agents of "Russia" – they had not heard of the Soviet Union – and that the ANC was no more than a front for the Communist Party.

He explained that our activities, most of which took place during the period of the Soweto uprisings starting on 16 June 1976, could only have served to fan the fires of revolt. The implication was almost that we had been responsible for the events of that time and were a major factor behind the riots. Our defence objected that he was exaggerating the consequences of our activities because the number of pamphlets we had disseminated increased manyfold after 1976 and had in fact corresponded to a decrease in unrest.

Colonel Broodryk was called again by the state to support an application for the identity of the next witness, Mr X, not to be revealed. He said that in the past state witnesses testifying in similar trials had been threatened and, in some cases, assassinated. A quotation was read from one of our leaflets that supported his point: "Smash the traitors and stooges – we shall harass the enemy, its police and its spies." At least they were admitting that Mr X was a traitor and stooge. Stephen's advocate, surprisingly, opposed the application but mine, in his usual collaborating way, said: "I just wish to say at this stage that I do not oppose the application nor have I ever done so." The courtroom was cleared of spectators, the press and our parents before Mr X was brought through a back door of the court to the witness stand. He eyed the court like a frightened dog to make sure no one would recognise him and then stood to attention to obey his masters' instructions.

He began his pitiful tale of how he had gone to Maputo to seek work. There he had been press-ganged by the ANC into joining its "terrorist wing" (Umkhonto we Sizwe). From Maputo he was sent to Tanzania where he claimed he had fraternised with the ANC leadership. Oliver Tambo, the president of the ANC, and Joe Slovo, the alleged mastermind behind all communist plots against South Africa, he knew well. So far Mr X had got his lines right.

From Tanzania he claimed to have been sent to Russia where he was taught "terrorism": how to make bombs and shoot with an AK-47 rifle. In Russia he had also learned to speak Russian. We were surprised when he did not reveal that he was mates with Brezhnev. Next, he was sent to Angola where he was given explosives, guns and money. From there he was infiltrated back into South Africa through Botswana, but as soon as he got into the country, he realised that what he was doing was futile and that he could not beat the police. He suddenly "saw the light" and as a responsible citizen gave himself up and handed in his weapons. Now he was working for the police and making life better for his people that way!

The story was so transparent and close to the usual propaganda tale that it was doubtful if even the judge and his assessors took Mr X seriously. It was no wonder that his testimony was given *in camera*, as the press would have made mincemeat of it. However, the point of the appearance was merely to emphasise to the court the state's contention that the ANC was really just a gang of nasties and that all its operatives were acting in the interests of Russia and not in the interests of South Africa's black population.

I wrote on a slip of paper the words "I do not understand Russian" in Russian and handed it to my advocate with a note asking him to give it to Mr X to test whether he could actually speak and read Russian as he had claimed. But he was not prepared to cooperate. He felt that such a step would not be necessary as he believed the judge did not accept Mr X's story. That was probably true, for when the judge asked Mr X to tell him what the devices in front of him were used for (the leaflet bombs), Mr X, after contemplating the objects for a good few moments, replied that they were for "demolishing installations". He was promptly hustled out the door from which he had appeared. I wonder if he was awarded the few cents he had been promised.

The day following Mr X's testimony there was a lot of whispering from the galleries below. Apparently, some new evidence had turned up and the state wanted to make another point before closing their case. Before announcing the new evidence, Prosecutor Louw summarised the state's case and argued for our conviction on the grounds that we had admitted to preparing the documents before the court, posting them and constructing and placing the leaflet bombs. He selected and read out the juiciest quotations from the leaflets to show that we had without doubt incited people to commit acts promoting the aims and objects of unlawful organisations. Needless to say, he was not impressed by our literature and considered it to be bordering on treason. One leaflet dealing with the defeat of the apartheid army in Angola in 1975, he called a "poisonous bit of literature". Clearly, he was a victim of the propaganda that turned the racist army's defeat into a victory.

And then he announced the new evidence: a letter I had written (to Robin) had been intercepted in the post. The letter contained sure evidence that I was not the least bit remorseful for my conduct, pre-empting what they assumed would be the strategy of the defence, which was due to present its case next.

The letter was one I had smuggled out in my prison washing and had been rewritten by my mother. I had written the letter using Robin's name because my mother had informed me that a friend of hers was going to Britain and would post it there. But at the last moment the friend had postponed the journey and could not take the letter. Not understanding the dangers of doing so and in good faith, my mother put the letter in the mail. It might not have been intercepted had she not also enclosed a bunch of press clippings of the trial.

My mother, naturally, felt terrible and started to blame herself for ruining my chances and for probably adding many years to my sentence. I tried to console her by explaining that the letter was but a mere pinprick compared to what I was being tried for and would not adversely affect the judge's opinion. It was just the state trying to score a political point. I'm not sure if she understood.

Having made its points, the state closed its case. Our defence declared that it was not calling any witnesses to lead evidence in answer to the charges and thereby closed the defence case. Then followed a lot of legal mumbo jumbo. Something about duplication of charges, something else about the two charges being the same transaction showing the same intention et cetera, et cetera.

Stephen and I had indicated to our legal advisers that we wanted to be called to answer the charges but they thought that doing so would only worsen our case. They were not interested in political statements and were only concerned with ensuring that we received the minimum sentences. Politics, slogans and raised fists would only annoy the judge and add years to our sentences.

Instinctively both of us felt that it would look bad if we made no political comment at all. Although we knew that we were no longer allowed to make statements from the dock, we felt that they could have thought of some way to get us up front. It was not that we wanted our words recorded for posterity; it was just that we were experiencing a psychological need to say something. We could not go through a whole trial without uttering a single word, as if we were no more relevant to the case than the wooden panelling on the walls.

Unfortunately, as I've already explained, our desire to escape left us insufficiently motivated to press the point and resist our advocates' appeals for moderation. We should have known from our studies of political trials that length of sentence was not determined by what you said in court but by legal precedent. If someone else before you got x years for doing more or less the same things, and that had not served to deter you, then your sentence was calculated by the formula $x + 20$ per cent of x.

The trial was postponed for a few days after the two sides had closed their cases. When the court reconvened, the state prosecutor summarised the state's case: From 1 August 1975 to 2 March 1978 the accused did "wrongfully, unlawfully and with intent to endanger the maintenance of law and order in the Republic" commit certain acts. These were listed in detail: so many pamphlets sent through the post, so many leaflets disseminated by leaflet bombs, and the displaying of an ANC banner.

To prove that the pamphlets and leaflets had or would have had one or more of the all-embracing effects of "terrorism" as defined by the Terrorism Act, long sections of most of our publications were read out in the court. This went some way towards helping us overcome our shame of not having said anything to the court – they were doing it for us! We felt proud of what was being read out to the large crowd gathered there, although we knew that it could not be reported in the press. Nonetheless, many people heard the message and that was what was important.

The state's object was to prove that by the dissemination of the documents, we had "without doubt incited, instigated and encouraged others to commit acts to promote the aims and objects of the ANC, the SACP and Umkhonto we Sizwe". This object they achieved, for immediately afterwards Acting Justice Nel pronounced his verdict: both guilty on count one and not guilty on count two. The not guilty verdict on count two was a purely technical matter relating to duplication of convictions, or something. We were now statutory terrorists.

After judgment, Prosecutor Nel took centre stage again and asked the court to impose a "heavy sentence" on both of us but a particularly heavy sentence in my case, as I was the "leading figure" in the events that led to the trial. He described the offences as "very serious indeed" and as amounting to high treason. Treason! Taking part in a struggle that has the support of the majority of the people and against a system of society that has been declared a crime against humanity, is treason? These servants of apartheid were the traitors; they were the ones who were really guilty.

The court was handed over to the defence to call witnesses to give evidence in mitigation. My advocate in his opening speech reiterated that we were not "terrorists" in the "ordinary sense of the word". We had to be sentenced for what had been set out in the indictment, and "this boiled down to pamphleteering and nothing else". The pamphlets contained "crude political claptrap" that did not call for specific acts of violence and for the most part "fell on deaf ears". The word "bomb" was an emotive one and inappropriate to describe the devices exhibited.

While agreeing that he had to play down the significance of the pamphlets, this was going too far. We were proud of those damned pamphlets and took offence at the crude insults of someone who was supposed to be on our side.

The first witness to be called was a cousin of mine who was a psychiatrist at a Cape Town hospital. He was persuaded to plead on my behalf at the last moment because my lawyers thought it would not be a good idea to call my father in the light of the intercepted letter posted by my mother. Initially several people, including my boss from ISD, had offered to give evidence on my behalf but when it became clear what the charges were about, they all got cold feet. That left only my father.

The cousin was a total embarrassment. He explained in his psychiatrist's jargon that my "burning desire to help the underprivileged" was the result of a "personality defect". The "extreme views" that I "vehemently held" were common of insecure people. As my personality needs changed so my views would "settle" and, presumably, I would then be cured of this affliction and revert to being a "normal", apathetic, racist, white South African.

What an insult! So one's beliefs and actions spring from dark psychic and emotional defects and have nothing to do with any genuine political motives; to throw in your lot with the oppressed and join the struggle against apartheid was an illness, a perversion, abnormal.

Thank goodness I only had one "witness". Poor Stephen had to contend with his parents, a Roman Catholic chaplain and a family friend. The parental plea was shameful. Stephen's father explained that as a young lad Stephen was sent to boarding school because he was in danger of becoming a "softy". At university he was corrupted by the "left-wing radical element" and his previously strong religious views were destroyed. The anti-capitalist tendencies he picked up there were expected to wear off and appeared to do so as he matured. But this never really happened as he merely began to harbour his views secretly. Stephen was "over-anxious to please whatever group he found himself in and adopted the attitudes and mores of any group in which he found himself in order to be popular". Stephen's normally ruddy complexion turned bright red; he could not lower his head far enough below the dock railing to hide his embarrassment.

The very strong implication in his father's plea was that I was the ringleader and had influenced his son to break the law. Mr Lee finished with an impassioned plea for leniency, as a long sentence would turn his son into a "hardened, bigoted terrorist".

The other witnesses pushed much the same line: Stephen was basically a decent sort of a chap who used to attend mass regularly but who had been corrupted by others because he was an idealist and easily influenced. By the end Stephen's face had turned bright scarlet. The security police must have been laughing in their jackboots.

Sentence was passed on 15 June. The judge's summing up was brief: Accused number one had carried on his illegal activities for two years and seven months and accused number two for about two years; In that time they prepared and disseminated 17 different pamphlets with the clear intent of undermining law and order; They were mindful of what they were doing and of what sentences others who had engaged in similar activities had received; There was no evidence that accused number two felt any remorse for his conduct while it was obvious from the intercepted letter that accused number one was wholly unrepentant. Without a pause or change in tone of voice he sentenced me to 12 years' imprisonment and Stephen to eight.

That was it. All over. The court turned to see our response, but it had not registered on our faces. I could hear the words "12 years" ringing in my ears but couldn't associate them with myself. I swore at the judge under my breath and looked at Stephen. He was looking at me. Suddenly we were grabbed from behind and jostled down the stairs by abusive orderlies; we were now *bandiete*, prisoners, and defiling the respectable ambience of the court. We had not even raised our fists in defiance or shouted any slogans. Our reticence was partly influenced by the adjurations of our lawyers not to do such things after being sentenced, as they would only jeopardise our chances of appealing against our sentences.

In the cells below, the two of us felt sick. Not because of the sentences just imposed, but because we had failed to even raise our fists and shout *Amandla!* – "Power!" – as is fitting and proper for political prisoners to do when sentenced. Why had we succumbed to the appeals of our miserable lawyers? We felt conned!

The security police graciously permitted us a few brief moments with our families to say goodbye. Weeping mothers were consoled and the hands of shocked brothers, sisters and fathers shaken. It was an unhappy scene, as we all knew that it would be a long time before we'd be able to see each other again without physical barriers between us. It would also be a long time before the two of us would be able to have physical contact with a loved one. I tried to cheer my mother by saying that we would soon be out because we were going to escape, but it was the wrong moment. She feared that we would be caught and then our sentences would be prolonged and she would not be able to bear the consequences. I assured her that it was just "prisoner talk"; I wouldn't do anything foolish.

To make sure that our valuable "chargers" stayed in place in case we were immediately carted off to Pretoria where we expected to be sent, I relieved my mother of her supply of aspirins, which we swallowed to make ourselves constipated.

The cops called an end to the sad little party and cleared the cell. They handcuffed our hands behind our backs and led us out to the awaiting police cars – they were taking no chances that we would defiantly raise our fists to the eager press photographers waiting outside.

The security police accompanying us back to Pollsmoor feigned surprise at the severity of our sentences but couldn't refrain from remarking that we should have expected what we got. Why had we done it? Just look at how we had ruined our lives now. Couldn't we see how much good the government was doing for the blacks – more than the ANC could ever do! The money-filled torpedoes in our guts gave reassurance at that heart-sinking moment.

Now we were real prisoners and joining the more than one hundred and twenty thousand others who daily inhabited South Africa's prisons. At that time, it was said, South Africa had the highest per capita prison population in the world. The country's network of prisons was filled mostly with the victims of apartheid, "criminals" without victims. During the apartheid era there were very few black

South Africans who did not in the course of their lives experience one of those institutions, for the "crime" of infringing one of the multitude of apartheid regulations that governed their lives.

Included in the one hundred and twenty thousand were the hundreds of political prisoners who officially did not exist. The regime claimed that there were no political prisoners in South Africa – only what it called "security prisoners". These, it said, were ordinary criminals who had been found guilty in the courts of law for crimes against the security of the state. In practice, however, they were forced to recognise the existence of a group of prisoners that was different from other prisoners. These prisoners were kept strictly apart from all others and had their lives governed by a different set of regulations from those that applied to ordinary prisoners.

The attitude that met us in the prison reception office was completely different to what we had experienced up to then. No longer were we unconvicted prisoners who could demand a modicum of respect; we were now prison property and they were free to do with us as they pleased. After signing our names in a register, we were told to remove our clothes and hand in all possessions for safekeeping. The warder in charge pointed to a pile of rags on the floor and told us to get dressed. The rags were our "uniforms" – probably the cast-offs of some prisoners who had just been released. The shoes were four sizes too big, the shirt and trousers about double my size. Too bad, you'll just have to get used to them.

Fortunately they did not search us as they did black prisoners who became convicted prisoners. They were forced to dance the *thawusa*, an undignified naked leap into the air with legs apart to show that they had nothing concealed up their rectums. This did not happen to white prisoners – especially those considered "respectable" like us.

First task – haircuts. A large, brutal-looking convict found much pleasure running a pair of clippers through our hair. He left only stubble.

Stephen's beard was shorn off like sheep's wool and he was made to remove the rest of it with an implement that he did not know how to use – a razor. When they had finished, he looked like a young boy.

We were shoved into large adjacent cells that were completely bare. In mine, some workmen had been welding up the windows that looked onto the passage and the area surrounding the plumbing below the two sinks in the one corner. The workmen had obviously taken a break as their tools were still lying about and the job had not been completed. Out of curiosity I looked below the sinks to see what they were welding there. The space was ideal for hiding things and it appeared that they were removing the wooden panelling that previously covered the area, and replacing it with sheet metal. As I looked closer, my eye suddenly caught sight of a glint from the pool of water that had collected in the concrete surround below one of the sinks. I put my hand through a gap in the panelling and grabbed hold of a heavy metal object. It was a large handmade dagger, complete with leather sheath. I put my hand in again and pulled out another, and another, and another – five in all.

The knives were beautifully crafted and had obviously just been hidden there by the prisoners who had been turfed out of the cell to make way for me. I quickly hid them in the metal lockers attached to the wall. The welders returned after a short while and completed their job. An hour later a gang of coloured prisoners brought in a bed, a real bed with a foam rubber mattress. They must have wondered who this *larney* (posh guy) was who was getting a real bed, alone in a ten-man cell.

The next day when the head of the prison came on his inspection round, I beckoned him towards the lockers. I opened one, took out a dagger and placed it in his hand. He stared at it speechless. The sergeant in charge of the two of us, who was standing behind the chief, was completely stunned and his mouth agape. The chief rebuked him for not searching the cell properly, but the sergeant swore that he had checked all the lockers. I assured the chief that the cell had not been properly checked and to prove my point I went to the second locker and took out the second dagger. The sergeant's mouth dropped even further open. The chief became agitated and asked if there were any more. I opened the third locker and removed the next one and then the fourth and the fifth. The sergeant just stood there not believing what he was seeing. How could he have missed five large daggers in five separate lockers?

I gently reminded the chief that he had to be careful of us "terrorists" as he could not tell what we would get up to with a set of daggers. No, he assured me, they trusted us and did not believe we would use daggers in the prison; only *skollies* (delinquents) did that.

To cap it all, the sergeant immediately launched another search of the cell and found a sharpened spoon hidden on a ledge inside one of the lockers that I myself had missed. I was surprised that he was allowed to keep his job after that.

The incident shook our minders so much that every day after that the sergeant came into both our cells and tapped every bar, window frame and pane of glass with a little hammer to check that we were not cutting our way out. Every hem of each sheet, blanket and item of clothing was checked, and the lockers, especially, were searched for "dangerous weapons". The deviousness of "terrorists" could not be overestimated!

They held us in those cells for about two weeks before transporting us to Pretoria. It was a lonely period, much like being in solitary confinement. We saw each other for only half an hour each day, when taken out for exercise on the roof of the prison. Otherwise we could not communicate. Our toilet pipes did not connect and our outer cell doors were kept locked. We thought of developing a code so that we could tap messages on the wall between our cells like prisoners did during the war but then decided it was too romantic. In any case we would soon be together in our destination prison and then we could talk as much as we wanted.

As newly sentenced prisoners we were allowed only one visit by one person for half an hour per month, which we both took in those two weeks. At his visit, Stephen's father brought the bad news that the regime had just announced that it was about to introduce a new set of currency notes. This meant that after a time the notes we had just smuggled in would cease to be legal tender. It was as if they knew we had the money and had deliberately decided to change it so that ours would be rendered invalid!

There were of course no more food parcels and no way of smuggling in any more contraband. The only "entertainment" permitted during those weeks were three books that were brought to us from the prison library each week. The rest of the time we spent having showers or just pacing madly round and round our oversized cells.

The trip to Pretoria was a nightmare that we will never forget. Without prior notice, they told us late one afternoon to pack our few things. This was no reason to suspect that we were about to be taken away;

a move to other cells seemed more likely. The issuing of a blanket and a brown paper bag containing two pieces of dried-out chicken, two boiled eggs and a few slices of bread confirmed that something more significant than a change of cells was about to take place. They led us through the administrative section and, very curiously, out of the front door of the prison to an armoured prison van parked in the street outside.

On each of us, they shackled a long chain between our left and right ankles and then pointed to an open door at the rear of the van. We looked through the door and thought they were pointing to something they wanted us to get out of the tiny compartment behind it. No, they wanted us to get into it. We looked at them disbelievingly, thinking that they were playing a game with us. No human being could surely be expected to travel all the way from Cape Town to Pretoria in a tool locker! *"Nee! Dis jou plek. Klim in!"* – "No! It's your place. Get in!" Against the back wall of the compartment was a narrow ledge on which we were meant to sit and at neck height a square metal tank with sharp edges protruded beyond the ledge, making it impossible to sit up straight.

The door was slammed shut and we could hear them locking padlocks on the outside. There was barely sufficient space to turn around, and to make matters worse there were two large milk churns on the floor: one containing fresh water and the other nothing. Presumably the empty one was for relieving ourselves. From the main compartment of the van we could hear the voices and chains of other prisoners.

With a sudden jerk the van set off, and through a small chink in the door we could see that a small Prison Service panel van was following us. The sun was beginning to set, but against the red winter sky we could still see the beautiful outline of Table Mountain. Both of us sadly acknowledged that it would be a long time before we saw that amazing and homely sight again.

As it grew darker it became colder. It was midwinter and we knew that our route to Pretoria, if indeed that was where we were being taken, passed through the Karoo, the dry central plain of South Africa, which becomes bitterly cold at night. Temperatures often drop to well below zero. We sat close to each other for warmth and wrapped ourselves in the single blankets we had been given. They were not very effective in keeping out the cold, as above us in the roof was a ventilator that blew a stream of cold air directly onto us. To make matters worse, the water in the milk churn splashed over the brim every time the van braked, cornered or accelerated and in no time our blankets and clothing were dripping wet. The problem was partially solved by removing some of the water with the metal dixies we had been allowed to bring along.

The cold became so intense that I felt like vomiting. Stephen developed diarrhoea and was forced to use the churn directly in front of me. With one hand he had to prevent his "charger" from discharging into the depths of the churn and with the other he had to grip onto the cabin's framework to prevent himself falling over. He was most embarrassed but I assured him I was out of the room under my blanket.

The van travelled at high speed through the night and stopped a number of times at distant police outposts, but the prisoners were never allowed out to stretch their aching limbs. Several times I almost knocked myself unconscious on the sharp edge of the water tank above our heads as the van lurched from side to side. On through that icy night a van-load of frozen prisoners were crying out.

It didn't warm significantly for a long time after sunrise. By that time our bodies were wracked with the intense pain of sitting in that cramped space coiled up in a ball to conserve warmth. The van stopped for an hour at a prison somewhere, where the drivers and guards got out – probably to stuff their pot-bellies with hot breakfast and morning coffee. The prisoners got nothing. Then on and on it went and Stephen's stomach grew worse and worse. He began to worry if he would ever get his "charger" back in place.

After midday the van passed through Johannesburg and sped on to Pretoria. We wondered where they would eventually deposit us. All long-term, white, male prisoners usually first went to Pretoria Central Prison for assessment. From there they were sent to other prisons, depending on the nature of their crimes. Would they send us there or would we be dropped off immediately at Pretoria Prison, the special prison for white, male political prisoners?

Part Two

Getting Out

Chapter Six

We Meet the Comrades

It was to be Pretoria Prison, "New European Section" – the special prison for white political prisoners. We thanked our stars that they did not take us to Pretoria Central. We couldn't face another bout of solitary, and had a prison to get out of.

When they opened the back of that prison van and we dismounted, uncrinkling ourselves from being cooped up in that damp, icy cage, we immediately felt that something was strange, at least as far as our limited prison experience could inform us. At Pollsmoor most boarding and alighting of prison vehicles took place inside the prison, behind massive steel doors. Now we didn't appear to be in a prison at all. We were standing in a street exposed for all the world to see, and in front of us stood a building that did not look very much like a prison at all. True, there was a high wall to our left but in front of us was a door, a varnished wooden door that would not have looked out of place on any suburban home. There were no barred windows or other signs that the building we were about to enter was a prison.

Two warders received us in the street. They unshackled the chains and threw them back into the compartment out of which we had just emerged. The sunshine felt marvellous on our frozen bodies and pale faces. They led us through the front door of the building, which wasn't even locked, but once inside we could see that indeed this was a prison. In front of us was a long passage with a great number of metal grilles across it. The first magically opened by itself: it was electrically operated. Another new experience. We passed through several more grilles and finally into a small room near the end of the passage.

A lieutenant in the room introduced himself and asked us to sign our names in the register. He took down our details and in return assigned us our prison numbers, which were to be used in all official and other communications he explained. My number was 393/78; Stephen's 394/78.

The atmosphere was relaxed and almost welcoming after Pollsmoor and the nightmare journey from Cape Town. There were no queues of black prisoners waiting to be signed in, no shouting and swearing, no rude warders rushing to and fro and no rattling of keys. It almost felt homely, quite unlike what we had expected.

The warders standing around eyed us up and down with curiosity as if they had never seen a prisoner before. It was a rare occasion that new prisoners were admitted to that prison, and all who were came for a long stay.

They asked us what size shoes and clothes we wore. Stephen and I looked at each other in disbelief. At Pollsmoor there was no asking. What seemed the right size to them was just thrown at you and you had to fit the item rather than the other way around. A warder brought our clobber from the store and deposited two neat piles of fresh clothing on the table in front of us. We discarded the badly fitting Pollsmoor "uniforms" for what appeared to be much cleaner, newer and better fitting outfits. A warder scooped up the stinking Pollsmoor rags from the floor, put them in a bag and was told to take them out to the waiting van. We dressed in our new rig, thinking to each other that this, dear friend, is how we are going to look for the next so many years. Get used to it!

The lieutenant gave a brief lecture about prisoner/staff relations. We were to address all warders, irrespective of rank, as *Meneer* – Mister. "*Ja Meneer!*" we responded. Relations were good and if we left them alone, they would leave us alone; if we caused trouble they would too. As simple as that. "Yes, yes. Sounds reasonable enough. We have no reason to give you any trouble, *Meneer.*" Then a snorting monster shuffled into the room, handlebar moustache and all – the notorious Captain Schnepel, we were to learn, the head of the prison.

Disrupting the lesson in prison etiquette he shouted: "Stand up straight! *Ja Kaptein!* when I speak to you, do you hear?" A few more strange gruntings and snufflings and then the beast disappeared. Obviously just some old buffoon trying to show who is boss around the place.

They took us up to our cells on the first floor. On the way we passed a door through which we could hear the sounds of cowboys shooting at Indians. The other prisoners were watching a film, they said, but we would have to wait for three months before being allowed to see any, and then only if we behaved ourselves.

A door was flung open and before us was our section – our home for the next so long. It was quite unlike Pollsmoor: the corridor was short and light with cells on one side only. I was put in cell 17, the first cell in the section and Stephen in cell 18, the second. A warder asked if we'd had anything to eat, to which we replied that we hadn't. A short while later a relatively decent meal of chicken legs and vegetables arrived. I shouted to Stephen that maybe things weren't going to be so bad after all.

We inspected our cells. They were light and airy, although a bit cramped: about three metres by two metres. They were larger than the cells at Pollsmoor but not really large enough for pacing up and down – an important consideration for prisoners. Pity. The roof was high: about 3 metres. The door was to the one side of my cell and as Stephen's cell was the mirror image of mine, our doors were close together and we could pass things to each other through the bars of our locked grilles. As at Pollsmoor, our cells also had outer panelled steel doors, but they were left open that afternoon.

The bed was hard, but not uncomfortable. At least it was a proper bed, not a mat on the floor. It was neatly covered with a blue bedspread. At the foot of the bed was a toilet. It was of the type we had grown accustomed to, with two curved pieces of wood fastened to the rim of the bowl on which you sat, but so uncomfortable that you couldn't sit on it for very long. The only difference was that it had a cover. On the wall was a push-button that flushed endless cascades of water – very handy for getting rid of contraband, we had come to learn. Next to the toilet on the far wall was an ordinary porcelain hand basin with two taps. I wondered what the second tap was for. Real hot water! What next? It felt hot enough to make coffee.

A shoulder-high cupboard was fixed against the wall opposite the bed. Out of the middle of it projected a shelf that could be pulled out and used as a table if you sat on the edge of the bed. Above the bed was a bookshelf and, in the corner, next to the basin a stool. That was all as far as "furniture" and "conveniences" were concerned.

At the far end of the cell above the basin was a large window and next to the door looking into the corridor another but smaller window. There were no bars in the windows as such: a number of narrow, vertical windows closed onto frames that served as the bars. The windows could individually be swung open but the space between the frames was too narrow to fit your head through. Rumour had it that inside the frames were indestructible tungsten bars, but this was probably just a story circulated by the prison authorities to stop prisoners trying to find out. We were amazed at the thickness of the outer wall. There was enough space to crouch sideways on the window ledge on the inside and an equal space on the other side of the window.

Outside was an extraordinary sight. Instead of just bare concrete, as there had been at Pollsmoor, there was a well-tended garden with a central concreted area marked out as a small tennis court. On either side of the court were large patches of well-trimmed lawn. At the far end were several trees, one so tall that it obscured the view of the warder pacing up and down a roofed catwalk on top of a high wall. The left-hand end of the catwalk was glassed off, forming a shelter for the warder on duty. The warder carried an automatic rifle. Along the right-hand side of the yard was a tall corrugated iron wall that appeared to be a temporary structure, and about halfway along its length a door that seemed to lead out of the prison. "The way out!" was our simultaneous first thought.

We were left to survey our new world for about two hours before we met the comrades. With a loud clang the section door flew open and in they trooped. The comrades congregated in front of our grilles to take a look at the "new guys" in their cages. We shook hands through the bars and exchanged names with each of them in turn. They were clearly excited to see some new faces but we were a bit apprehensive because we weren't sure who they were and how many there would be. As it turned out, most of those whom we had expected to be there were there. Only two we had never heard of before.

The person who had been there the longest was Denis Goldberg, one of the Rivonia Trialists who had been sentenced with Nelson Mandela and other ANC leaders in June 1964. He had received no less than four life sentences for allegedly "campaigning to overthrow the government by violent revolution". Denis, like us, was from Cape Town and had been an engineer before his capture. He was a young man of 30 and father of two at the time of his arrest in 1963. When we met him that first time he was 45.

Next was Dave Kitson, who had been inside for just a few months less than Denis. He was sentenced to 20 years in December 1964 for his part in the early sabotage campaigns, for furthering the aims of "communism" and for being a member of the High Command of Umkhonto we Sizwe. Like Denis he was also an engineer, but came from Johannesburg. He was 59 and had divorced his wife when he was imprisoned, "to give her her freedom".

John Matthews was sentenced to 15 years in the same trial as Dave Kitson. It was alleged that he assisted in obtaining materials for making bombs, but I never found out exactly what he had done that deserved such a long sentence. In his trial he had grounds for appealing against his sentence but refused to do so, claiming that he was proud to be sentenced along with his co-accused. Johnny had been a bookkeeper and father in Johannesburg and was 65 years old. We had not heard of him or Dave Kitson before.

After them in date and length of sentence was Alex Moumbaris. He was sentenced in June 1973 to 12 years' imprisonment for, among other things, "conspiring with the ANC to instigate violent revolution in South Africa", aiding guerrillas to enter the country, distributing ANC literature and reconnoitring the Transkei coast to find places for the sea-borne landing of guerrillas and arms.

Alex was 40 when we met him that first time. He was the only prisoner who was not South African and as such was to South African propaganda the archetypal "communist". According to this view all communists were, firstly, white, then foreigners or acting on behalf of some foreign power (usually Russia) and thirdly, but not necessarily, Jewish – which Alex was not. He was born in Egypt of Greek parents. His family emigrated to Australia when he was young, but he left the place when he was 16 because, in his own words, it was "the arse-end of the world". After that he spent a number of years in France where he married his wife, Marie-José. He then moved to London where he worked for about nine years before getting involved with the ANC.

He was arrested in 1972 with Marie-José while trying to enter South Africa from Botswana. Because she was pregnant at the time and because of pressure from the French ambassador, Marie-José was not charged but promptly deported to France.

Raymond Suttner was sentenced to seven and a half years in November 1975 for "taking part in the activities of an unlawful organisation" by distributing ANC literature, and "undergoing training or inciting or encouraging others to undergo training, or obtaining information which could be of use in furthering the achievements of any of the objects of communism or any unlawful organisation". Before his arrest he was a senior lecturer in law at the University of Natal in Durban. He was 32.

David Rabkin and Jeremy Cronin, who were mentioned earlier, were sentenced in September 1976 to ten and seven years respectively. David, who was 30, was working as a sub-editor for the *Argus* newspaper in Cape Town when he was detained with his wife Sue. From here on Dave Rabkin will be known as Dave R so as to avoid confusion with Dave K.

Jeremy, who was 28, had been a lecturer in political science at the University of Cape Town. His wife, Anne-Marie, died shortly after his imprisonment due to a brain haemorrhage and he was denied permission to attend her funeral.

The person last sentenced before us was Tony Holiday, who was also mentioned before. He was given six years in November 1976 for establishing an underground cell with three others, receiving money from the ANC, publishing ANC literature, receiving "subversive" training while working in Britain, training recruits to evade surveillance, all with the aim of "promoting the policies of a banned organisation". Tony had been a senior reporter on the *Cape Times* at the time of his detention and before that a political reporter for the Johannesburg *Rand Daily Mail*. He was 38.

In a way the comrades were heroes to us. They were all people who had inspired us with their dedication to the cause and with their selfless actions that had got them into prison. They reminded us while we were working underground that there were other white South Africans who were prepared to cast aside their privileges and throw in their lot with the oppressed; that we were not mad and that there were others doing the same sort of work as us.

The older comrades, Denis, Dave K and John, were all imprisoned before we became politically involved. They were of another generation. But Denis was one of Mandela's compatriots and as such one of the names we held in highest esteem. The detentions and trials of the others we had followed with great interest and had been inspired by the brave statements they made from the dock. The trials of Raymond and Dave R and Jeremy had provided us with much information about how they had run their cells and how the police had tracked them down. Their imprisonment had angered us no end and spurred us on to even greater activity, not deterred us as was intended.

We had expected the comrades, especially those who had been in prison for 15 years, to be somewhat oppressed by their condition. But that was not the case. Although obviously not happy to be where they were, they were a group of people full of spirit and as committed to the cause as they were on the day they were arrested – some of them probably even more so.

Denis, in particular, was an inspiration and made us feel ashamed of feeling sorry for ourselves. He had been in prison since we were young teenagers and had no release date to look forward to. People had come, served long sentences, and gone out. He would still be in prison after we had served our sentences, yet the prospect did not undermine his strength and commitment. It should have been us helping him but it was he who helped us by reminding us that our sentences were just "parking tickets"!

At the time of our arrival, Pretoria Prison was part of a giant prison complex known incorrectly as "Pretoria Central". In this complex were actually three separate prisons or prison clusters: Pretoria Central Prison proper, Pretoria Prison and a third known only as "Maximum" or "Beverly Hills". Also in the complex were warders' houses, a prison shop, a shooting range and sporting and other recreational facilities for the warders.

Pretoria Central proper consisted of a number of separate prison buildings. In keeping with South African apartheid "tradition": one for white males, one for black males, one for white females, one for black females, and so on. Central was a "national" prison and a reception centre where many prisoners started and ended their sentences. Pretoria Prison was Pretoria's local prison and consisted of "non-white" sections for ordinary prisoners; possibly separate "white" sections for ordinary prisoners, and a maximum-security section, which was our prison. "Maximum" was a special, high-security prison for recidivists, habitual escapees, the "State President's patients" and the condemned.

Ours was not a large prison. It was a single building consisting of only 52 cells and built in the late 1960s specifically for white male political prisoners. At no stage had there ever been more than 22 political prisoners in the prison, with the average complement being about ten. For this reason, the remaining cells were used for housing awaiting-trial prisoners, known in prison language as *"stokkies"*, from the Xhosa word *isitokisi*, which means "prison".

The prison building was L-shaped (*see photograph*) and three storeys high. The ground floor of the long wing of the "L" consisted of administrative offices; the short wing contained our dining room, storeroom, workshop and a toilet. The door to the street – through which we had entered the prison – was at the far end of the administrative section. Apart from the gate leading out of the prison yard – which actually led into prison property next door – there were no other exits from the prison.

The first and second floors consisted of cells. Ours were on the first floor of the short wing; the *stokkies* occupied the rest. Each wing of cells was sealed off from the other wings and parts of the prison by panelled steel doors, making them into self-contained sections. Each section consisted of 10 or 16 cells, all of them facing the yard. The outer walls of the "L" had no windows or exits at all.

In the middle of each section were two shower rooms with two showers in each. At both ends of all sections were stairways leading into the yard. The stairway at the far end of the short sections had been sealed off as its ground floor entrance no longer led into the yard but into the property next door. This was as a result of the positioning of the temporary corrugated iron wall along the side of the yard a few metres inward of the old wall, leaving the entrance outside the yard. This was a temporary arrangement while construction work was going on next door. The stairway in the bend of the "L" was strictly reserved for us political prisoners; the *stokkies* used the stairway at the far end above the front door.

The prison yard was on the inside of the "L". As explained, at the far end of the yard opposite our cells was a catwalk, known to the prisoners as the *"pos"* – from the Afrikaans word for "post". The entrance to the *pos* was through a door at the base of the wall, also on the outside of the corrugated iron fence for the same reason as the sealed-off door at the bottom of the disused stairway. The vast part of the yard was reserved for our use but about a quarter of it below the *pos* was fenced off by a 2-m high corrugated iron fence for the *stokkies'* use. The political prisoners were allowed to enter the *stokkies'* yard through a gate that was never closed, provided there were no *stokkies* in it.

In the centre of the yard was our tennis and volleyball court with the two patches of lawn alongside it. Along the base of the corrugated iron wall was a flower-and-vegetable bed and dotted around the yard several smaller flowerbeds. Around the yard too were a number of shrubs and trees. The tallest one, which obscured the view of the warder on the *pos*, was grown by the comrades from an avocado pip. Several of the other trees were also fruit trees.

The prison workshop was entered through a door opening onto the yard. Next to it was a toilet and next to that the storeroom where we kept our books and sports and gardening equipment. The storeroom door also opened onto the yard but at the back of the room, behind the toilet, was a door leading into the workshop. This door was never unlocked (by the warders, that is). Next to the storeroom a door led into our dining room. A double door at the other end of the dining room opened into the prison at the bottom of the stairs we used to reach our section. This door was also normally kept locked.

Our prison had no kitchen facilities so our and the *stokkies'* food was brought to us in pots from the kitchens in the main part of Pretoria Prison behind our prison. There was a stove in our dining room but it was meant for heating the food, which often arrived cold. We were also allowed to use it at weekends to cook foods that we could buy with our allowances.

The only other objects in the yard worthy of mention were a dog kennel for the dog that was placed in the yard at night, and two searchlights – one mounted on the *pos* wall and the other on a tall pole in the middle of one of the patches of lawn.

The prisoners' day started at five thirty in the morning when a bell rang and the night-warder switched on the cell lights. The prisoners had to be up, dressed, shaved and have their beds made and cells tidied in time for inspection at 7 am when the cells were unlocked. The section was not opened at the same time because we were required to sweep the passage, empty the dustbins and dust the window ledges before being released into the yard to await the arrival of our breakfast at half past seven.

To pass the time until breakfast, most of us kept fit by running around the yard, otherwise we walked up and down the tennis court and discussed the day's prospects.

Breakfast was followed by workshop duty for most of us. Our work consisted of assembling and finishing various items of prison furniture that had been prepared at the main workshops at Central – things like bookshelves, tables and benches. Those who did not work in the workshop were responsible for tidying and cleaning our part of the prison.

In the carpentry workshop, the warder on duty shouted "time" at 10 am. This oft-repeated and much-hated word signalled the start of the 10-minute morning tea break, when we drank the weak black tea prepared for us by Denis. A similar "time" would signal its end. At eleven thirty a gang of black prisoners with a white warder in attendance arrived with our lunch, carried on trays, sedan-car style – a scene that reminded us of colonial explorers marching through darkest Africa with their black porters carrying their equipment and supplies.

After lunch we were locked in our cells from noon to 1 pm while the prison staff took their lunch break. During this period a heavily censored recording of radio "news" was relayed to us over loudspeakers mounted in the passage. Later, the speakers were mounted inside our cells so you could turn them off if you didn't want to listen to the "news". After that it was back to the workshop until two, when there was another tea break. At three thirty another "time" announced the end of the day's work session. Up to the section again for a quick shower and back down to the yard to wait for supper, which arrived at about four. At suppertime, letters, library books and study assignments were handed out. The final "time" of the day was called just after half past four when the warders locked us in our cells for the night.

Shortly after lock-up, the day-warders went off duty and a single night-warder took over. He played us another "news" broadcast and, until 8 pm, a selection of music from our large collection of records on our record player in his office. Lights out for the *stokkies* was at 8 pm, when the night-warder carried out an inspection tour of the prison. For us lights out was at 11 pm, marking the end of the day. At ten, a guard came on duty on the *pos* and at midnight there was a change of night-warders.

There were some variations to this basic routine. On Fridays there was no workshop duty. Instead, in the morning we were required to scrub down our part of the prison. On a rotating basis some comrades washed the passage floor of the section while others washed the floor of the dining room. This did not take long and for the rest of the morning we were locked, unguarded, in our section with our cell doors open. During this time, we were meant to clean our cells but since most of us maintained them in a respectable state it became a much-valued period for holding discussions, playing cards, chess, Scrabble and other games, and for doing other things.

Friday afternoons were set aside for the showing of films. During our first six months they only showed movies once every two weeks, but later on this changed to every week. When there were no movies, we played tennis in the yard or just lay about reading and chatting.

Saturdays and Sundays were reserved for sport – mainly tennis. We were allowed to remain in the yard until the lunchtime lock-up and after that until suppertime, which was an hour earlier. Lock-up was also an hour earlier. There were occasional variations to this routine if there was a shortage of warders or someone in authority visited the prison, but in general this was the pattern of daily and weekly events.

Chapter Seven

First Approaches

It was on our fourth day in Pretoria Prison that Stephen and I decided to tell the comrades about the money we had smuggled in. Before our arrival we had decided to wait until we had sussed everyone out before revealing our secret: we did not want to have someone go straight to the authorities with the information. But it was soon obvious to us that the comrades were not sell-outs. They conducted themselves with integrity, seemed to be united in their convictions and there were no obvious antagonisms. As Denis appeared to be the most senior of the prisoners, we decided to tell him first. He would be able to advise us when or whether we should tell the others and how and where to hide it. To avoid losing all our cash if it went wrong, Stephen and I decided that he would reveal his stash first; if it worked out okay then I would reveal mine at a later time.

During the pre-breakfast walk up and down the tennis court, Stephen broke his news to Denis. Predictably Denis was amazed and excited, probably a bit suspicious too. But that was to be expected, for it must have seemed a bit odd to an old lag to have a four-day-old prisoner come sidling up to him and claim to have a couple of hundred rand stashed up his arse. After Denis had recovered his composure, Stephen asked him for advice on how to hide the money. Probably thinking it the best thing to test Stephen's credentials, Denis offered to take the money and hide it himself. After all, if Stephen had been given the money to trap Denis, it would have been a bit difficult for the authorities to claim that he had been sitting with it for the previous 15 years.

Denis took the money and concealed it inside a spare tube of toothpaste he had in his cell. To us this seemed a bit dicey but he assured Stephen that as far as he could remember his toothpaste had never been violated. Denis also spread the news among the other prisoners.

A few days later, after deciding with Stephen that it was safe to do so, I too approached Denis. We were walking in the yard and when I revealed my secret he came to an abrupt halt and stared at me in astonishment. What are these new guys up to, he must have been thinking. Money in prison, as he knew full well, can be used for three things only: bribery, smuggling and escaping.

Three hundred and sixty rand would have seemed a lot to any prisoner at that time, but to Denis it must have sounded even more as he had never had a chance to come to terms with the prevailing notions of inflation. In his amazement at the revelation, he could do no more than advise me to do the same with my money as he had done with Stephen's. The toothpaste tubes turned out to be good hiding places for the money, as it was never discovered.

In the course of our first days, Stephen and I discussed with each of the others the question of escaping. This did not raise their suspicions as escaping is the most natural thing for prisoners to talk about, especially new prisoners. Everyone said that they had of course thought about it, but none of them came up with any concrete or viable ideas of how it could be done. This both amazed and disappointed us as we had expected them to have had some pretty thoroughly worked out plans or at least some good ideas, as some of them had been in prison for a very long time. It made us think that perhaps we had been naïve to imagine that we could escape from one of South Africa's most secure prisons. Perhaps we really would have to serve our full terms. That thought was demoralising in the extreme.

Denis, in particular, had given the question a lot of thought and had actually attempted an escape while in detention before he was sentenced. The only time a collective escape had seriously been considered – many years earlier when the comrades were housed at Pretoria Local, the first prison in which they were held – it had been betrayed by one of the prisoners, Raymond Thoms. Thoms was the only white political prisoner who was thoroughly broken by the prison experience. He went a bit mad and started narking on the others, who naturally sent him to Coventry. He committed suicide sometime after his release.

Denis himself considered the chances of getting out of the prison to be fairly good but did not believe it would be possible to get away from the prison, off the terrain and out of the country without outside assistance. Naturally, any thinking he had given the problem involved making an exit via the prison yard. He could only offer suggestions, not a thoroughly worked out plan. He believed that the security situation around the prison was thoroughly sewn up.

I approached Alex separately because he seemed to be a little aloof from the others. Surprisingly, the others had not shared the news with him that we had brought money in with us. I told him about the money, how we had brought it in and what we had done with it but did not say that our intention was to use it for an escape. Later that same day he came back to me and said that if any escape plans were being hatched, he would definitely like to be one of the chickens. His response singled him out from the others, none of whom drew the conclusion that we had brought the money in for the specific purpose of escaping. I asked Alex if he had any bright ideas how an escape might be pulled off, but he didn't have any. He did point out, however, that whatever plans were contemplated they would all involve the making of keys. How we could make them he didn't know as there were no obviously suitable materials around out of which to make them. I said to him that I thought it might be possible to make a key out of wood but he contemptuously rejected that idea. The giant prison locks, he insisted, would require keys of a much more robust material to turn them. I believed otherwise.

In our first weeks at Pretoria, Steve and I carefully studied the layout of the prison to see if there were any obvious cracks in the prison's security. From our initial observations, all escape routes had their origin in the prison yard. It was reasonable to think that way, for once you were in the yard the only barrier between you and freedom was the yard wall. Any other starting point meant that you were placing more barriers in front of yourself, not fewer. You could take your cell as the point of departure but once out of it you had to get out of the prison building, and that meant into the yard. There were only four doors leading out of the actual prison building, and three of them led directly into the yard. The fourth, the front door, led directly into the street but that was totally out of the question because the only way to get to it was by passing clean through the administrative section where the prison staff hung out, and opening a great many doors and gates on the way.

How to get out of the prison yard was another question. The yard gate, although it led out of our prison, opened into prison property next door – into the site of the old Pretoria Local that was about to be demolished. That was not very useful, but as the demolition progressed, we thought it might begin to offer some prospects.

The opportunities for traditional escape methods, such as digging tunnels, making holes in walls and crawling through ducts and pipes were nil. Our cells were on the first floor so there was nowhere to dig to. There were no opportunities to dig a tunnel from the yard as it was mostly concreted and visible to the guards. Anyway, where would the tunnel go and where could we hide the rubble? Our prison was in a prison complex, so if we could have dug a tunnel it would have come up somewhere in prison property.

Nonetheless, we believed that it would be possible, somehow, to get over or under the yard wall and into the street. There had to be a way. We would eventually discover it – it would just take time.

The security arrangements that had been installed indicated that the prison authorities also recognised that if an escape was to be attempted it would have to start from or go through the yard. There were searchlights that illuminated it at night like a football stadium, and after lock-up a large, ferocious guard-dog was placed in it. The dogs were of a breed that would have torn apart a prisoner on the loose. The *pos*, with its armed guard, eliminated the possibility of prisoners making a dash for freedom during the day.

We did, however, notice a few cracks in the security: the dog was never placed in the yard exactly at lock-up (four thirty) and sometimes up to an hour later; between lock-up and 10 pm there was no guard on the *pos*. This meant that if we could get out of our cells shortly after lock-up and into the yard before the dog arrived, it might be possible to scale a wall to get into the street. The prospects did not look brilliant but there was some hope. One thing was clear: we could not rely solely on cracks in the security arrangements to get out – we had to develop our own capabilities to exploit them and expose others.

To be able to get into the yard after lock-up, or to be able to do anything at all for that matter, we needed keys. But how could we make them? How could we get the dimensions? Between us we knew only a little about how locks worked. I had once removed and opened the lock of the back door of my parents' home to see how it worked, and had made a pick with a piece of bent wire. The giant prison locks looked more formidable than anything we had experienced in civilian life. Still, we couldn't allow ourselves to be intimidated by their size. Inside they were probably the same as any ordinary locks of a similar kind.

For several nights I sat on my bed and stared at the lock on my grille. It was completely accessible as it was right there, bolted to the frame. I could even see right through the keyhole and get my hand around the other side of it because there was a fair space between the grille and the outer door. I *had* to make a key for it, but I didn't know where to start. Since the warders never left their keys lying around for us to take measurements or impressions, there was no alternative but to work it out for myself.

I dared not tell anyone apart from Stephen that I was planning to make a key, for we had no idea how the comrades would respond if we raised the subject first. We knew that it would be a different matter to announce that we had made a key that worked.

After two weeks I decided to stop staring at my lock and get down to the business of finding out its secrets. I lit a match to see inside the keyhole, but all I could see were the scrape marks against the inner faces of the lock where the key had turned. The levers were above the keyhole and so out of sight. Then it occurred to me that simply by measuring the parts of the lock around the keyhole I could obtain most of the dimensions of the key. By measuring the diameter of the round part of the keyhole with a ruler, I got the diameter of the key shaft. The length of the key shaft that went through the round part of the keyhole was obviously the same as the thickness of the lock on the outside.

The width of the head of the key, or the "bit" in locksmith's lingo, and the shape of the ward cutaways in the side of the bit I established by inserting a piece of paper through the keyhole and creating an impression on it by pressing it against the keyway with my bread knife. The internal measurements of the lock I took directly from the indentations on the paper.

The final and most crucial measurements were the depths of the "cuts" on the top of the bit. These are what make a key unique. They lift the levers inside the lock to the correct heights in order to open an internal "gate" that permits the locking bolt to slide in and out. I had noticed that there were five cuts on all the warders' keys, meaning that the locks had at most five levers inside them. By dividing the width of the bit by five, I worked out the widths of the individual cuts. As the keys had to be symmetrical in order to work from both sides of the lock, I only had to know the depths of half of the cuts, meaning in practice three of them because there were two cuts on either side of the middle one. And because those two cuts were the same depth, there were in fact only two cut depths that I needed to know. (*See diagram*)

Simply by measuring the distance from the centre of the round part of the keyhole (the axis of the key shaft) to the outer radius of the scrape marks inside the lock, I established the absolute heights of the two outer cuts (1 and 5). Once I knew that, finding the depths of the inner three cuts (2, 3 and 4) was made easier because I only had to know their depths relative to the height of the outer cuts 1 and 5. Fortunately on this first key, the cuts were all of the same depth relative to each other. In other words, the middle cut (3) was as deep relative to the inner two (2 and 4) as these were to the outer two (1 and 5). This actually meant that there was only one dimension that I needed to know, as the depth of cut 3 was simply twice the depth of cuts 2 and 4.

The only way to establish the depths of the three inner cuts relative to the outer two was by staring at the warders' keys and making an estimate based on eye judgement. This might sound incredible but there was simply no other way of obtaining the measurements, short of waiting – probably forever – for an opportunity to physically measure them when a warder inadvertently left his bunch of keys lying around. At every opportunity I stared at the warders' keys, and there were plenty of opportunities as they derived a sense of power by displaying and jingling them in front of us. I also watched very carefully when they were locking and unlocking my doors right in front of me.

I estimated the two inner cuts (2 and 4) to be 2 mm deeper than the outer two (1 and 5), and the middle one (3) to be 2 mm deeper than 2 and 4 (in other words, a total of 4 mm deep). I drew a life-size diagram of the key on a piece of card, and then cut it out and tried this two-dimensional "key" in the lock. Of course it did not turn the bolt but it did not jam in the keyway, indicating that at least most of the dimensions were correct (*see diagram*). The key looked good on paper but how to turn it into a real, working key was altogether another matter.

In the absence of any other suitable materials, I decided to try making the key out of wood. I searched the workshop for some hard wood and found a number of off-cuts from an earlier job carried out by the comrades. Stephen and I roughly cut out the pieces of the key from the bits of wood I had found. There were three pieces: the shaft, the bit and the handle.

The reason for making the key out of three separate pieces of wood instead of carving it out of one solid piece, was to take advantage of the strengths offered by the different directions of the grain of the separate pieces of wood. A key carved out of a single piece of wood with the grain running parallel to the shaft was strong for the twisting action of the key, but the bit would break off easily because the pressure of the key against the levers would snap it across the grain. A separate wooden bit mounted at right angles to the shaft was much stronger. The vertical grain was unlikely to break off when lifting the levers and turning the bolt.

Cutting the pieces in the workshop did not arouse anyone's suspicion, as they bore no resemblance to the parts of a key. Everyone made odds and ends for themselves, and as new prisoners they expected us to be making all sorts of things for ourselves, such as stands for our shaving mirrors, boxes for pens, hangers for clothes and suchlike.

The next step was to assemble the pieces and turn them into a key. I could obviously not do this in the workshop so we had to figure out a safe way of getting the pieces and necessary tools up to my cell. We had noticed that the others smuggled things up to their cells by unscrewing the bottoms of their Thermos flasks and hiding them around the glass inner container. We were allowed to take flasks up to our cells at night with tea, coffee or soup. This seemed a good way, so one afternoon I hid a small triangular file, some pieces of sandpaper, a sachet of wood glue and the pieces of the key in the storeroom next to the workshop. At suppertime I secreted them into the bottom of my flask and at lock-up took them up to my cell.

As soon as the day-warders knocked off duty I set to work. First, I rounded one end of the square shaft until it fitted and turned in the keyhole and went right through the lock. Then I filed a rebate in the bit and glued it into a slit in the end of the shaft I had just rounded, and glued the handle into a slit in the other end of the shaft. When the glue had set, I cut the bit to size, filed the ward cutaways into the side of it and the cuts into the top of it according to the dimensions I had worked out (*see diagram*).

After shaping the key, I tried it out. To my absolute astonishment, it worked the first time! Not only did it work, it turned with such ease that I thought it had broken inside the lock. I got such a fright that I withdrew it immediately and hid it under my clothes in the cupboard. I sat on the edge of my bed with my heart pounding and hands trembling. "Soon there will be a troop of goons marching up here to drag me off for attempting to escape", I thought. I started imagining hidden video cameras peering down at me through tiny holes in the ceiling; microphones that had heard the lock turning and secret alarms signalling the lock had been tampered with. Such are the effects of a guilty conscience!

After I had calmed down and no warder had come up to question me, a peculiar sense of defiance and achievement crept over me. It was a feeling that I was to experience many times later on, a feeling that is difficult to describe but one that anyone who has cocked a snook at authority will know.

I retrieved the key from its hiding place and tried it again. True enough, it really had worked. As the key had to be turned two full revolutions for the bolt to be turned fully in, I slowly turned it round once and then half the second turn. I dared not turn the bolt all the way in and swing the grille open, as I feared that for some reason it might not relock. If the lock was found to be only half-locked that could be blamed on a careless warder, but there would be no way of explaining a fully open door with its bolt turned right in.

The next morning, I took the key and file downstairs in the same way as I had brought them up. I hid the key behind a bookshelf in the storeroom and later returned the file to the workshop. In the workshop I broke the good news to Stephen, which he greeted with such excitement that the others demanded to know what we were so elated about. But we had agreed not to tell anyone until we had made a key for door number two – the outer cell door. We thought that premature announcement might result in us being regarded as provocateurs.

The success of the first key proved that it was possible to make keys out of wood. The reason why we had at first thought that wood might not be suitable medium was because whenever a warder opened a lock, he did it with such gusto that we were led to believe that the lock mechanism offered a lot of resistance to turning. The opposite was in fact the truth. The vigorous turning was no more than part of the warders' need to demonstrate their power over us. Our keys could have been made of metal, and later were as we perfected our methods, but wood had certain distinct advantages: it was readily available in the workshop; the pieces of the keys could be roughly shaped more or less openly (the warders would never have imagined that a key could be made out of wood and if they had spotted one of us cutting a piece of key it could easily be explained away as something else); a wooden key operated relatively silently; it did not leave scrape marks inside the lock; it was easily disposed of; key jams left scrape marks on the wood, indicating where more filing was necessary; and the final shaping and measuring could be done in the cell after lock-up.

Now that we had found a material out of which to make keys and had developed a method of constructing them, we could proceed with the next ones until we had all the keys needed to get ourselves into the yard and out of it. But making the keys turned out to be more complicated than we had at first thought. The double-locking action of the locks confused us. As far as we could see, the doors could be locked with two completely different sets of keys: one set by the warders during the day and one set by the night-warder. According to our fellow prisoners, the day-keys were master keys that could turn the locks both turns, while the night-warders' could only turn them once. The logic for this, they explained, was to make it pointless for a prisoner to attempt to persuade the night-warder – through bribery, force or collusion – to be let out, as his keys would not be able to unlock the mastered cell doors. The section doors through which he needed access were not mastered. The night-warder was in fact locked inside the prison by the departing day-warders and was let out the next morning when they came back on duty.

The second key turned out to be a much greater obstacle than the first. Door two was a panelled steel door with only one keyhole – on the outside. As such, the major dimensions of the key could not be obtained as easily as the first key's. But as key two looked pretty much the same in overall size as key one, I guessed that its main dimensions would be the same: the diameter of the key shaft, the length of the bit and the depth of the neck. As can be seen from the diagrams, the ward cutaways were extraordinarily complicated and the shape of the cuts also much more complicated.

The main problem with door two was that we seldom had access to the outside of it. When we were due to be locked into our cells, the warders usually brought us smartly from downstairs and locked us up immediately. The only times we could get to look at the keyhole was during shower-time – when we were usually left unattended in the section – and on Friday mornings when we were locked in the section to clean it. Shower-time was not really suitable as the time was short and a warder could come into the section at any moment; Fridays were a better prospect as we were left in the section unattended for several hours with our cell doors open. The main problem in the beginning was that if Steve or I started peering into locks, the others would straight away see what we were up to. As we didn't want to be seen doing anything that might arouse suspicion, it was clear that in order to proceed we needed to tell the others.

After making a blank key for door two based on the measurements of the first key and guesswork, I broke the news about the first key to Jeremy one afternoon in the workshop. I decided to tell him first, not just because I worked right next to him but because he was the most approachable and Steve and I had judged that he would be more interested in participating in an escape than the others. We did not know what to expect, but to our relief he responded with considerable excitement and interest. I told him of the problem we faced with door two and asked him if he would be prepared to assist by asking Dave R if we could test the new key in his door the coming Friday. We wanted to use Dave's door because it was the last in the passage and furthest from the section door; mine being the first and hence the worst. Jeremy agreed to do this and later in the day informed me that Dave had agreed.

Before the Friday I also told Alex about the first key. He found it hard to believe that I had managed to get a wooden key to work but was most excited about the prospects. To prove it for himself, he took the key from me and tried it in his grille at lunchtime. Clearly it worked as well in his lock as it had in mine, for that afternoon in the workshop, with a broad grin on his face, he hollowed out a piece of wood, put the key in it, glued another piece of wood over it and planed the two pieces to make it look like a single block.

That Friday we tested the number two key, but it did not turn at all because the ward cutaways in the bit were incorrect. At that early stage we were not entirely sure of the function of ward cutaways and did not realise that they were there only to clear circular ridges or obstructions (wards) in the keyway that blocked the use of incorrect keys, and that the bit could simply have been cut away on its sides to clear all the wards.

I was bitterly disappointed at the failure as I had expected the key to work the first time like number one. I was planning to tackle the third door – the section door – that weekend and for us be out in the next few weeks. After the first success it was difficult to reconcile myself to the idea that the job of making keys was not going to be quite as easy as I had at first imagined, and that it would be longer than a mere few weeks before we were free. It was also difficult to cope with the knowledge that we could do absolutely nothing more with door two until the next Friday. I had not yet adapted to prison time, which is different to outside time in that it lacks the distance dimension. The next Friday seemed eternally far away.

Testing with a new key the following Friday resulted in our first disaster, and also our first experience of extremely good luck. Having become bolder, and because everyone now knew, I tried out the key in all the number two locks. It turned part of the way in all of them, indicating that the ward cutaways were now correct but that the cuts were not, as it did not bring out the bolt in any lock except mine. I should have realised that this meant something was wrong but the excitement of seeing the bolt move out blinded me – I wanted to see it come out and go back in again. At first, I was worried about turning it all the way out for fear that it might not return, but I could not contain my curiosity and gradually turned it out completely. I then tried to turn it the second time to master lock it but it would not turn any further. The realisation of what I had done suddenly hit me like a blow to the head. I tried desperately to turn the bolt back in but it would not budge. I began to panic and tried to force it in, but all that happened was that the key broke. Fortunately, it did not come to pieces inside the lock and I was able to extract the damaged implement. It was also fortunate that the door was open, as it would have been more difficult to explain a door that had locked itself closed. Unable to do anything about it, there was simply no option but to leave the door with the bolt sticking out and hope for the best. I broke up the damaged key and flushed the pieces down my toilet.

Luckily, when the warders locked us up after lunch, they said nothing about the bolt being out and even started to blame each other for not being able to unlock doors properly. All that we could conclude from the incident was that it must have been possible for an overzealous warder to jiggle his key out of the keyhole and accidentally turn out the bolt. The key had worked in my lock and not in any of the others' because when I turned it, my bolt must have been partially out and the levers already lifted up. Turning the bolt fully out caused the levers to latch, preventing the bolt from moving in again.

After this near-disaster it was unanimously decided that all future testing of number two doors was to be done when they were locked. This presented a huge problem, as the only time they were locked was when we were inside our cells and thus when we had no direct access to the keyhole. How can you unlock the door from inside a safe?

The narrow panes of the passage windows opened sufficiently to allow you to stick an arm through, but at full stretch your hand was still at least a metre from the keyhole. Obviously, we needed to make some kind of device to help us reach it. Several schemes were devised, the first of which were inordinately complicated and would have involved using a series of pulleys and ropes. These proved too difficult to implement and were unrealistic in that they required bringing a load of equipment into our cells.

While contemplating one of these schemes, I needed to measure the distance from the window to the keyhole. I looked around for something to use as a "ruler" and spotted my broom. I unscrewed the brush and stuck the broomstick out of my window. Using a mirror, I could see that the end of the broomstick easily reached the keyhole. As I looked at it touching the keyhole, it suddenly occurred to me: Why not fix the key to the end of the broomstick somehow so that it can be inserted into the keyhole to open the door?

I retracted the broomstick and contemplated it further. The solution suddenly became obvious and I wondered why I hadn't thought of it before: simply create a wooden crank handle with one end attached to the broomstick and the other end holding the key. All I had to do was drill a hole in the end of the broomstick ("so that it could be hung up") and cut a piece of wood to serve as the crank and key holder.

Next morning, I discussed the idea with Alex, and when he suddenly visualised it he also couldn't understand why he hadn't thought of it before. It seemed so obvious and, like all good ideas, it was simple and elegant. Alex immediately cut a rectangular block of wood and chiselled a square hole through the one end to accommodate the square part of the wooden key handle. To prevent the key falling out, he drilled a hole in the side of the block for a small retainer screw. At the other end of the block he inserted a large screw, sufficiently long enough to go through the broom handle (*see diagram*).

That night I tested it. I removed the brush from my broomstick and assembled the device. The block and key dangled from the end of my broomstick. To the brush end of the broomstick that I was holding, I fastened a piece of string and tied the other end around my wrist so that I couldn't drop the whole thing onto the corridor floor. To reach the keyhole I passed the whole contraption out of my side window, and to see what I was doing I held my shaving mirror out of the window at the correct angle with my left hand. I simply inserted the key in the keyhole and was then able to crank it around with the broomstick like a crank-handle on a steam-engine.

This method of unlocking our number twos proved very successful, mainly because it was so simple and did not require bringing any special equipment into our cells. I even left the block with the screw sticking out of it openly in my cell. It became a secondary "clothes hook" hanging from my jacket hook on the wall.

It was about August 1978 when I started attempting to open my outer door using this method. I did the testing at night after the eight o'clock inspection round when the music had ended. This was the best time as it was easier to hear the movements of the night-warder after quiet had set in. Fortunately, my cell was in the best position for this as I could easily hear when the warder moved out of his office and passed through the doors and up the stairs leading to our section.

At this time, Alex one day presented me with a piece of hacksaw blade that he had found sometime earlier after the plumbers had been working in our section. He had kept it for a rainy day and in the end, it became our most valuable key-making tool, without which the making of the wooden keys would have been much more laborious and risky. It was a short piece, about eight centimetres in length, which I kept hidden between the sole and heel of my shoe for the entire duration of my stay at Pretoria.

We also had access to all the files for metal and wood that any prisoner could dream of. These were kept in a "security" tool cabinet in the workshop and were provided for use whenever needed (for jobs in the workshop, of course!). The tools were seldom counted and whenever a count was due to take place, ample warning was given. This allowed us to return any "borrowed" tools we might have had out. I kept one file hidden in the hairs of my broom for many months while making the first wooden keys. This hiding place proved adequate for the most thorough of *skuds* – shake-ups (searches). Later on, we made keys that enabled us to enter the workshop and open the metal cupboard whenever we required something, doing away with the need to keep such dangerous items as files in our cells.

Several other locksmith's requirements were procured in various ways. Denis managed to order a pack of epoxy glue under the pretext of needing it to repair broken teacups. This he passed on to me, which I used for various jobs including the building up of key-cuts that I had filed too deep and, later, for gluing together the pieces of the metal keys we made. To speed up the curing time of the epoxy, I made an Allen key out of a large nail so that I could open the cover of my cell lamp, which I could reach by standing on top of my cupboard. Glued objects placed inside the lamp cover set in no time under the heat of the bulb.

* * *

The impression might be given in the following pages that the escape preparations were responsible for generating a certain degree of antagonism between us political prisoners. This was not so. While there were differences – some of them severe – over the planning of the escape or whether it should go ahead at all, we remained comrades to the end. The very escape was testimony to this comradeship, for had it not existed no escape could have taken place.

We were not in prison for criminal offences but for our political activities and beliefs. This had a profoundly uniting effect and helped us avoid the dog-eat-dog individualism that characterises prisoner relationships in ordinary prisons. We were all members of the ANC and therefore shared the same views on the political situation in our country, and bore the same attitude towards our captors. Most important of all, as members of a revolutionary organisation we were disciplined and shared in our suffering collectively. No one sought advantages over others or privileges that others did not have.

Our unity was the prime reason they kept us separated from other prisoners. If we had been brought together with ordinary prisoners, our example of struggling collectively for improvements would have undermined prison authority. The only way that prison bosses can maintain control in an ordinary prison is by promoting individualism, competitiveness and disunity. This is easy to achieve because imprisonment is a uniquely personal experience that naturally brings out the worst forms of individualism in prisoners. Division was reinforced with additional institutional measures. In South African prisons, as in most other parts of the world, there was a system of rewards or privileges in the form of a grading or classification system. There were also promises of parole and remission. Prisoners who behaved themselves were promoted to higher categories that conferred increased privileges in the form of more letters, visits, spending money and the like; persistent co-operation and obedience was rewarded with remission and parole. To us these things meant nothing, as those who had earned greater privileges shared them with those who hadn't. And for us there was no remission or parole.

Had we been placed among ordinary prisoners we could never have contemplated escaping. At that time there was a standing reward for information leading to the prevention or exposure of an escape attempt. In ordinary prisons there was little need to apply this as there would always be some prisoner wanting to ingratiate him- or herself to the authorities in the hope that it would bring remission. From us they had no hope of getting to know about a planned escape. For us an escape was a political act, not an individual flight for freedom. It was this implicit trust in each other as comrades that made the escape possible.

Our comradeship also gave us the strength to withstand the conditions imposed on us. It was not easy to live at close quarters with nine or fewer people for years on end. Inevitably small things about your fellow prisoners got on your nerves. In an ordinary prison such irritations and frustrations are relieved through aggression but in our prison a structure had been developed by the comrades to deal with frustrations and irritations without resorting to violence or personal attack. This was our "recce" – short for "recreation committee".

"Recce" had nothing to do with recreation of course and was so titled because we did not want the authorities to know of its existence. It consisted of a democratically elected committee of two, each of whom had the responsibility of discussing matters of mutual concern with four others. It served as an anonymous conduit for complaints by one or more prisoners to the others. It was also the body through which our collective demands were formulated and presented to the prison authorities. This was an additional reason why it had to remain a secret – the governors were not interested in any collective demands, only in personal "complaints and requests".

A prisoner who wanted to raise something, spoke to his representative who then discussed it with the three under him and passed it onto the other "recce" representative. In this way we passed on complaints and formulated demands and requests without holding open meetings. If there were any matters that required thorough or urgent discussion then general meetings were held. These were frowned upon by the officers, but never in my time did they openly intervene to stop one. They preferred to deal with gatherings in a sneaky way by having our favourite bushes and trees uprooted, which forced us to hold our meetings in the often-unbearable sunshine, but this never deterred us.

While at Pretoria, Denis was the accepted "leader" of the prisoners when it came to approaching the authorities. He had over the years won their respect and they considered him the most senior of the prisoners. The commanding staff in any case preferred to deal with one prisoner rather than face a united front because they liked to think that requests were coming from an individual rather than from a collective: they never wanted to appear to be giving in to group demands.

While our unity and comradeship were our greatest source of strength, they were also the source of the controversies that arose over the planning of the escape. A failed attempt, everyone knew, would lead to severe disruption and threaten the unity that gave us our strength. The differences arose out of this: some felt that the preservation of unity was paramount, while those bent on getting out found it difficult to accept that others did not display the same drive and determination as they did.

But despite the agonising over the escape plans, we remained good friends underneath it all. We shared in each other's ups and downs and offered each other comfort and advice. When a prisoner was refused a visit, did not receive an expected letter or had a problem with a girlfriend or wife, we all knew about it and commiserated with him. The strength of our friendship was such that at no point was there any doubt that our plans would be compromised. More than anything else it was this that made the escape possible.

Chapter Eight

The Escape Group Expands

B y August 1978, apart from Alex, Steve and myself, only Jeremy
had expressed any interest in the escape project. At that point
in time we had not formulated any concrete plans, as we first
wanted to improve our ability to open locks. Jeremy approached the
matter from an altogether different perspective: he insisted that we
first work out a detailed plan so that our energies were not wasted
on experimenting with keys that might never be needed and only increased the security risk. This difference in approach led to considerable tension and controversy, especially after others joined the escape
group.

We believed that getting out was essentially a practical problem,
and as the comrades professed to be believers in the unity of theory
and practice, it surprised us that some of them looked at it as a purely
theoretical problem. Theory, as we understood it, was to inform
practice but practice had to serve as the basis on which the theory
had to be constructed. Many of the comrades believed that the entire
escape could be planned beforehand in the mind without knowing if
or how it could be achieved in a practical sense. A purely theoretical
approach made no sense to us, as what we were faced with was a
hugely complex practical task with many uncertainties. Besides, none
of us had any experience of escaping so how could we possibly know
how to do it before even trying. *Papillon* provided only general advice

but could not inform us how to get out of *our* prison.

Without wishing to divide ourselves into "pragmatists" and "intellectuals", our approach proved in the end the folly of trying to concoct complete escape plans before knowing everything that lies before you and the limits of your own capabilities. In August 1978, and for many months after, no one would have dreamt of escaping in the way that we finally did. The route eventually taken was not even considered as a remote possibility; it would have required thinking the absolutely unthinkable. It was only after a long, frustrating process of experimenting and testing that we were able to overcome the barriers across our path. Our developing technical abilities suggested the route to take, not some abstract thinking about the possibilities.

Some of the schemes put forward by the others would have led to certain disaster. One suggestion was for us to sneak through the yard gate while the captain was conducting his morning inspection of the *stokkies* in their yard. While inspections took place, the armed guard on the *pos* stood to attention and it was thought that he might not notice a handful of prisoners making a quick getaway through the yard gate. Another plan proposed waiting for a summer thunder shower, and then when there was no warder in the yard and the *pos*-warder was sheltering in his enclosed corner, we would casually sneak out of the same yard gate.

At this early stage most of the comrades were reluctant to identify with us because they believed that our dabbling with locks and keys was but an expression of frustration and anger at the long sentences we had just received. They told us later that they had expected us to carry on experimenting and looking for escape routes for a short time and then either get bored or give up when we discovered that in fact it was impossible to get out. Our fanaticism was expected to wear off in due course.

For this reason, there were at first no attempts to formalise the escape: no suggestions of establishing an escape committee or of planning the necessary steps collectively. In a sense this made our activities "undemocratic" because they were carried on without consultation with the others. But from very early on we realised that if we took each problem to the "yard" (i.e. to everyone) the day of departure would have been delayed and the screws would have been alerted. Besides, our problems at that stage were purely technical and none of the others were capable of offering much assistance in that department.

The comrades' reluctance to participate was buttressed by the fear that these "new guys" were going to upset things by getting themselves caught. These fears were reasonable enough, especially from those who had been inside for a long time. It had taken them 15 years of hard struggle to achieve the conditions that prevailed in the prison. The "privileges" that had been won over the years could easily be removed, and then it would be back to square one. The stable relationship with the prison staff, which at best was no more than a precarious state of truce, could easily be reversed. They could not stomach the thought of having to fight all the old battles again.

From August until November 1978, practically all escape-related activity was spent on attempting to open door two. For more than a month I struggled for up to two hours a night to open my outer cell door. I had made about six number two keys in the hope of getting one to work by trial and error. There was no other way to do it. I tried each key, filed it a bit or built it up with epoxy and then tried again, over and over. Each evening I was forced to stop, not by impending inspections, but by an aching arm caused by holding the crank out of my passage window for too long.

During the day I made every effort to stare at the warders' number two keys in an attempt to capture a mental image that I could then "measure". But I couldn't see any difference: our keys looked exactly the same as theirs. After a while I began to wonder if there was some hidden secret we couldn't see. Alex persuaded me not to get superstitious.

Towards the end of October, I finally managed to get key two to turn in my door. It was almost annoying how smoothly and easily it suddenly turned, as if there had been no problem all along. It could at least have jammed or nearly turned to let me know that I was getting close. The excitement combined with relief as the crank effortlessly turned the key was exhilarating. I felt dizzy with success and couldn't stop myself dancing a jig on my bed that night.

Keeping in mind the earlier disaster with number two, I turned the key one-and-a-half turns only and then relocked it. Fortunately, it relocked all the way. If it had not done so it wouldn't have been too serious as the door would still have been locked one turn. They wouldn't have been able to blame me for it being un-mastered and even if the warders had suspected something, there would have been no evidence that I had tampered with the lock as I would have disposed of the keys down my toilet.

To make sure that it had not been a fluke that the key had worked, I immediately filed all the other number two keys to the same dimensions as the one that had worked and tried them out. All worked with equal facility. I shouted to Alex and he stuck his shaving mirror out of his window to see what I was carrying on about. When I gave a thumbs-up – the agreed sign for a success – he shouted back to congratulate me for achieving the long-awaited breakthrough. He was so overjoyed at the news that for a long time afterwards I could hear him, the atheist that he was, praising the Lord!

The excitement was short-lived though. The following night Alex tried the keys in his number two and found that none of them worked. This had us completely baffled because we knew that the warders used the same key in his number two as in mine. Why the keys should then have worked in my door and not in his we could not understand.

I took the keys back the next day and made some alterations for him to try the next night. Again, none of them worked. Disappointment on top of the recent success caused a serious ebb in morale, but we kept at it. One night Alex tried out some of the keys while I modified the others; the next night he tried out the ones I had altered while I changed the ones he had tried the previous night. This procedure went on for another month. It was a slow and tedious process, but eventually he got one to turn. I knew, because I could hear him singing in his cell that night.

I tried the successful key in my own door the following night and found that it turned as easily as the one I had got to work a month earlier. I then cut all the other number twos to the same dimensions as the successful one and found them to work in both our doors. At last we were certain that we had got the measurements right.

The problem as far as we could work out was caused by not having the absolute heights of the key-cuts correct. The relative heights had been established when the first one worked in my door, but the key would not work generally until all five cuts were at the correct overall height. There seemed to be some tolerance in the overall dimensions but there was no way of knowing this at the time, forcing us to employ the trial and error methods that we did. As our keys were made of wood and the shape of the number two keys imparted fragility, our dimensions had to be one hundred per cent correct. Metal keys allowed a greater degree of inaccuracy as any resistance could be overcome by forcing.

We had noticed early on that not all the number two doors used the same key. Starting from my cell at the beginning of the section, each alternate cell used the same number two key that had given us so much trouble; the others used a number one key. Why this was so we could never figure out. Perhaps it was to confuse new warders, who found it inordinately difficult to get the sections unlocked.

This duplication of keys actually simplified matters for us because it allowed us to use our number one keys, of which we had made several, on every second number two door. The number one keys were of a much simpler and robust design than the complicated, warded number twos. It was also possible to test them during shower-time and on Fridays from the open-door position. All appeared to work, but as experience had taught us, there was no certainty they would work from the door-closed position.

Stephen's was one of these number-one-key number two doors but the prospect of having to go through the same rigmarole to test it that we had gone through to test our own, drove us to think of an alternative scheme.

During October, those prisoners who were allowed to study could remain in their cells over weekends to complete their studies before exams. Alex was one of these "students" so he requested to be locked in his cell one Saturday "to catch up on some work". The usual practice when this happened was for the grille to be locked but for the outer door (number two) to be left open. Stephen happened to "fall ill" on the same day and asked to be locked in his cell. He requested that his outer door be locked "to prevent drafts". I remained in the yard – the normal place to be on a Saturday – to signal to Alex when it looked like the warders were relaxing and unlikely to enter our section. When I gave the all-clear by lifting from the ground the book I was pretending to read, Alex opened his grille with the number one key he had with him, came out of his cell and crept down the passage to Stephen's cell and tested his number two lock with the same number one key. It worked perfectly.

After successfully opening our number twos, Denis and Dave K wondered if the keys would work in their doors. We were sure they would but our earlier experiences informed us that to be certain, they had to be tested. Since both had doors that used the problematic number two key, they had to be tested with the crank from the door-closed position – i.e. at night. We gave Dave K the crank and a couple of keys to try out one evening. Our hearts thumped when he missed the keyhole trying to get the key in with the crank. Eventually he managed to get it in but he couldn't get it to turn. I was sure that he was trying to turn it in the wrong direction but he swore that he wasn't. Alex and I watched with our mirrors as he struggled for a long time to get the key out. After what felt like a heart-seizing eternity, the key suddenly shot out and he pulled the crank back through his window and into his cell. Almost as he did so the night-warder came into the section on an unscheduled inspection round.

After that we decided it would be less risky for Alex or me to come out of our cells one night and test the locks directly. As Denis's and Dave's cells were closest to mine and because I had the most experience in opening doors, the task fell upon me.

It was not a difficult mission but it required more courage than I imagined I possessed. Actually coming out of my cell involved a much higher level of risk than merely sticking a broomstick out of a window. How would I explain to the night guard why I was wandering around the corridor if he happened to come into the section? It would have been the end, as there would have been no way of turning it into an escape.

But all went well. I opened my doors after the music had stopped – as I had done many times before – came out of my cell when all was quiet downstairs and headed down the corridor towards Denis's and Dave's cells. It was an eerie sensation as I stood in the corridor: I was experiencing a situation that many prisoners had dreamed about but none in that prison had ever experienced.

I tried the key in Dave's door first and then in Denis's – it worked perfectly in both. Then back into my cell, where for the first time I felt happy to be securely locked in my private tomb. The whole operation had taken less than a minute, but more than a year off my lifespan.

By the end of 1978 there was a feeling among some of the comrades that we were just messing around and not concentrating on developing a proper plan. Perhaps in an attempt to ensure that the escape planning took a more collectively inspired course the "Washing Committee" (WC) was set up, ostensibly as an escape committee to coordinate activities and liaise with the comrades. A point had been reached where it was evident to all that we were serious about our intentions, and doubts about our motives had been dispelled. The yard therefore decided that a committee should be set up to bring our activities under the mantle of its democracy. This did not mean that henceforth every move had to have the blessing of the entire yard, but that the yard wanted some connection with the escape group and some say in affairs that would affect everyone in this regard. It was never clear exactly what the mandate of the WC was and it seemed to vary with time and depending on who was considering its functions. However, after a time its functions became accepted and its mandate became structured by practice rather than by a formal constitution.

Alex, Steve and I were at first not too pleased that our wings had been clipped, but eventually welcomed the formation of the WC because it seemed to give our activities, if not approval, then at least an air of acceptance. The committee finally accepted by the yard consisted of Alex and Dave Kitson. One member of the committee had to be one of the three of us, and this fell upon Alex because he was the most vociferous. I was more involved with the technical side and as everyone knew, not much of a negotiator.

Despite what was ever intended for it, the WC served in practice a vital function – especially at a later stage when more people were involved in the plans. It became responsible for informing the yard that particular escape activities were about to take place and that everyone should be on their guard. It also served as a focus for ideas and suggestions and for spreading these to other members of the escape group.

* * *

Before going on to discuss the first concrete escape plans that were contrived before the end of 1978, it is important to describe in more detail how we went about making our keys, how we managed to smuggle the necessary bits and pieces into and out of our cells and how we concealed the contraband.

Only seven of the ten of us worked in the workshop. Dave K was the official gardener so he was excused from workshop duty. Denis used to be one of the best carpenters and even passed a trade test in carpentry while in prison, but was excused by the doctor because he had a gammy back. He had injured it in his youth while playing rugby, and standing behind a bench for several hours gave him severe backache. He was the chief dishwasher, tea-maker and cleaner, but these were not particularly arduous tasks. Tony assisted him in this important work, so the chores were quickly done and the two of them were able to get on with the more important job of keeping themselves amused. Tony was excused from workshop duty because he had a coordination problem and could not handle tools at all. A short test proved that he would have severely damaged prison property, that is, himself.

In the workshop were four workbenches. Raymond and Dave R worked at the first one next to the door and where the warder usually sat; I worked alone at the second; Jeremy and Johnny at the next and Steve and Alex at the last. Alex, fortunately, had the prime position for making illicit items. Not only was he against the back wall of the workshop and facing forward, but between him and the back wall was a tall rack of shelves on which were kept the wooden parts we had to assemble for the prisons. The shelves and piles of wood gave him excellent hiding places for contraband.

Each bench had its own locker of woodworking tools that was unlocked at the beginning of the day by the warder on duty, and in theory should have been locked by him at the end of the day after checking that all the tools had been replaced. In practice it did not work like that. The prisoners closed their own lockers and seldom were there checks for missing tools.

The "security" cupboard containing the files and hacksaws, among other things, stood in the corner next to the door leading into the storeroom. The warder opened it on request if something was needed out of it, but it was easy enough to return less to it than had been taken out.

While the rest of us dutifully sanded our items of prison woodwork, Alex was more often than not busy cutting out the bits of wood needed to make keys. He propped up the piece of furniture on which he was meant to be working in such a way that it obscured what he was really doing. He also had an uncanny ability to appear to be doing the prison's work while actually doing something else. He did take twice as long as everyone else to complete his quota but he had always been the slowest so they did not suspect he was up to anything.

None of the objects Alex made on the side were recognisable to the warders, so even if he had been caught, there would not have been serious consequences. In fact, he, and for that matter all of us, were regularly "caught" by the warders making personal things. So long as you had a good excuse, such as that you were making chess pieces or a pen holder, they didn't mind. Sometimes the warders even got us to make or mend things for themselves. Johnny, who had proved himself over the years to be a competent fix-it-all, spent most of his time repairing damaged prison items and doing odd jobs for the warders.

For the warders, duty in the workshop was a singularly boring task as it involved sitting doing nothing for three hours in the morning and two and a half in the afternoon. Usually the sessions were totally uneventful: only occasionally did one of us speak to them and then only to comment about rugby, the cost of living or some other inane topic. We were generally well behaved and got on with the work, which was probably not the case in most other prisons.

Most of the warders took a turn at workshop duty but one particular warder was assigned more or less permanently to the post. His name was Van Loggerenberg, or "Loggie" as we called him. He was a fat, lazy, hulk of a man with a drooping moustache and pointed pixie ears. I always said that if one were to attach an electroencephalograph to his head there would be an absolutely straight line, except for a slight bump every now and then when he sucked on his pipe. He is the only person I have ever known who could sit dead still staring into space for three hours. He must have been asleep with his eyes open. Sometimes he really did fall asleep but he had a well-tested method of ensuring that this had no serious consequences. He placed his chair in front of the opened door and held onto the door handle, and when he collapsed into his empty stupor his hand dropped off the handle and it snapped up and woke him. Loggie was totally disinterested in what was going on in the workshop, and for his "assistance" in this way we are eternally grateful. Thank you Loggie.

The bits and pieces Alex made during the day were taken out of the workshop before the end of the afternoon work session. They were deposited either behind the flush tank of the toilet next door or hidden behind some books in the storeroom. At suppertime I retrieved the pieces and concealed them inside the bottom of my Thermos flask. The space in the bottom of my Thermos was large enough to hold the pieces of key as well as sandpaper, files and whatever else I needed for an evening's key-making session. Sometimes when there was too much to carry up in this way, I made "key sandwiches" out of the five or so slices of bread we were given at supper. In the mornings the reverse procedure applied: I sealed the items in the bottom of my Thermos and then hid them in the storeroom or downstairs toilet for later dispersal. I flushed sandpaper and other debris down my toilet in the morning before open up.

At first, I kept the completed keys behind a book rack in the storeroom, then in a tin of sugar or bottle of lavatory cleaner in my cell. These were not very good hiding places compared to some of the places we later used, but they proved adequate at the time. When there were too many keys for these hiding places, I hid them in tins of sugar in the dining room and in "unopened" boxes of soap powder. When there were just too many for all these places, Dave K buried some of them in the garden. They were first sealed in plastic bags, then placed in old jam or coffee jars and buried under particular plants so that they could be found again later.

* * *

The peaceful relations that existed between prisoners and prison staff were an important factor in the success of our escape. As I've indicated, a *modus vivendi* existed, based on the principle of "you leave us alone and we'll leave you alone". Had any other form of relations prevailed it is doubtful if an escape could have been pulled off. As the authorities had for a long time not been given reason to suspect that the prisoners were up to anything mischievous, they had allowed their watchfulness to lapse. Relations had been peaceful for so long that they were under the impression that all we wanted to do was read our boring textbooks and talk our intellectual and unintelligible things. They had observed that when they left us alone, we gave them no problems and responsibly got on with our affairs.

This state of affairs had not always existed. In the early sixties, when the first comrades were brought to Pretoria Local, relations between the prisoners and staff were very strained. Vindictive warders made life as difficult as possible by rigidly applying a multitude of petty rules and regulations. The policy was to make the prisoners' lives hell and it appears that to a certain extent they succeeded. Political prisoners were kept for years in the very lowest classification grades, conditions were harsh, and privileges and hours out of cells were few.

On Robben Island the black prisoners were frequently beaten, overworked and starved. Conditions were never quite so bad for the white prisoners, mainly because they were white, but also because most had access to prominent lawyers and the press. The publicity for the regime would have been too negative if they had violated the prison regulations too seriously. In any case, because of their prejudices, they found it more difficult to assault and mistreat white prisoners than black prisoners – not that they had any great sympathy for "communists", as they saw us.

Over the years the warders' attitudes matured. They learned that by being harsh on the prisoners they made life more difficult for themselves. Bad publicity resulted and the working day was unpleasant. Warders are generally lazy creatures and at that time joined the prison service to get out of military service or because they couldn't find employment elsewhere. To spend the time chasing prisoners meant less time to read comics and newspapers, sit and smoke pipes or do nothing. They also learned that if they were more relaxed the prisoners were more relaxed, caused fewer problems and were less inclined to want to get out. A relaxed atmosphere also meant that the prisoners would get on with their affairs openly and not resort to subterfuge.

None of us kowtowed to our jailers but neither did we seek confrontation. Our policy was to maintain a relationship of distance and least contact. This meant seeking a balance between obsequiousness and outright defiance. Some of us tended more towards the one extreme and some to the other. Alex was the most aggressive and defiant, Dave K the least. But on the whole, we obeyed the prison regulations and related to our captors in a spirit of firmness and dignity.

In prison situations where the conditions are extremely harsh, there is a case for confronting your jailers aggressively and defiantly, especially if there is nothing to lose by doing so and those outside can derive succour from your stand. But where the conditions are not so severe or there is little chance of the outside world hearing about your struggle, a permanent state of war becomes counterproductive. No one's nervous system can take the strain of confrontation for years on end and anyway there is no point in destroying yourself for your jailers' delight. Major political victories are difficult to achieve inside a prison.

As disciplined members of a revolutionary organisation our duty was to do whatever was best for our organisation, and this was not to destroy ourselves for publicity's sake. We had to ensure that we would be of value to the movement when we got out and this meant keeping ourselves healthy both physically and mentally. We had to keep ourselves informed of the current situation as best we could and advance our knowledge in such ways that would make us useful to the revolution later on.

Our attitude towards the prison staff paid dividends in that they accorded us a certain measure of respect and treated us as partly civilised humans rather than as animals, which was how they treated ordinary prisoners, especially black prisoners. They knew it was unlikely that they would ever be assaulted by one of us and for this reason some of the usual security measures that applied in other prisons did not apply in ours.

Searches, for instance, were seldom and perfunctory. Sometimes the only sign that they'd been through your cell was a ruffled bedspread. They never found anything illicit so searches became a matter of mere routine. Never, while I was there at least, were we subjected to a thorough or humiliating body search. Occasionally they went through our pockets, but even when they did, there were indications beforehand that something was afoot.

This trust in us had other small consequences that made life just that much more bearable. Ours was probably the only prison in the country where the prisoners were allowed to eat with knives and forks off normal crockery. In other prisons the prisoners were forced to eat with spoons out of steel dixies, and in some of the most dangerous prisons even the handles of the spoons were removed. We were allowed to prepare food for ourselves from purchases made with our allowances, and generally possess all manner of objects and substances normally considered dangerous.

As we were generally well mannered and well behaved, the warders did not find it necessary to watch over us very closely. In the mornings, after opening our cells, they left us alone in the section before letting us out into the yard. This gave us time to hide any contraband we'd had out for the night. Most times while we were in the yard there were only one or two warders in attendance. They paid scant attention to what we were doing and preferred to spend their time talking to each other or dreaming about their cars and girlfriends. In the workshop only one warder watched over us, and as they were not required to give any advice or assistance – and were usually incapable of doing so anyway – they invariably fell into a trance or stood in the doorway looking wistfully out into the yard.

There were seldom warders in attendance during mealtimes but if there were, it was not because they were intent on watching us eat but because it was too hot outside or they got bored watching nothing in the yard. At shower-time and on Friday mornings while cleaning our section, there were no warders in attendance at all. These periods on our own provided us with ample opportunity to get on with our "subversive activities".

Our "good" behaviour fooled our jailers into thinking that we were all totally reconciled to our fate. Some of them even believed that as "communists" we were proud of being in prison and were using our imprisonment to show the world that we were strong and could cope with any adversity. Stephen and I attempted to appear more resigned than the others but we had an advantage in that we did not have any past history to weigh us down. We kept our cells clean and tidy, dressed neatly and generally avoided giving the warders any reason to criticise us. It was important to make them feel that you respected and feared their authority.

The urge to tease and taunt had to be suppressed, and responses of anger, rudeness and arrogance avoided. When they spoke to us, we pretended to be intimidated, and obediently carried out orders or instructions given to us. Alex, unfortunately, had a bad reputation among the warders and officers. He was often rude and visibly displayed his reluctance to respond to orders. He laughed at new warders who attempted to throw their weight around or who tried to discipline him. He refused to keep his cell clean and tidy and his appearance was generally scruffy. For this reason, he had never been promoted beyond "B" group in his six years in prison, while others had reached "A" group within two. Not that this mattered a damn to Alex but his attitude had to change if he was going to give the impression that he was at last "settling in" and not thriving on thoughts outside the prison.

After the escape idea had taken hold of him, Alex pulled up his socks: he began to dust down his cell and be polite to the warders. Within a few months his change of heart was noticed and he was "rewarded" with a promotion to "A" group. They thought that their magnanimous gesture had won him over, that he had been reformed, that he was going to give them no more trouble. Little did they know.

For the first nine months of our sentence Captain Schnepel was the head of the prison. He was a bumptious old dog who imagined he instilled fear into everybody, but whose bark was worse than his bite. He was so grossly overweight and unfit that he had to take a break to catch his breath when he walked across the yard. His face turned bright red and his handlebar moustache twitched up and down in time with his panting. Most often we could not make out what he was saying under his snorting and puffing. To get his message across he resorted to shouting, but his mind was slower than his voice. He could never tell if the prisoners were having him on or not.

Captain Schnepel – "Schneppie" we called him – was of the old school of warders. He believed that a *bandiet* was a *bandiet* and a "communist" was a "communist". He had contempt for the young guard who believed that you could look at a regular prisoner other than as a *bandiet* and a political prisoner other than as a "communist". He had been in charge of the politicals more or less from the start and had only become more lenient towards them because it was in his interest to do so, not because he had softened towards the "communists".

Why Schnepel was placed in charge of political prisoners I could never understand, because the question of political prisoners was a very sensitive one for the regime, and he did nothing to make it easier for their reputation. He had an abrasive personality and had annoyed countless visitors with his caprice, unreasonableness and irrationality.

Perhaps his tenure had something to do with the internal politics of the Prisons Service, a residue of the old guard in a battle for ascendancy by the new school with their degrees and university theories.

In the first half of 1979 Schnepel was replaced by a sour-faced dwarf of a captain by the name of Venter. Captain Venter had a face that had spent most of its life contorted into a scowl. The grimace had become permanently engraved so that even when he was smiling, he looked miserable. He was a more constant personality than Schnepel and for this reason Steve and I guardedly welcomed the change. We had found it almost impossible to communicate with Schnepel, but the older guys said that they'd learned to handle him and that they preferred to stick with the devil they knew.

The advent of Venter brought rumours of "big changes". We wondered what these would be. Had he been brought in because the authorities had got wind of what we were planning? Would he scour the prison to start off on a clean sheet? Would he introduce new security measures? Only time would tell.

Within a month or two it became clear that nothing of the sort was about to happen. The atmosphere became more relaxed and the governors became more responsive to our demands and requests. While Venter tried to appear firm and in control, he was really a weak man. Clearly he had personal problems, for he would often reek of alcohol. It did not take long for the prison staff to nickname him "Half-Jack".

The change of captains was not the only change in staff during our time: there was a tremendously high turnover of warders. Twice a year there was an influx of pimply-faced youngsters fresh from prison college. Some of these new recruits were only 18 years of age and found it difficult to address us by the stipulated surname only. Sometimes one of them would preface a name with a "Mister" and we would laugh them out of our presence in embarrassment.

Warders who served in our prison were thoroughly briefed on how to handle the "communists": there was to be no talking to them except to give instructions and they were to be watched extra carefully because they were *slim* – treacherous. It took a few months for them to learn that we were not monsters but ordinary people, not at all like the criminals and gangsters they'd been taught about at prison college.

This high turnover of staff had both advantages and disadvantages for us. It took a while to get to know the whims and habits of particular warders and consequently we felt more at ease with those who had been around longer. New warders were unpredictable and some deliberately did things to try to catch us out. The obverse applied from their perspective: older warders knew our behaviour better and were able to detect changed patterns; new warders didn't know what to expect. We were able to use both these factors to our advantage. For instance, we only tested our number twos at night when warders whose behaviour we knew well were on duty. Later on we took advantage of newly arrived warders to do things that would not have been contemplated had older warders been on duty.

It is probably true of warders throughout the world that they are not the brightest of creatures. This is no doubt due to the fact that the job is one without much status and hence does not attract the nation's geniuses. Some of the specimens who worked in our prison were close to borderline cases. There was one warder, unfortunately named Van der Merwe (the butt of dunce jokes in South Africa), whom Alex nicknamed "Mongo" after a particularly thick character who rode an ox in the American comedy-western, *Blazing Saddles*. Van der Merwe was definitely half-man, half-brute. When he was on duty on the *pos* he marched up and down with his arms flailing to the accompaniment of his own voice shouting "left, right". He was once discovered in the toilet attempting to see how far he could stand from the urinal for his stream of piss to still reach the wall. It must have been a world record. Another time he was found having fisticuffs with a grille and challenging it to hit back.

On the whole it was difficult for us to judge the warders correctly as they were not really in their element. Most of them were Afrikaans-speaking and could not understand English properly. Although most of us were fairly fluent in Afrikaans we were not familiar with their everyday topics of conversation. Also, ours was not really a prison in the sense in which they had been trained to serve. They were instructed to treat us differently to ordinary prisoners and avoid human contact as far as possible. As such the job was extremely boring and soul-destroying for them, which accounted for the high turnover of staff.

Although the warders were just doing a job as regular order-followers, they were wittingly or unwittingly playing a political role. This applied especially to the officers who knew what the game was all about. They in particular were responsible for keeping some of our best people behind bars for a very long time. How many years of people's lives did they waste? How much did they contribute to the continuance of apartheid? We knew and didn't forget.

Chapter Nine
First Plans

It was towards the end of 1978 that we began to consider escape routes that did not start from or pass through the prison yard. The initial observation that there could be no other departure point than the yard had straitjacketed our escape-thinking until then. The realisation that there could be another way brought forth an explosion of fresh ideas. Although we had neither the technical means nor could we visualise how to do it, our recent successes suggested that a route taking the front door as the departure point was not entirely inconceivable.

We had looked at all possibilities involving the yard, but none of them seemed very satisfactory. Any escape going that way would have involved either going out through the yard gate into the prison property next door or scaling a wall.

The prospects of using the yard gate had improved slightly from the time when Stephen and I arrived, as the old Pretoria Local Prison next door was being knocked down and excavations for a new building had started. As such "next door" was a deserted building site at night, not a well-guarded prison precinct.

It was common knowledge that the yard gate used a number one key but the main problem was deciding what would be the best time to get out through it. During the day when we had access to it, getting out was impossible because the warder on *pos* duty could see the gate directly and would have used us for target practice if we had attempted anything. After lock-up, we would have had to break out of our cells, capture the night-warder, tie him up and then make our way outside. The guard dog was placed in the yard within an hour of lock-up, introducing another obstacle that we would have to overcome. We would also have been in full view of the *stokkies* in the other wing directly opposite, who undoubtedly would have seen us in the yard and raised the alarm.

These were not seen as insurmountable obstacles. We could have made our exit before the dog was placed in the yard or, if it was already there, it could have been lured inside the building or poisoned. And if we were dressed in civilian clothing, we would have looked like *stokkies* to the *stokkies*, not like escaping political prisoners. These were, however, complicating factors that could easily have caused the plans to go awry.

To escape over the wall into the street presented the same problems. There was one weak link, however. This was the short piece of wall next to the front door that joined the main building to the *pos*. Here the wall was not as high as the rest and climbing over it there landed us in the street and not directly in other prison property, as would have been the case had we climbed over anywhere else. The problem of the dog could have been solved by closing the *stokkies'* yard gate, which we would have reached by passing through their section and out of their yard door.

A serious problem with this plan was that if there had been any *stokkies* in the cells above ours, they would have seen us in their yard and scaling the wall, and most definitely would have raised the alarm. When there were only a few of them signed in, the cells above ours were not used but it was difficult for us to find out if they were in use or not. If we could have found a way of answering this unknown, this route may have become the chosen one. And of course, there was the danger of being seen by pedestrians on the other side. What do people who are climbing over a high prison wall look like! This climbing-the-wall option was only realistic while there was no guard on the *pos* in the evening. It was later eliminated when one was placed there permanently.

Considerable thought and experimentation were devoted to some of these plans. Alex and I carried out a number of tests to find out if the dogs would accept food thrown to them. It was claimed that they were trained not to accept food from anyone but their handlers. This seemed to be partially true but there were some dogs that accepted whatever food was thrown at them. As only a limited number of dogs were used, we could simply have waited until they used one that we knew would accept food. Then we could either have poisoned it or lured it somewhere where it would have been out of our way.

But it was in the face of all these complications and as a result of the confidence we had gained from our practical achievements that we started to entertain the inconceivable by turning our attention towards the front door. Apart from the yard gate that led into the prison next door, the front door was the only formal exit from the entire prison. Prisoners came through that door on the day they started their sentences and left by it on the day of their release, but it had always remained in the realm of the unthinkable for us because it was only accessible by passing through the administrative section and at the far end of a corridor blocked by many, many barriers.

The initial plans involving this exit were a bit wild, but that was to be expected because we didn't know exactly what lay in front of us. Forcefulness substituted for thoughtfulness. One scheme involved capturing the night-warder, tying him up, taking his keys to get out (we did not realise at this stage that he was locked into the prison and only had keys to enable him to move from section to section), taking his car keys and weapon (if any) and making a getaway in his car that was parked outside.

Although we assumed that the night-warder would have the keys to enable us to open all the doors on the way to the front door, we were not certain. What if the keys were stored in a locker, for which he did not have a key? To avoid finding ourselves in an embarrassing situation on the day of escape, we decided to develop our door-opening abilities to the extent of being able to open any door, even when confronted by it for the first time. This meant perfecting our lock-picking skills and making keys for the workshop so that we could at any time get hold of the tools we might need: hammers, levers, chisels, screwdrivers, hacksaws and so on.

We took advantage of Loggie's laziness here. Most days he found it too much bother to get up from his seat to open the metal tool-cupboard where all the "security" tools were kept. Many times, against the rules, he handed his bunch of workshop keys to us in order to get the tools we needed. On the bunch were the keys for the metal cupboard, the tool lockers and for the two workshop doors. It was easy enough to take impressions of them on a piece of soap while pretending to be searching for something in the cupboard, and then to make our own keys.

The metal cupboard had a small pin tumbler lock (commonly called a Yale-type lock) while the workshop doors had ordinary, small mortise locks with normal lever tumbler keys – miniature versions of our cell keys. It did not require much skill to make a replica of the cupboard key out of a small piece of aluminium found in the workshop. The two door keys were easily crafted out of wood, in much the same fashion as the larger number one and two cell keys.

Having these keys was a tremendous boon because we then had access to the workshop and all the tools we could possibly want, whenever we needed them. We could get into the workshop through the interior door at the back of the storeroom, out of the sight of the warders. One of us sat at the entrance to the storeroom and watched for signs of approaching warders while the other entered the workshop and helped himself to all the tools that were needed. We did not bother making keys for our own tool lockers because during the day we could simply leave out any tools we needed and then retrieve them on entering the workshop after it was shut. Our bench lockers did not in any case contain much of value for key-making or door-forcing.

The tools I required for evening key-making sessions were usually retrieved from the workshop at suppertime. I secreted them up to my cell in the usual way in the bottom of my Thermos flask and replaced them the next morning before breakfast while the others were getting dressed for their morning run and exercise.

After making keys for the workshop we decided to make keys for every other door to which we had regular access. We knew that there would probably never be a need for most of those keys but we had learned that each time we made a key it provided more options for our planning. The keys were for the two doors to the dining room, the door leading into the yard at the bottom of the stairs to our section, the storeroom outer door, the visiting room door, the awaiting-trial prisoners' yard door and door number four (the metal grille at the start of the administrative section). Door number three, our section door, used a number one key, obviating any further effort there.

The measurements of the keys for the dining room outer door, the door at the bottom of our stairs and the awaiting-trial prisoners' yard door were obtained by taking soap impressions when warders inadvertently left the keys in the locks. The warders did not bother too much about the security of these doors as they did not lead anywhere of importance and were just ordinary wooden doors with small mortise locks. The measurements of the key for the storeroom outer door were obtained by removing the lock one Saturday while the others were playing tennis. I opened the lock and cut an already prepared blank key to the correct measurements there and then. This I did in the dark recess at the back of the storeroom while Alex or Steve stood guard at the entrance.

The measurements of the key for the visiting room door I obtained one day by catching a quick glimpse of the key when I entered the room for a visit. The key was in its lock and when I entered, there was no warder or visitor in the room. I quickly pulled it out, looked at it, and put it back in. Its measurements were simple: like a number one key, only smaller. I made a key from our large stock of blanks, and one showery afternoon while there was no one in the yard, Dave K and I took shelter in the doorway. Behind my back I inserted the key and turned it. I pulled the door handle and the door opened.

The key for the dining room double-door at the bottom of our stairs was normally handed to Dave K on Fridays so that he could open the door to bring through the film equipment that was kept in a small cupboard under the stairs. The only measurement that needed to be taken was the height of one of the outer cuts relative to the key-shaft; the rest could be obtained by sight.

Key four was also a cinch as it had a very simple shape. We frequently got a chance to see it when taken into the administrative section. Its bit was flat along the top except for two shallow cuts, each about one millimetre deep. I prepared a key to the same basic dimensions as keys one and two, filed the cuts as I had seen them and tried it out one day while passing the grille on the way down to the yard. It failed to work the first few times but by lowering the overall heights of the cuts a fraction each time I eventually got it to turn. Key four was also the key for door five, the next grille down the passage on the way to the front door.

Regular trips out of and back into the prison by the comrades helped us build up a thorough picture of the number and types of doors on the way to the front door. Quite often someone would go out – either to a dentist, a doctor or an optician – and be issued with instructions to look for this or that crucial detail.

Having made the key for doors four and five we knew that we only had to make two more of the large-type prison keys – for doors six and seven. Door six was a panelled steel door the same as our outer cell doors; door seven a grille. Door eight was also a grille but was electrically operated. We knew that the button to open it was in the main office where the night warder sat during his shift – you could see the warders pressing it as you were taken out. Doors nine and ten were ordinary wooden doors like the others in the prison and used the small-type mortise keys as used in all the other wooden doors. Door ten was the front door, the door to freedom. It was also a wooden door in a wooden doorframe.

The door that gave us the most worries was door six because no one had ever seen its key. Whenever a prisoner went into the administrative section during the day it was open and hooked back against the wall. But Denis remembered from an occasion some years earlier, when he was brought back from hospital very late one night, that door six had been closed. From this piece of information, it made sense to assume that it was only locked at night – by the departing day-staff – to lock the night-warder into the prison. This turned out to be the case, as we later found out.

Occasionally someone got a glimpse of key seven, so we had a vague idea of its shape. But this gate did not worry us much as we knew that we could, if necessary, tackle it another way – by cutting the bars or dismantling its lock. That left only keys six, nine and ten about which we knew nothing.

If you do not have the key for a lock the only other ways to open it are to smash it or pick it. Smashing locks was not our style so we set about training ourselves to become master lock pickers. Our knowledge of how locks worked had grown considerably so it was not too difficult to figure out how to make suitable lock picks. The greatest advance was made one night when I managed to smuggle a shifting spanner and screwdriver into my cell, which I used to remove and open my number one lock. The lock was held to the frame by four bolts, the ends of which were hammered over to stop the nuts being turned off. But with the help of a small triangular file from the security tool-cupboard, I was able to restore the thread and loosen the nuts. I removed the lock from the grille, dismantled it and measured its internals in minute detail. To understand the geometry of the lock and reveal possible hidden secrets, I also made accurate tracings of the levers onto a piece of paper.

If I may say so myself, we made some quite ingenious lock picks from pieces of bent wire after that. We spent hours practising how to use them on the inner workshop door and on our number one locks, and in no time became quite adept at picking the prison's locks. One of our picks was actually a special shaftless key with adjustable cuts for opening the smaller locks in the wooden doors. Once the vague shape of the key was known, this device worked as effectively as the real key. What were formerly barriers became openings; what was solid became paper.

From the tracings of the levers, I made a set of paper "levers" by carefully cutting them out with a pair of scissors. When these were stacked on top of each other in the correct order and arranged in the "open" position (i.e. in the position that the key would have lifted them to allow the bolt to slide in or out), I could measure the relative heights of the "levers" on the edge that the key would have lifted them. This revealed the relative heights of the cuts in the key bit. In short, from the paper levers I could work out the shape of the key. I knew this exercise would be useful later, and it certainly was.

In the end we had more keys than our jailers, which presented us with a massive security problem – where to hide them all. With such a vast amount of equipment, finding some better hiding places became urgent.

As luck would have it, we were presented with the perfect hiding places just when we most needed them. One day, after the plumbers had been to repair one of the hot water geysers in our shower room, we noticed that the door to the closet in which it was housed had been left unlocked. Inside the closet the round geyser fitted tightly in the square space, leaving two vertical gaps behind it in the corners – the perfect place for hiding our contraband. If we could make keys for the closets – there was one in each shower – we would have two massive and secure storage spaces.

So, one shower-time I removed the lock of the unlocked door and hid it in my cell over suppertime. Risky? Not at all. The warders never had a shakedown during supper: the time was too short and they were readying themselves to go home. That evening I took a blank that I had prepared beforehand and cut a key to open the lock. I replaced the lock the next morning before we were let out of the section for breakfast.

The following Friday I easily picked the lock of the other closet because I knew exactly how it worked. I left the door unlocked to see if it would be noticed. It wasn't, so a few days later I made a key for it in the same way as I had made the first one. All our gear was then placed in sacks and dropped down the triangular spaces between the geysers and the corners of the closets in which they stood. A piece of string was attached to each sack so that it could be pulled up again. To keep the strings out of sight, a piece of black cotton was tied to the end of each and led over the pipes at the back of the geysers and hidden there. To retrieve a sack, you first had to find the piece of cotton, then pull up the string and finally the sack.

The geyser closets proved to be the ideal hiding places and were used to the end. They did give the occasional problem, such as the time when a leak occurred in one of them and the plumbers had to be called – but that is a story for further on.

Also, at this time – the end of 1978 – our thinking began to turn towards getting our hands on civilian clothing. So far, the only non-prison garments we had were two pairs of short socks – not exactly enough for a whole gang of convicts to break loose in. These had been retrieved from the rubbish bin in the *stokkies'* yard.

Alex, in his usual pioneering way, put in an order for two white T-shirts for "sports use" – the first time anyone had done so. Inexplicably the order was granted without question and two more items were added to our wardrobe. I ordered some coloured drawing inks via Denis to dye one of the shirts for myself. After this, everyone ordered T-shirts for themselves – for both legitimate and illegitimate purposes.

For trousers I took one of my voluminous pairs of prison trousers and modified them to look like a pair of khaki bell-bottom jeans (they were in fashion at that time and khaki was trendy!). Everyone had proper running shoes (trainers) that were quite suitable for escaping. Alex, who always scratched around in rubbish bins, later found a pair of shorts in one of the *stokkies'* bins. Only the fly zip was missing but he soon replaced that with one from an old tobacco pouch. I made three belts from an old piece of canvas someone had found in the workshop and Alex carved three buckles out of wood for them. We made these openly and Alex even wore his belt to assist in the everyday job of keeping his oversized prison trousers around his waist. Steve and I made caps – modelled on Denis's tennis cap – out of surplus prison shirts, a few pairs of gloves and some balaclava-style "terrorist" hoods out of surplus vests. All this was ultimately stashed in our cache behind the geysers.

Prison is not good for much, but I'm thankful for the various skills that I learned during my short stay. I picked up a few tips about carpentry, but most of all I'm now a proficient "seamster" and locksmith (read: lock picker).

* * *

According to traditional penological theory, a prison sentence is supposed to serve five purposes: it is punishment for the offender; it is to rehabilitate the prisoner; it is to act as a deterrent to others; it prevents the offender from committing the same or other offences, at least while he or she is in prison; it protects society from the offender. In political cases there are two other purposes in imprisonment: the political purpose and the retributive purpose.

Starting from the last: the vengeance inherent in political imprisonment is not aimed at the individual; it is aimed at the organisation that has had the temerity to challenge the state's authority. To the state, the individual prisoner is nothing – just a number. Vengeance is closely allied to the political purpose of imprisonment.

The political purpose itself has several dimensions. First of all, the state uses it to demonstrate to its opponents that it still has power and that it will use that power when and how it pleases in order to preserve its authority. It also uses it to demonstrate to its followers that it is still in control; that its opponents will not get far.

Political imprisonment in apartheid South Africa, while it "protected" whites from the "offenders", did not protect the majority of the people for they did not want to be "protected" from those imprisoned for political reasons, but rather from the state itself. Political prisoners were seen as freedom fighters, and those who were involved in armed actions against the state, in particular, were seen as heroes and protectors of the people.

Political imprisonment does, of course, prevent prisoners from engaging in the activities for which they were imprisoned, but in the long term it serves to encourage others to take up where the imprisoned left off. In the same way, political imprisonment fails as a deterrent. While it does deter some, others take the imprisonment of their comrades as added cause to challenge the state.

There is no way that political imprisonment can serve to rehabilitate a political prisoner. For a political prisoner, "rehabilitation" means re-education and in South Africa at that time it would have meant adopting the ideology of apartheid – hardly likely even for prisoners broken by the experience. If the authorities had attempted to "rehabilitate" political prisoners they would have resisted it with everything at their disposal. The authorities knew that, and for this reason did not try their hand at it. All they could hope for was that the experience would serve to mellow the prisoners or sap their resolve to fight apartheid when they got out. It usually did the opposite.

Finally, for imprisonment to serve as a punishment it has to be perceived as such by the prisoner. The prisoner must show some remorse, feel guilty and at the bottom of it recognise that what he or she has been committed to prison for is considered by society to be "wrong", a crime, anti-social and worthy of punishment. In political imprisonment the prisoners show no contrition. Their imprisonment convinces them that they were absolutely correct in doing what they did and only makes them regret not having done more. In South Africa, only supporters of "the system" agreed to the imprisonment of the opponents of apartheid; to the oppressed majority those convicted for fighting apartheid had committed no offence at all. The only offence was the imprisonment of the alleged offender by the state.

The punishment inherent in imprisonment is the loss of freedom itself. Anything over and above this is vindictiveness. For this reason, we as political prisoners could not help feeling victimised. Our punishment went way beyond the normal loss of freedom associated with imprisonment. Special conditions applied to us that made life very difficult. This was intentional, as our captors wanted to inflict their vengeance on us. We were the political enemy, "communists", "terrorists" and in their eyes not worthy of recognition as human beings. They knew that we could not be "rehabilitated" and so had to ensure that when we left prison we were broken and no longer desirous of "making trouble". The only way of doing that, they thought, was by ensuring that we were kept permanently demoralised; that we were cut off from events in the real world as effectively as possible by being denied news of anything in the political realm. They knew as well as we did that our morale was influenced by developments in the political world, not by the conditions of our immediate existence.

What this meant in practice was at first a total blackout on news, and later, as they became more sophisticated, only the transmission of news that they considered to be "good news", that is, what we interpreted as "bad news". The total ban on news applied until 1978. Before that time there were no newspapers, no radio broadcasts, no news magazines – nothing. The prisoners were not allowed to discuss anything apart from family news with visitors and the same applied to letters. The authorities were so obsessed with this issue that the only periodicals they allowed were a handful of family, entertainment and sports magazines. Even these were subject to rigid censorship and often had huge sections removed from them. The censor meticulously searched through everything in the pursuit of anything that smacked of "news", or "sex" – the other bogey. If something was found, the whole article was excised, not just the offending line or paragraph.

The lengths to which the censors went to remove the news drove the comrades to desperation and in 1977 they made a court application for an order to ease the restrictions placed on them. The prisoners' request was that they be allowed to receive newspapers and magazines of their own choice, to have less censorship of their letters, and to have freer conversations without interference during visits. In their application the comrades claimed that the deprivation of news was "cruel, inhuman and unnecessarily harsh treatment". They asked no more than that they be treated in the same way as other prisoners.

During the court case, which the comrades were not allowed to attend, the prison authorities confirmed that the withholding of news was their way of "rehabilitating" political prisoners. The state representative said, "The individual propensities of these so-called political prisoners could be cured by not allowing them to know what is going on". The comrades' lawyer argued that to live without any real knowledge of the world was cruel, vindictive punishment.

The judge dismissed the application. In summing up he said that to grant the order would fetter the discretion of the censors and would mean the end of the prison authorities' right to exercise the function entrusted to them. He clarified the state's view by commenting: "News is not necessary for me. The last thing I want to do is look at the news." The comrades appealed against the judgment and lost that too. In the end, however, they won a moral victory because the absurdity of the efforts to keep political prisoners in the dark was exposed to the world. Shortly after the appeal, the rigid censorship began to break down. Within a short time letters began to be left largely intact, interference in conversations during visits became less frequent and the comrades were allowed to receive a wider range of periodicals. Not only had they achieved an actual improvement for themselves, the prisoners on Robben Island – who had been conducting a similar campaign over the years – were granted the same "privileges" as well.

By the time that Steve and I arrived at Pretoria heavily censored SABC news broadcasts – which were highly censored versions of the truth in the first place – were being relayed over the loudspeaker system twice daily. Virtually all news about South Africa was cut out except for sports news and the most trivial items that displayed the regime in a good light (from their point of view). Foreign news was also heavily censored but the censor, not being too enlightened, often did not know what was "good" or "bad" news from their narrow viewpoint. Sometimes the most startling items came through. For instance, for long periods we heard about the advance of the Nicaraguan revolution and events in Afghanistan. The censor had obviously never heard of these places.

The radio broadcasts were a step forward – not a big one, but a foot in the door. Like all "privileges" they could be removed or the threat of their removal could be used against us. But we gradually wore down the rigidity of the censor. In 1979 we were allowed to receive *Time* magazine – censored of all reference to South Africa – and shortly after we escaped, political prisoners were allowed uncensored daily newspapers.

Despite the blanket ban on news, the comrades had managed to keep themselves amazingly well informed over the years. One important source of news was from new prisoners who came to the prison. They were "debriefed" by the others and every ounce of information squeezed from them. Another source was the representatives of the International Committee of the Red Cross who visited us and all other political prisoners in South Africa once a year. They filled us in on events during the preceding year and give us their analysis of current developments.

The major source of news, however, was smuggled newspapers. Extraordinary as it may seem, for long periods we read newspapers, or parts of them, every day. The smuggling worked like this: black prisoners, who were brought to the prison each day from the black section of Pretoria Prison, cleaned the administrative area of our prison. Part of their work was to empty the rubbish bins inside the prison into the main bins in the *stokkies'* yard, and to take these out of the prison for emptying. The bins were taken out through the yard gate, emptied somewhere, and then returned through the same gate. The cleaners often found newspapers thrown out by the warders or *stokkies* in smaller bins inside the prison. This we knew because occasionally we found pieces of newspapers in the bins in the *stokkies'* yard, where we emptied our own bins. The "worker" prisoners could also bring newspapers from their own prison.

To initiate the smuggling act one of us went to the toilet next to the workshop while the black prisoners were waiting in front of the yard gate to be let out with the bins. From there he could mimic the action of reading a newspaper and point to the *stokkies'* bins, meaning that if they got hold of any papers, they should leave them in the bins. He then mimicked smoking and pointed again to the bins, meaning that we would exchange tobacco, the prison currency, for any newspapers.

The black prisoners understood exactly what we wanted and indicated agreement of the trade with a thumbs-up disguised as a scratch of the head with a thumb. They were obviously skilled smugglers themselves and understood prison sign language and needs even better than we did. Sometimes they indicated that they wanted other things apart from tobacco, such as a pack of cards, soap, aspirin or other medicines. We were amazed – and shocked – that they couldn't get these basic things that we took for granted.

The system worked perfectly for months at a time. The tobacco was wrapped in a piece of dirty brown paper and deposited in the *stokkies'* bins by Denis or Tony when they emptied our kitchen bin each morning. The newspaper was retrieved later in the morning when the kitchen bin was emptied again. If it was a good chunk of newspaper the reward was greater the next day: half a bag of tobacco for a page or two, a whole bag or more for several pages or a whole paper.

The newspapers were hidden in the storeroom during the day and taken up to our cells at shower-time inside a completely gutted Thermos flask. At shower-time the paper was split in two, one half for the five cells on the one side of the shower and the other half for the other five. The papers were passed on to the next cell by means of an ingenious device made from two long rulers. The rulers were joined together with a rubber band and then pushed under the door in the direction of the next cell. The rubber band would cause the first ruler to spring under the next door instead of just following the bottom of the wall. The next comrade then grabbed the end of the first ruler and pulled in the second, to which was attached by a piece of string an envelope containing the folded pieces of newspaper. The following night the two halves were swapped over. The last comrade on each side to receive the piece, finally disposed of it down his toilet.

In this way we were able to keep ourselves reasonably well-informed, but the system had its dangers and broke down several times – sometimes for as long as two or three months. When this happened, we really felt the pressure of our enemy's attempts to "rehabilitate" us!

Occasionally the warders discovered a piece of newspaper on one of the black prisoners, or found the tobacco or a piece of newspaper in the *stokkies'* bins. Then there was pandemonium. The entire gang was punished or changed for a new group. Each time a new group of prisoners was brought in, the system had to be set up again and if the prisoners had been threatened not to engage in smuggling with us they were very reluctant to cooperate.

Nevertheless, practically the whole time we had newspapers to read. The authorities probably knew that we were smuggling but could do little to stop it. They were reluctant to tackle it from our end as they didn't want to upset relations. Constant searches would have fouled the air too much and if one of us had been caught, punishment could only be imposed after an internal trial. Since it was within our rights to request a lawyer on such occasions – the comrades had always done so in the past – the bother and embarrassment of having to hold court with a skilled lawyer present was usually too much for them.

We knew their feelings on this matter and for that reason took no extra-special precautions about transporting and reading the papers. They were stored and carried up to the section in the gutted Thermos and read after lock-up when there was little chance of being caught. If a warder came while you were reading a paper, you simply threw it under your bed. If the warder did catch you reading, you could calmly tear it up and flush it down the toilet in front of his eyes as he had no access to the cells. If there was a "trial" it would only be his word against yours. However, it was not advisable to get caught, as it would only make it more difficult to keep the system going.

There were other ways of getting news of the world and details of our immediate surroundings: from visitors, letters and warders. Strictly speaking, the only matters that we were permitted to discuss with visitors or write about in letters were family affairs and news of friends. But all of us got around these restrictions by developing code words with our most regular visitors and correspondents that referred to certain political figures or countries. Stephen and I were ahead of the others in this respect as we had agreed with our parents, while awaiting trial, on a set of code words to refer to various countries and political organisations. For example: Angola was Angela; Mozambique was Mary, and Frelimo was "her boyfriend"; Rhodesia – Roger; Namibia – Nancy, and SWAPO "her boyfriend"; ANC – Anthony; Britain – Aunt Bertha; USA – Uncle Sam; and so on. Although the need to use this code seldom arose, it came in useful when the newspaper smuggling broke down or if there was an urgent need to know the latest on some major international development.

Denis and the others had established similar codes with their visitors over the years, some of these through the assistance of departing prisoners. Denis's code in particular was sophisticated enough to enable him to make contact with the movement in connection with the escape.

Stephen and I had other letter codes that we had set up while awaiting trial. One of these could be used to describe conditions in the prison and our own treatment. It involved writing the letter according to various formats, each configuration conveying information about the degree of edibleness of food, of the nature of our treatment, and so on. Another less descriptive code could be used to convey a short, accurate message. We never used any of these codes, as the clamp on talk about conditions was not as tight as we imagined it would be and we never thought it advisable to inform our families about our real intentions.

The prison staff themselves were a major source of information about the prison and surroundings. Although they were instructed not to talk to us about such things, some were quite willing to answer questions that seemed totally innocuous and were fond of bragging about the "impenetrable" security barriers on the terrain. From warders we were able to extract information about such things as dog patrols, dog handlers and their dogs, security arrangements, sentry duties, shifts, changes in routine and security, morale, who hated whom, which warders were corrupt, and other things such as whether the old currency (like the money we had brought in) was still legal tender.

These questions were asked in much the same way as we would ask them of our visitors – not directly but as requests for comments on something about which you pretended to know already. For instance, we often heard dogs barking at night and to try to find out where they were stationed, we would say something like: "I can't work today, *Meneer*, because the dogs were making so much noise last night. Why must they have dogs in the empty yard next door? They just keep us awake." One particular warder named Moreby, who was much hated by the prisoners, was also despised by the other warders. To ascertain the level of antagonism towards him we said to another warder: "It's good when you're on duty in the workshop, *Meneer*. You know, when *Meneer* Moreby is on duty here he walks around looking at our work so much it puts us off and we can't get on with the job." Inevitably they would also have something disparaging to say about him, and get the message that if they wanted to be liked by us, they shouldn't inspect our work too much!

The warders were also a source of news about the world in general, although not a reliable one. Sometimes, after reading something in a smuggled newspaper and then not finding out the outcome we would ask a warder – provided it was not the censor – to comment on the matter. For example, we once read that there was going to be a by-election but then never found out the result. Someone then asked a warder what he thought about a particular party winning the election – the party thought least likely to have won. The warder responded indignantly that the traitorous party just mentioned had not won the election. The Nationalists, the party of apartheid that he obviously supported, had scored a landslide. To clear the matter the prisoner who had asked the question then said: "Oh, I must have heard it wrong on the radio broadcast."

Chapter Ten

First Escape Date

By the end of 1978 the first plan of escape had taken shape. It was the product of countless hours of debate and dispute. With hindsight it can be said that the plan contained a large element of adventurous ideas, but at the time we weren't aware of the many pitfalls that still lay before us. It was not a complicated plan: it involved leaving our cells shortly after lock-up (at 5 pm to be more precise), quietly moving downstairs, passing through door four, jumping the night-warder in his office, tying him up and taking his prison and car keys.

Door six remained a major problem but we had thought of various ways to tackle it. We hoped that one of our many keys would fit its lock or that we would find the key for it in the possession of the night-warder. If not, there was a contingency plan that involved going out into the yard, entering the visiting room, smashing the window separating the two halves of the room and then re-emerging in the passage beyond door six but before door seven.

Door seven wasn't considered much of an obstacle because we could cut through its bars with a hacksaw, or dismantle its lock with a spanner. Door eight would be opened by pressing the button in the warder's office before going out into the yard. If none of our keys worked in doors nine and ten, we could easily smash them open because they were wooden, or their hinges could be dismantled because they opened inwards and were thus exposed. Then we would all jump into the warder's car outside and drive off into the setting sun. Simple as that!

With hindsight we know that this plan would have been suicidal, but based on our knowledge of the prison and terrain at the time, it seemed feasible and was the general consensus. I felt a bit ambivalent about it because Papillon's ghost kept reminding me that it was always best to not have to accost guards and leave traces of how you got out. Capturing, stealing, cutting, dismantling and smashing were all against the "rules" of escape.

By January 1979 both Denis and Dave K were fully behind us and prepared to come along on the first date, which had been set for a Saturday in early February. It was not surprising that Denis showed an interest, as he had everything to gain by escaping. He had spent 15 years in prison and had no release date to look forward to. As we began to show that the prison doors were not as impenetrable as he had always believed, his attitude grew increasingly positive. Dave K had always shown an interest in the escape project, even though he had not at first displayed any keenness to participate. He looked at escaping in much the same way as we did: as a technical problem.

Although those of us in the escape group were determined to break out, there was an air of unreality about the whole affair. We had a plan but no one we spoke to had real faith in it. Privately, we somehow could not see ourselves tiptoeing down to the warder's office and pouncing on him there; we could not see ourselves tying him to a grille and fastening a gag around his mouth; we could not see ourselves casually hopping into his car and driving off to freedom. That was the stuff of movies, not reality.

As the escape date approached, Denis rightfully began to raise a number of objections and problems. Then two days before the date, Denis reported that his outside contacts had responded to a request for escape assistance and could provide transport, a safe house and all the rest if we would give them more time and further details. Denis had conveyed the request in a letter code established through departing prisoners many years previously, and enhanced it to cover new situations through subsequent releases.

A vote was taken on the issue and it was decided to postpone the attempt until help could be arranged. Those participating felt that in view of the increasing number of people showing an interest in escaping, our chances would be infinitely improved if we could be assured of outside assistance and did not have to rely solely on our own resources to get away. It would also then not matter so much if the actual breakout was not a clean one, as we would be able to get away from the mess quickly. Only Alex voted against postponement. Looking back, it was a good thing that he was defeated on that one occasion.

We realised that it would take some time to arrange assistance and for some reason – probably impatience – assumed that two months would be sufficient. From our point of view we considered this reasonable: when you have all the time in the world to contemplate one thing only, it is difficult to understand how it could take others longer to think about the same thing. We tended to forget that those outside were planning and executing a revolution and that our little request could not have been high up on their agenda. Even if it was, it would take months to assemble a team to carry out the task, acquire suitable vehicles and safe houses, let alone carry out all the detailed planning.

A second escape date was set for mid-April and a letter was sent off to the contact. The reason for the choice of the April date was because the presence on duty of a certain night-warder, a Sergeant Vermeulen, was vital to the success of the then-existing plans. He was going on a two-month holiday from just after the initial (February) date and was due to return in April. The new date was on the first weekend after he was due back on duty after his holiday.

Vermeulen's presence was necessary, not because we had struck an arrangement with him, but because our plan involved taking a warder's car, and we knew what sort of car he had and where he parked it. Not only that, the man had been on the early night shift – at his own preference – for almost 11 years and was thus thoroughly reliable and consistent in his movements. For instance, he was supposed to inspect the cells every half hour or so but we knew that he never came into our section until 8 pm, when he was required to come up to the first floor to turn off the *stokkies*' lights. And when he did come into the section, he never looked properly into the cells. Most nights he went straight to Denis's window to chat about rugby or air his gripes. Other warders, in most cases being younger and newer on the job, grew bored and restless as the evening wore on. They performed inspections at whim, just for something to do. Some looked carefully into the cells and some stopped for a chat. Others even played tricks by coming into the section very quietly and then trying to trap prisoners doing something embarrassing or against the rules.

During this two-month wait we made some of our greatest technical advancements. We developed our lock-picking abilities and improved our adjustable picking device to enable us to open doors nine and ten, as well as all the other wooden doors to which we had access. The period also gave us time to recover from the effects of the nervous strain that the preceding months' activities had inflicted upon us. Everyone had been affected by the stress of carrying out these activities under the noses of the warders, and it helped those of us intimately involved in the preparations realise why some of the others had become nervous about the escape preparations.

I cannot speak for the others, but the stress seriously affected my sleep. Every night I lay awake for hours, with my mind's cursor jumping from one idea to the next. Shapes of keys flitted across my consciousness, I dismantled imaginary locks and escaped from the prison in a hundred different ways. When I concentrated too deeply, my heart would pound heavily as if I had received a fright. I frequently broke into cold sweats and was completely unable to relax. Even during the day when I had a moment to rest, my heart beat faster than normal, stuck in a state of chronic excitation.

Memories of the university physiology class came to mind and the "fight or flight" reaction of the autonomic nervous system. What had been purely theoretical then was now being demonstrated to me in the most practical way. The hours awake were not wasted though, for mental work like that can be productive. Many problems were solved during those late-night insomniac sessions. And if we had made a breakthrough it would ensure that I got no sleep at all that night.

Despite the agony caused by the fear of being caught, there was no question of reconsidering or stopping what we were doing, or of being stopped. The preparations had taken on a momentum of their own, and drove us forward remorselessly. We began to live the escape, sleep the escape and see everything in terms of the escape. Nothing else mattered; nothing else existed. It forced those of us at the core of the exercise closer together, but further apart from those who were not. Our combined obsession was turned into an inexorable force. Papillon would have been proud of us.

It was during this period of waiting that David R, Jeremy and Raymond became interested in the escape project and asked if they could join the group. David joined after the February postponement because he could see that our technical capabilities had progressed to a point where the chances of pulling off an escape were becoming increasingly good and that there was a likelihood that outside assistance would be forthcoming. He also had a very long sentence ahead of him. The reasons for the others joining were similar, although they were encouraged to an extent by Dave's joining. The earlier criticism, that we were wasting time by making too many keys before working out a plan, was raised no more. The keys in hand were shown to be more effective in opening doors than brainwaves.

All welcomed the added participation and the others were integrated into the group. Although these new recruits greatly increased the logistical problems, the political impact that would be made if, say, eight prisoners got out of prison at one time, made them worth it.

This period was one of good comradely co-operation as well as intense debate. Dave R took an active part in preparing clothing for himself and others. Dave made himself a canvas shoulder bag while the others ordered T-shirts, inks to dye them and felt pens to draw on them. After "civilianising" them, the shirts were stored behind the geyser with all the other gear.

Dave R discovered another hiding place for forbidden wares – in the space between the two sides of the corrugated iron yard wall. The wall ended just below the far side of his outer cell window. From his window he could reach the top of the wall and hang a bag down the middle from a piece of string attached to a nail. The string could not be seen from inside his cell so it was quite safe. It had two disadvantages however: he could only get access to it late at night and it was open to the weather. Nonetheless, the bag he made was wrapped in plastic and stored in the place until the end.

A rather amusing incident concerning the acquisition of civilian clothing happened at this time. To continuously wash the floors of our part of the prison we needed a large supply of rags. Usually we were provided with discarded bedspreads that could be torn into useful-sized rags. One day, after a request had been made for more rags, it was found that there were no old bedspreads available. In order to avoid the floors not being cleaned – something the governors could not tolerate – none other than Captain Schnepel gave us some old clothing left behind by *stokkies*. Amongst the jumble was a perfectly usable pair of blue denim jeans. As they happened to be Stephen's size, he took them, washed them, mended the loose hems and repaired the zip. Since the jeans were "legal", they were washed openly and hung on the washing line in the yard to dry. One of the warders saw them hanging up and asked where we had got them, thinking he had stumbled on a misdemeanour. When told that they had come from the captain and were for cleaning the floors, he expressed surprise but could do nothing. The jeans soon disappeared into our cache.

Soon after this, Alex made a windfall discovery of a mine of disused civilian clothing. For a long time a large wicker basket had stood under the stairway to our section, which everyone knew to be full of old linen and blankets. One day, out of curiosity, Alex put his hand into the basket and lifted up the sheets and blankets to see if it contained anything else. At the bottom of the basket he discovered sufficient socks, shirts and trousers to dress a battalion, cast-offs that had been left by departing *stokkies*. Over a period of weeks, we removed everything of value and hid it in the cache. The items were washed and repaired, and altered to the respective requirements of those participating.

With a full wardrobe of escape garments, we began to think of other ways of disguising ourselves. In the storeroom was a shoebox-full of old spectacles discarded by the comrades over the years. Alex found a pair of weak, old-fashioned glasses that hardly affected his normal vision at all. He looked quite ridiculous when he put them on but that was the whole idea. Stephen ordered a pair of sunglasses because he found the Pretoria sun "too bright" for his sensitive eyes.

I could not wear any of the old specs because I was short-sighted, so I set about thinking how I could get another, different-looking pair for myself. I normally wore a pair of clip-on shades over my glasses because I really did find the Pretoria sun too bright. But I couldn't wear those while escaping because the prison staff had got used to me looking that way. So I put in a request to see the doctor and complained to him that I was getting terrible headaches because I believed there was something wrong with the prescription of my glasses. I was taken to an optician who – what a surprise – found nothing wrong with my prescription. But I insisted that I be given a new pair of glasses. Maybe the distance between the focal points of the two lenses had been ground in the wrong place, I suggested. After much wrangling and having to put up with accusations of complaining about headaches just to get a ride into town, they eventually relented. I could choose a pair of frames paid for by the state or pay for frames of my own choice. I chose the state frames because they were dreadful – thick, dark and heavy. They thought I was mad because I had "lots of money" and the frames did not suit me at all (even they could tell that!). I explained that in prison it did not matter how I looked and that I would rather spend my money on records and books when eventually I was allowed to buy them. When the specs arrived a week later they went straight into the cache and I never wore them until the day of the escape: I did not want the warders to get used to seeing me with them on.

After much thinking about the difficulty of organising help using established codes with people who could never appreciate the problems we faced in getting out of the prison, a contingency plan was worked out in case on the day of the escape there was no help waiting for us outside. This plan was based on the strange fact that Jeremy had in his possession, in his cell, his "Book of Life" – an identity booklet carried by all white South Africans at that time. It contained various licences such as driver's licence, marriage certificate, gun licence and so on, as well as personal details. Through some curious bureaucratic bungle, the security police had handed him the document so the commanding staff never questioned his keeping it. Noting that he had a driver's licence stamped in it, we realised that if we could get to a place where there was a car-hire facility it would be possible for him to hire a car that we could use to drive ourselves to the border.

The plan that emerged out of this was that if we managed to get outside and there was no assistance waiting for us, we would all climb into the warder's car parked outside the prison and drive from Pretoria to Jan Smuts Airport (now O.R. Tambo International Airport) near Kempton Park, where undoubtedly there would be car-hire facilities. There, Denis, Dave K and Raymond would split from the rest of the group, take the airport bus into Johannesburg and fend for themselves. At the airport the rest of us would dump the "hot" warder's car and hire a car from one of the car-hire firms. From there we would drive as rapidly as possible to the northern Lesotho border. We estimated that this would take between five and six hours, beyond the time it would take for our absence to be discovered, but hopefully before the police could mobilise roadblocks that distance away. This contingency plan had the second-level contingency that if the warder's car was not outside the prison, we would take the airport bus from Pretoria to Jan Smuts.

Only the five of us would use the hire car because it was felt that it would be impossible to drive all the way to Lesotho with eight people in one car. Besides this, Denis and Dave K claimed to have friends in Johannesburg who would "put them up" and felt it wisest anyway not to make for the border immediately but to wait some time for the heat to cool off. Raymond, it was decided, would accompany Denis and Dave because he was the last person to join the group and had stated that his coming was conditional on there being assistance. There was also an understanding that he would have to find his own way once we got out.

Alex and I were unhappy with this plan as we felt it would be better to make for Swaziland rather than Lesotho. We considered the time factor to be more important than the intensity of the border guard. Our estimate was that it would take between three and four hours to reach the Swazi border, in the region of a town called Amsterdam in the Eastern Transvaal (what is now Mpumalanga province). This would give us sufficient time to be over the border before the police were able to mobilise themselves and set up roadblocks. Our objection to the Lesotho route was that it would take too long to reach the place and the police would already have been alerted by the time we got there. Also, we did not like the idea of eight people climbing into one car directly outside the prison, let alone driving all the way to Jan Smuts. Lastly, we felt that Lesotho would be too vulnerable, being completely surrounded by South Africa, and there would be nowhere to go should we not be welcome. By going to Swaziland, we could pass immediately to Mozambique, where we definitely would be welcome. Since it was vital that our getaway be made with the warder's car and because we had to rely on Jeremy, the two of us had no choice but to go along with the Lesotho plan.

Another major dispute broke out over the question of taking arms, if we could lay our hands on any. It had been observed that when the *pos*-warder came on duty at 10 pm, he first collected his FN rifle from the night-warder in the office. The latter passed the rifle through the office window to the other who stood in the yard, while the dog-minder held the dog on a leash. There was no exchange of keys so it was legitimate to assume that the night-warder had free access to the rifle, and thus we would too. In addition, we thought that the night-warder would either have a small pistol on his person or have one lying about in his office, or have keys to the gun room or a locker in the office.

Alex and I argued that we did not plan to shoot our way out of the prison, but if someone who did not represent too great a menace accosted us at the last moment, the weapons could be used as a threat. We envisaged, for instance, that there might be a guard on the gate outside the prison and that we would have to force him inside where we could tie him up.

Others argued that if we got away and it was discovered that we had taken weapons, we would be regarded as "armed terrorists" and shot on sight. This was a fair assessment but we believed (perhaps naïvely) that the police would prefer to capture us alive rather than dead. They knew that we were not an inherently violent lot. In any case we felt that it was more important to think how we could gain our freedom rather than waste our thought power on how they would recapture us.

Whether in retrospect the arguments for or against taking arms seem more sensible, our attitude on this point reflected our single-minded determination in contrast to the others' greater sense of caution. The arms question was finally decided by the vote and it was agreed that no weapons would be taken. The three of us were in a minority at that time and had to abide by the group's decisions.

Alex, Stephen and I had expected the outcome and had prepared ourselves for it: we had begun to construct a wooden model of a pistol that would substitute for the real thing. To this project (known only to myself, Alex and Stephen) we gave the name "pea", short for "pea-shooter".

In an old *Reader's Digest,* we found some really good profile photographs of a Beretta 7.62 mm pistol. The pictures were in an article about a murder and were of the murder weapon. They were perfect side, front and oblique views – a bit like the mug shots of a criminal from a police record. I made a tracing of the side-view photograph and a number of accurate enlargements from this using a grid. These shapes I then cut out for the three of us to study so that we could choose the one that seemed to be the most life-size. Once we had chosen one, I cut it into its major components and made accurate drawings of the other smaller parts.

Alex stuck the paper cut-outs of the body and breech of the gun to suitable pieces of wood and cut out the outline shapes in the workshop. Between us, we cut out all the other visible parts to be stuck to the body of the gun. This we did not only so that the finished product would look more realistic, but also as a safety precaution in case a warder found a part on one of us. Before the parts were properly shaped, they looked like nothing at all and could easily be explained away as something else.

The barrel was made on a "lathe" created out of a large breast drill. This we did openly in the workshop and explained it as a pencil-holder in the making. I carved the parts of the gun to shape in my cell at night, one at a time. I carried them up and down in the same manner as I had done with the keys, in the bottom of my Thermos flask or in a tin of sugar. Our trusty piece of hacksaw blade came in most handy for this job, but for the finishing touches I borrowed small files from the "security" cupboard. To make the gun look authentic, I sanded each part with fine sandpaper and then coloured them with a very soft drawing pencil. To prevent the lead rubbing off, I sprayed the parts with artist's fixative that Denis had ordered for me. He explained to the warders that he needed it for "protecting his old university drawings".

When all the parts were completed, I assembled the pea. There were many parts: the body, sliding breech, barrel, trigger, magazine, hammer/cock, safety catch and two side panels for the handle. I glued all the parts in place with epoxy, and when completed it looked extremely realistic. It even fooled the comrades when I showed it to

*Court orderly
displaying exhibits*

*Policeman removing the ANC banner in
Cape Town – September 1977*

View of the prison from the "pos"

LET US ADVANCE OUR LIBERATION STRUGGLE

It is now a year since the police massacre of demonstrators in Soweto which triggered off the greatest mass upsurge against the white fascist state in recent times. Thousands of our heroic sons and daughters paid a dreadful price for their defiant stand against the brutal terror regime. Their deaths have not been in vain for they have made us more determined and have strengthened our resolve to smash the apartheid monster. We have convincingly shown Vorster that 20 years of ruthless application of the laws of apartheid have failed completely to secure our co-operation and submission.

Vorster in his turn has shown us that his trained killers have not the slightest restraint in gunning down innocent bystanders, including women and children. We have learnt too that spontaneous uprisings alone cannot destroy the enemy and that future actions must be linked with the broad strategy of our liberation movement headed by the African National Congress of South Africa. The Liberation Movement, through Umkhonto We Sizwe, the armed wing of the ANC, has as its immediate task the launching of armed struggle in South Africa.

Brothers and Sisters! We must organise now for the armed struggle which will liberate our people. We must not simply take to the streets, where gunmen can pick off our organizers, and where informers can betray our leaders.

In the mines and factories we must organise secret groups that will attack when the moment is right, through strikes, through sabotage, or other tasks which the liberation movement will call upon the people to undertake. In the townships we must expose the sell-outs who look to government stooges as their leaders. We must learn to distinguish our true leaders from those who opportunistically use government-created institutions and bodies for their own ends. Above all, we must see that many so-called critics of the apartheid state are being used by the fascists to give the illusion of democracy to the outside world as well as to people inside the country who are easily fooled by these tricks. We know what happens to our true leaders when the state gets hold of them - if they are lucky, they are sent to jail. If they are not lucky, they are sent to the mortuary

FORWARD TO THE ARMED LIBERATION OF SOUTH AFRICA! POWER TO THE PEOPLE!

VOICE OF THE AFRICAN NATIONAL CONGRESS AND

UMKHONTO WE SIZWE

Radio Tanzania - External Service (Dar es Salaam)

on 15435 Khz   19 meter band

10 pm South African time

Sundays : Mondays : Wednesdays : Fridays

Location of Pretoria Prison

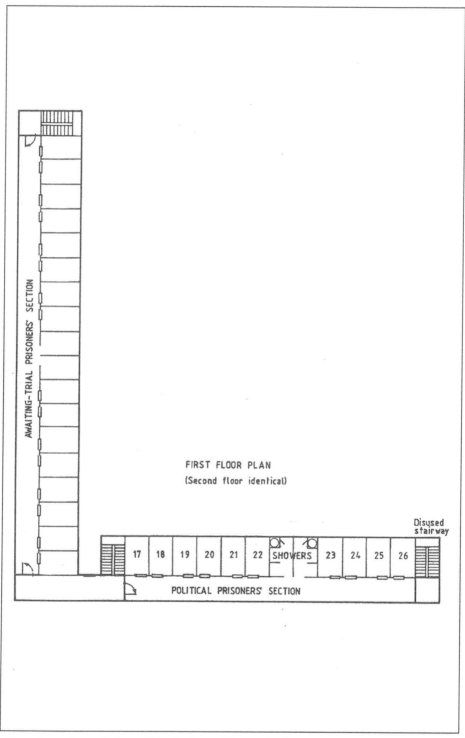

First floor plan of the political wing of Pretoria Prison

Plan of the yard and ground floor

YARD

WINDOWS

STOOL

BOOKSHELF
(Above bed)

TABLE
(Slides
out)

CUPBOARD

BED

1

GRILLE

BELL

2

WINDOWS

PANELLED STEEL DOOR
Keyhole on outside
only

LIGHT SWITCHES

PASSAGE

Plan of a cell

The inside of one of the cells at Pretoria Prison

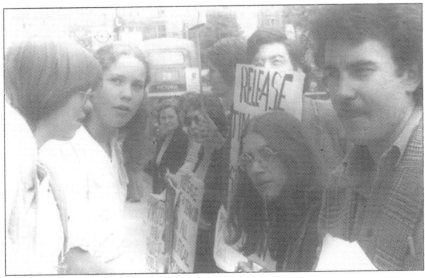

*Demonstrators, among them Robin, in front of South Africa House,
6 June 1978*

TO PASS ON NEWS ABOUT SURROUNDING AFRICAN COUNTRIES. IT CAN
BE USED IN CONJUNCTION WITH THE OTHER 2 CODES. IT WORKS BY
EMPLOYING CERTAIN KEY WORDS (NAMES) AND CRYPTIC LANGUAGE
IN ONE PARAGRAPH OF THE LETTER (NOT THE FIRST). THE KEY NAMES
ARE: ANGOLA = ANGELA   ;   BOTSWANA = BILLY
MOZAMBIQUE = MARY   ;   FRELIMO = HER BOYFRIEND.

NAMIBIA   = NANCY   ;   SWAPO = HER BOYFRIEND
RHODESIA   = ROGER   ;   P. FRONT = HIS GIRLFRIEND

SOUTH AFRICA = US (WE)   ;   ANC(SA) = ANTHONY
ZAIRE   = SARAH   ;   BRITAIN = AUNT BERTHA

USA   = UNCLE SIDNEY) ;
OTHER IMPORTANT W. NATIONS (FRANCE, GERMANY) = THEIR CHILDREN
(ie of AUNT BERTHA + UNCLE SIDNEY)
RUSSIA, CUBA etc = AUNT ROSE ;   UNITED NATIONS = UNCLE NORMAN

GUERILLAS, TERRORISTS = FRIENDS OF TERENCE
IF ANY OTHER COUNTRIES ARE OF IMPORTANCE MAKE UP OWN NAMES BUT
CHOOSE A NAME THAT GIVES A CLUE ABOUT THE COUNTRY
USE THIS METHOD TO DESCRIBE MOST IMPORTANT EVENTS OVER PERIOD
SINCE LAST LETTER. DO NOT DESCRIBE MINOR EVENTS.
AN EG OF HOW CODE WORKS:

HERE IS SOME NEWS ABOUT FAMILY AND FRIENDS' ABOUT 3 WEEKS AGO
WE WENT TO VISIT NANCY'S BOYFRIEND WHO IS STAYING WITH ANGELA. WE
WENT FROM NANCY'S SO YOU CAN IMAGINE THE SCANDAL IT CAUSED! WE
HAD JUST BEEN TALKING TO UNCLE SIDNEY AND FAMILY SO YOU CAN
IMAGINE THE STIR. ROGER IS STILL BICKERING WITH HIS GIRLFRIEND
SEEMS HE WOULD RATHER GET MARRIED TO HIS EX-GIRLFRIENDS BUT
I CAN'T SEE THAT WORKING OUT. SARAH HAS JUST HAD A VISIT
FROM TERENCE AGAIN, AT AUNT ROSE'S PROMPTING IT SEEMS.
POOR GIRL, IT WILL BE BAD FOR HER AND HER FRIENDS IF HE MANAGES
THIS TIME TO WIN HER FAVOUR. etc.

→ SA RAID ON SWAPO BASES IN ANGOLA, RHODESIAN REJECTION OF PF,
+ INTERNAL SETTLEMENT; GUERILLA RAID OF ZAIRE.

Codes devised by the prisoners to write letters

SEEING THAT P. DID NOT GET THE LETTER WHICH THE POLICE INTERCEPTED. PLEASE SEND MEE THIS ONE WHICH IS MORE OR LESS THE SAME AS THE LAST. THE LETTER MUST NOT BE POSTED IN G.A. IT DOES NOT MATTER WHEN SHE GETS IT SO WHOEVER LEAVES THE COUNTRY NEXT AND IS PREPARED TO TAKE IT, GIVE IT TO THAT PERSON. BEST IS, IF SOMEONE FROM THE FAMILY TAKES IT IN THE ORIGINAL TOILET PAPER LETTER, — SOWN IN A HEM OR SOMETHING. WHEN THEY GO OVERSEAS. ONCE OUTS. DE THE COUNTRY IT CAN BE POSTED OR HANDED DIRECTLY TO HER IF IN LONDON. I WANT HER TO KNOW ALL ABOUT THE LETTER THAT WAS STOPPED SO ADD A BIT YOURSELF EXPLAINING EVERYTHING. PLEASE LET HER KNOW ABOUT COMMUNICATION METHODS TOO.

IT WILL BE QUITE SAFE TO WRITE OPEN FRIENDLY LETTERS TO R. USING HER NAME. BUT IF YOU WANT TO SAY MORE USE OTHER ADDRESSES AND FALSE NAMES AS YOU HAVE BEEN DOING ALL ALONG. JUST DONT INCLUDE NEWSPAPER CLIPPINGS WITH LETTERS ! ONCE I AM SENTENCED THERE IS LITTLE TO WORRY ABOUT IN THIS REGARD.

REGARDING THE DOCUMENTS ETC. WHICH I WANT YOU TO GET TO R, IT IS BEST IF SOMEONE CAN TAKE THEM BUT IT WILL ALSO BE OK TO POST THEM AFTER. I AM SENTENCED. WHAT I SUGGEST YOU DO IS WRITE ▬▬▬▬▬ TO KENNETH + SAY YOU ARE SENDING COPIES OF DOCUMENTS TO HIM FOR HIS INTEREST (OR IN ANSWER TO HIS REQUEST) AND ASK HIM THEN TO PASS ON — OR MAKE ADDITIONAL COPIES TO PASS ON — TO R. SEND HIM HER ADDRESS TOO. WHEN YOU SEND THE DOCUMENTS DO NOT INCLUDE A COVERING LETTER. THERE IS NO PANIC IN DOING THIS AS ▬▬▬, I AM SENTENCED. PERHAPS YOU CAN EVEN THINK UP A BETTER SCHEME THAN THIS.

YOU CAN GET ALL DOCUMENTS ETC. FROM LAWYER. IF LAWYER GIVES YOU COPIES OF THE STATEMENTS I MADE TO POLICE ASK AGAIN DO NOT SEND THEM. THEY WERE WRITTEN UNDER DURESS AND I M MOST ASHAMED OF THEM. THEY LAWYER IF ANYONE DIRECTLY REQUESTS ANY DOCUMENTARY MATERIAL RELATING TO OUR TRIAL FROM HIM, HE MUST REFER SUCH REQUESTS TO YOU. USE YOUR DISCRETION WHETHER AND IN WHAT WAY YOU WILL ANSWER SUCH REQUESTS.

Letter written on toilet paper

Crank mechanism used to open door 2

Opening door 2 with crank

Diagrams of wooden and wire keys

Stages of construction of a wooden key

One of the dummies left in a bed on the night of the escape

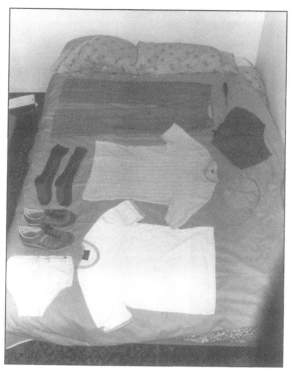

Clothing used in the escape

Vermeulen – the warder accused of assisting in the escape

Vermeulen in his office (picture presented at his trial)

Tim Jenkin in his escape outfit

Tim Jenkin, Alex Moumbaris and Stephen Lee in Dar es Salaam
after the escape

The escapees back in uniform

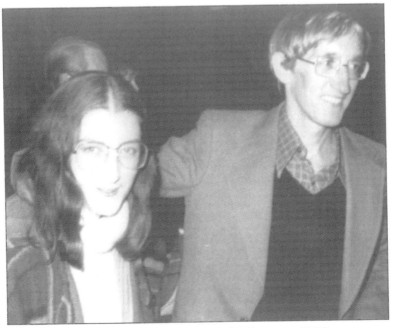

Tim arriving at Heathrow Airport on 21 January 1980

them. Finally, it was wrapped in toilet paper and plastic and stuck under the bottom of the metal tool cupboard in the workshop – probably the least likely place the warders would have looked for booty if they had decided to have a thorough search.

Despite the earlier opposition to arms, when the others saw the pea there was no opposition to its use and it even became included in the general plans. The idea was that it would be used for accosting the night-warder, which would make the job of tying him up somewhat easier. Some wanted the plan to include revealing to the warder after he had been tied up that the pea was a fake gun, and even leaving it with him so that we would not be regarded as armed fugitives. How the pea was finally to be used was never brought to the vote because the gun question got pushed into the background as other more pressing problems came to the fore. Later the escape plans were changed, such that the pea was no longer an important element.

* * *

In November 1977 the prison authorities announced that political prisoners could no longer study beyond matriculation level while in prison. Prisoners who were already studying post-matric courses (in all cases through the University of South Africa – South Africa's correspondence university) could complete their courses, but no new courses could be started.

This change in policy was said to have come about because some prisoners on Robben Island had abused the study "privilege" (as the authorities saw it) by using study materials to smuggle "inciting documents" to the outside. Rumour had it that one or more prisoners on Robben Island had written revolutionary slogans in a library book from the University of South Africa. Because of this alleged abuse by one or two prisoners, all prisoners had to pay the penalty.

The authorities are probably sorry now that they took away this right (as we saw it). The ensuing publicity was very bad for them and the first two prisoners to be affected by this ruling at Pretoria Prison decided, as they were forbidden from engaging in academic studies, to study something else – how to get out of a prison! I would not like to believe that our escape was the sole or even one of the main reasons for the reinstatement of studies shortly after we got out, but undoubtedly it must have been a factor in their decision making.

The real reason for removing the right to study, of course, had nothing to do with the "abuse" of the "privilege" by political prisoners. The authorities had for years been looking for a pretext to stop political prisoners studying. They knew as well as the prisoners that prison was regarded as the "university of the revolution".

On Robben Island Nelson Mandela and other ANC leaders imprisoned for life organised their fellow prisoners to study, much to the chagrin of the enemy. Many of the prisoners signed up for correspondence courses to complete their school certificates so that they could go on to study for degrees, while those prisoners who had been inside for a long time worked on their umpteenth degree. It is no wonder that Mandela and other leading figures were removed from Robben Island and sent to Pollsmoor where they were kept in isolation from the general mass of politicals.

The apartheid jailers grew jealous that their captives were able to receive funding from outside sources to engage in studies, and they were not. They despised prisoners who were more intelligent than themselves – especially black prisoners. Also, they believed that we "terrorists" only used our education for "subversive purposes" when released.

"Why allow the prisoners the opportunity to advance their cause while in prison? Their imprisonment is specifically designed to remove them from circulation so that they cannot subvert law and order. They should be allowed to rot, suffer for their crimes and be kept totally in the dark so that when they come out, they are broken and of no value to their terrorist friends." This was the real thinking behind the ending of studies, not the discovery of a few slogans in the margin of a book.

It is true, of course, that the prisoners did "abuse the privilege". They did so in every conceivable way, consistently, deliberately and cunningly. That was natural, for they used every opportunity they could to advance their knowledge, not only of current happenings in the real world but generally so that they could be of more value to the movement when released (just as suspected!).

The desire to study, at least in our prison, did not arise so much out of the wish to accumulate degrees but out of the need for books. The university had a fabulous library by prison standards and provided just about everything that could not be obtained in other ways. Library books were not supposed to be swapped but of course they were. At the beginning of the year it was decided collectively who would study what, so that the broadest possible range of library books could be obtained. Nobody ever studied the same subject in the same year – that was a wasted opportunity. The course on Comparative Literature, for instance, gave access to a great range of top-class literary works from many countries. We read all the most famous revolutionary novels as well as a number of progressive African writers. The censor was not equipped enough to be able to detect which carried ideological messages. The course on Comparative African Government gave access to virtually any books on Africa. Those who hadn't been able to keep up with developments on the continent because of the denial of news, could update their understanding within a year or two.

Science subjects were not permitted but the reasons for that were practical – prisoners could not get access to laboratories and workshops. The only arts subjects not permitted were law and the Russian language. Law studies could not be allowed, they said, because people with criminal records could never become lawyers. The real reason was that they didn't want us to know too much about the legal circumstances under which we were being held. Who knows what the prisoners might have got up to had they known more about the law! Of course, this prohibition was meaningless because there were usually one or more qualified lawyers among the prisoners and most of the others had studied some aspect of the law at one time or another. On top of that, we had the best lawyers at our disposal so there was little that the authorities could get away with on that score.

The comrades did not take the formal side of their studies very seriously – they were only interested in the library books. This doesn't mean that they did poorly in their assignments and examinations. On the contrary, among us were some of the university's best students. There was so much time for studying that the work could be left to the last moment and help could be obtained from those who had already studied the same courses. In any case, most of the comrades were graduates already and so found the courses very easy and treated them with cynicism because of their low standard and conservative content.

Not everyone was engaged in formal studies while we were there. Johnny, because he was not enrolled when the ban came into force, was not permitted to start a new course. Alex, although he was enrolled, did not study at all (formal studies, that is). His was a fake enrolment that allowed the others to order library books in his name. Everyone read the university library books, including those not enrolled. In addition, there were a vast number of textbooks that had accumulated over the years and these could also be read by all. There was even a complete set of Russian grammar books that one of the comrades had studied before the language was banned. In a way, those who were not enrolled had an advantage over those who were – they were not encumbered with essays, assignments and swotting. Everyone could also order any book they wanted – you just had to find someone whose course covered your areas of interest.

Most of the money to pay for the studies came from the International Defence and Aid Fund (IDAF) in London and was channelled through various prisoner relief agencies in South Africa. The Defence and Aid Fund was set up in South Africa in 1960 to look after the welfare of political prisoners and their families. The organisation was banned in 1965 and forced to set up office outside South Africa. To use this money to pay for fake studies, as Alex and others before him had done, was not unethical. In a sense practically everyone who was studying in our prison was engaged in fake studies as they did it for the books and not to learn what the courses were supposed to teach them. Most of those who sent in assignments and wrote exams only did so to keep up appearances. In the light of the total ban on news by the authorities, we felt justified in using the studies to keep ourselves informed about the world. We also had to ensure that our years in prison were not totally wasted and that our minds did not atrophy as our political opponents hoped they would.

The position on Robben Island was quite different. The black comrades had not lived the privileged lives that we had. Very few had achieved matriculation level and even fewer had obtained degrees. Prison gave them the opportunity – many for the first time in their lives – to receive a relatively acceptable education. It was reported that some warders had been heard saying that black prisoners deliberately got themselves arrested so that they could get a free education. Clearly this was a case of sour grapes.

Prison for the black comrades was much harsher than it was for us, but the opportunity it gave for study, in a sense, made it an experience with some value. The ending of university studies was a serious blow for these comrades; for us it was not so serious. For them it meant that they would never be able to progress beyond the school level; for us it meant the end of private studies in our own specialisations.

Our fellow prisoners did take their private studies quite seriously, however. A prisoner whose life is made less meaningful by being confined in a prison will grasp onto anything that gives life meaning and direction. Those who found that studies did this for them devoted a lot of attention towards it; those who were more interested in challenging the prison security system devoted everything to that.

Chapter Eleven

The Second Date

The date set for the second escape attempt was the 21 April 1979, a date we had calculated as one when Sergeant Vermeulen would be back on duty after his holiday. This was the date that Denis had conveyed by code to his contact. Our request for a car and driver were the minimum requirements. Our suggestion was that the driver should wear a yellow shirt so as to be easily recognisable, in case it was not possible to park the getaway vehicle directly in front of the prison.

No reply arrived by the April date and so without confirmation of outside help there was no choice but to cancel the attempt. A deep gloom set in. Those of us who were in more of a hurry to get out were annoyed that we had agreed to wait for assistance. By doing so, we felt that we were in effect keeping ourselves in prison. We believed that we were in a position to let ourselves out and had now placed ourselves at the mercy of unknown people outside with whom we had no direct contact.

A letter eventually arrived about ten days after the cancelled attempt, explaining that we had given insufficient time and details for assistance to be arranged. A general meeting of the escape group was called and it was decided that the onus of choosing a date should be passed to those giving the assistance. Another letter should be written explaining that we were prepared to wait until all the necessary arrangements had been made and that all we wanted to know was in which month the attempt should be made. To simplify matters, we would take as the date of our first attempt the first Sunday of the month chosen by the assistance group (a change from our earlier choice of a Saturday). If for any reason (ours or theirs), it was not possible to make it on the first Sunday, we would do it on the second Sunday, and so on until it succeeded. In addition, we should let them know that the escape group had expanded to eight persons but that the previous arrangements remained the same, that is, the minimum requirements including the person with the yellow shirt.

Another letter was sent. Each letter stirred Alex's, Steve's and my further impatience. It took two months from the time a letter was sent off until we received a reply. It was now May – nine months after the first key had been made and three months since we had first considered ourselves ready to leave. The reply would only arrive in July and even then, our helpers might not be ready. We felt that we had somehow relinquished to others the initiative of what we had started. We believed that every step taken should be towards bringing forward the day of departure, not pushing it further away.

Our impatience to get out was prompted by a number of other factors. After April it begins to get cold in Pretoria, where the winters can be bitterly cold. The approach of the cold season worried us because our civilian clothing was unsuitable for winter use. Our money too was becoming outdated, because it was then 10 months since the new currency set had been introduced. Each passing day also increased the chances of our cache being discovered.

The decision to change the day of escape from a Saturday to a Sunday was another of those decisions that revealed the differences between the participants in the escape group. From an early stage, everyone was of the opinion that it would be better to make a break over a weekend rather than during the week. This was because lock-up on Saturdays and Sundays was at 3.30 pm – an hour earlier than on weekdays – but the dog was placed in the yard at the same time as weekdays (about 5 pm). That would give us more time to put our contingency plan into operation should it be necessary. Also, on weekdays awaiting-trial prisoners were brought to the prison at about 6 pm, which meant that we would only have about an hour before the escape was discovered; at weekends no awaiting-trial prisoners were brought in because the courts only operated during the week. We would thus have about five hours before the escape was discovered. This was reduced to three or four hours on some weekends when a particular duty-bound officer inspected the prison at about seven or eight in the evening.

The basis of our differences regarding a Saturday versus a Sunday departure revolved around this occasional inspection. We had noticed that if the officer inspected on the Saturday he would inspect again at the same time on the Sunday. Those who favoured a Sunday argued that if the officer came to inspect the prison before 11 pm on the Saturday then we would not go on the Sunday but postpone it to the next weekend.

Alex, Steve and I felt that the officer was irrelevant to our plans because he never carried out his inspection before 7 pm, a couple of hours after the planned time of breakout. A Saturday departure would give us the advantage that the authorities would not be able to get our pictures in the papers the next day. (The Sunday papers were all printed on Saturdays and it would thus not be before the Monday that our pictures appeared, by which time we would be far away. TV did not count because it only operated for five hours in the evening at that time.) We also reasoned that there would be fewer warders around on a Saturday night, should there be a general alert and call up. By Sunday night, most of those who had been away for the weekend would have returned. A final reason we put forward was that petrol stations were closed on Sundays at that time, due to rationing, but open until 6 pm on Saturdays. This meant that we would still have time to refuel the warder's car if it was necessary. Later this argument fell away as petrol stations closed even earlier.

These were the arguments that we had originally put forward for a Saturday departure, and they had been accepted when the group consisted of only five participants. It was Jeremy who first considered the Sunday option to be the better alternative. After intense discussion it was Sunday that finally won the day.

Towards the end of May, Raymond was taken to hospital for a minor operation and for a week or two afterwards had to be taken daily to Central Prison for a bath. On one of his trips he spoke to an accompanying warder who claimed to work on gate duty in the street outside the prison. When he asked him what time he came on duty the warder told him that gate duty started at three thirty in the afternoon. On hearing this Raymond immediately announced his withdrawal from the escape project. Some of the others were influenced by what he had been told but the rest did not accept it. No one had ever seen a guard on duty outside the prison at that time of the day and we could clearly hear the gate squeaking and its chains rattling only after six in the evening.

Jeremy was one of those influenced by what Raymond had been told and a short while later he announced his withdrawal too. He had not lost interest in escaping and would reconsider joining again if it could be shown that the chances of success were greater than they appeared to be at that time. He asked to be kept informed of all developments.

We were disappointed at Jeremy's withdrawal because it meant the loss of a valuable participant. His allotted task of assisting in the jumping and restraining of the night-warder was not easily replaced – Jeremy was a brawny fellow and the rest of us not. It meant that we would have to subject our plans, as they then stood, to a radical redrafting.

Jeremy's withdrawal forced us to think of other ways of overcoming the night-warder. It was not an easy problem to solve because jumping the warder meant in practice stopping him from using the walkie-talkie he wore on his belt, restraining him and tying him up. The only replacement we could think of for Jeremy in this task was the pea. It would, we hoped, be sufficient inducement to persuade the warder to co-operate without needing to use physical coercion. But if his walkie-talkie was fitted with a panic button that he could easily press to send out a distress signal, the pea would make a very inadequate replacement.

The plan after we had removed or disabled the walkie-talkie and restrained the warder was to move him either to the "cage" between doors six and seven where he could then be handcuffed to a grille, or "encouraged" to drive us out of the prison complex in his car. A bit far-fetched? Perhaps, but who would have stopped a warder in uniform driving around the area with a group of respectable-looking passengers?

There was one major shortcoming with this plan: if we could not get through door six and were forced to put our contingency plan of going through the visiting room into operation, it would be extremely difficult to get the warder out of the prison to chauffeur us away. This observation made us realise that it was no longer good enough to rely on the hope that one of our keys would open six or that we would find its key in the prison – we had to be absolutely certain that we could open it.

The logical train of thought generated by this realisation led us to the conclusion that we had to find a way of testing door six. But how could we do that? It seemed totally impossible. The administration section was sacred, out of bounds, a zone occupied by prison staff and therefore in the realm of the unthinkable. Our thinking would not allow us to visualise ourselves walking through that area, let alone fiddling with or testing locks. Being in there meant disabling the night-warder, and that meant an actual escape attempt.

But necessity is the mother of invention, they say. For days we strained our brains to bursting and finally realised that it was just our own prejudices that were preventing us from getting any further. The area beyond door four was not inviolable: there had to be a way of getting in there to do what needed to be done without alerting the warder.

Separately and on the same night, both Alex and I thought of a plan to get to door six to test it. It was really quite simple. If we came out of our cells shortly before 8 pm and hid in the dining room while the warder was doing his inspection round, we could come out of the dining room, go through door four and down the passage, open five and test six. Then we could dash back to the dining room and wait for the warder to return to his office before returning to our cells.

After arriving at this plan it was only a matter of time before we realised that if we could somehow get to and open door six early enough in the evening, we could pass through it and test all the doors down the passage on the way to the front door and then return to our cells at eight. We could do this right under the warder's nose, as door six was a solid door that would obscure us from his view. Not only that, the actual escape could be made without the need to accost the warder at all, allowing us to choose a time of departure that would maximise the time before the escape was discovered.

So ultimately Jeremy's withdrawal gave impetus to the most

profound changes in the escape plan. In the same way that it helped us overcome our fears about going down to the administrative section to test six, it allowed us to eliminate the need to confront the night-warder to get beyond him. The benefits were enormous and gave the plan for the first time an air of realism. No longer did we need to resort to measures that were more in place in Hollywood movies than in reality; no longer were we ignoring Papillon's advice.

The plan that emerged out of all this was not complicated, but the way we had arrived at it reminded us that we could never have dreamed it up before we had the technical ability to carry it out, as some of the others had wanted us to do when the first preparations for escaping were being made.

No letter arrived during May and June confirming that help had been arranged. Alex, Steve and I became increasingly frustrated by the delay and realised that the longer we put it off the more problems we would have to face. The problems were not long in coming.

On 20 June I was taken to hospital for a minor nasal procedure. As I was climbing into the prison ambulance outside the front door, I noticed some building activity in the road outside. I did not give it much thought because it looked as if they were digging up the road to repair a broken drain pipe or sewer. Denis happened to be taken out two days later and noticed that the building activity was not going downwards but upwards: a new sentry post was in the process of being built, right outside the front door of our prison in the middle of the street. Several of the others were taken out at this time so we were able to monitor the progress of the new post. Even worse, they reported, the gate in the street was being moved about twenty metres closer to the front door of our prison, placing it about fifteen metres from the post-in-the-making.

It was clear that the post was going to be a sophisticated one. It was being constructed almost entirely of glass and was to consist of two sections or rooms. We guessed that it would probably also be equipped with phones and sirens. On either side of it heavy booms were being erected, that would presumably be operated from inside the post.

Alex, especially, became worried about this development, for it seemed logical to conclude that the post was being equipped for a guard to be on duty 24 hours a day. We couldn't help thinking that our jailers knew all about our escape plans and were quietly going ahead with measures to make the prison escape-proof. Alex began to agitate that we had to make a break immediately, before the post was completed, as it would be our last chance. A meeting of the escape group was called and after much debate, approval was given for the three of us to go if we wanted to.

The others were still waiting for word from the contact. Alex, Steve and I discussed the matter between ourselves and decided that we would make an attempt one night during the 8 pm inspection round. The plan was based on the scheme we had just arrived at but it combined elements of the previous plan because we were not certain if we could get through door six.

The plan was to move downstairs shortly before eight, hide in the dining room, and while the warder was upstairs switching off the lights in the *stokkies'* section, we would attempt to make our way through doors four, five and six.

If we got past six using our own resources, we would have all night to work our way through doors seven, nine and ten. Door eight would be opened by pressing the button in the warder's office before going through doors five and six. If we could not get six open, we would wait in the warder's office for him to return. Then we would threaten him with the pea, tie him up and take his keys if he had any. If he had no keys we would attempt to get into the visiting room and through it as we had planned earlier.

We realised that we would have to contend with a guard on duty at the gates in the street, but since the gates even in their new position were a short distance from the front door it would still be possible to exit without being seen. The plan was to use the pea to force the sentry into the prison where we could tie him to a grille.

In the end I decided the scheme was far too risky and refused to participate. The plan was a product of panic, not reason, I said. It would be too risky for the three of us alone to tackle the night-warder, the door-six barrier had not been breached and the situation outside the front door was too much of an unknown. I could not allow a plan that had been so long in the making to be hinged on the hope that the pea alone would ensure our freedom. What if the warders were not convinced?

Without unanimity, the plan was scrapped.

* * *

After the great burst of key-making activity in the early months of 1979, the period that followed until the next major phase of the escape was a period of reduced activity on the escape front. The activity did not stop, it just slowed down. We continued to prepare clothing, discuss options and details and work out new plans. The absence of overt preparations led to a general reduction in tensions and an improvement in relations all round.

The activities of the previous period had affected everyone, even those not participating. They were understandably growing weary of the constant fiddling with locks, hiding of gear and talk of escaping. There had been no let-up, resulting in an atmosphere of tension in the prison. And because everything was so secretive it made prison life very unsettling.

Those who were less determined to get out had tolerated our activities despite the disruption it had caused. But they were not the worst to suffer: our own merciless drive to get out rebounded on us. Alex's task of generating enthusiasm, of persuading the comrades that we should all participate and that it was possible to get out was far more onerous than mine of making the keys. Clearly it affected him because he would often complain of sleepless nights and regularly walk on his own, up and down the court with clenched jaw and furrowed brow, looking down at his feet. Stephen shared Alex's task. Regular visits to the medicine man exposed his response to it all.

I welcomed the few months of calm as a period of recovery for my nerves, which were beginning to show signs of strain. I had never "settled in" to prison life, in the sense of finding some form of non-escape-related activity that I could devote my attention to and that would help me relax. I had given everything to getting out, not to making life more bearable. Taking an interest in something else helped me understand how unsettling the escape project had been on some of the others. It was quite easy to become absorbed in something like reading, drawing, music or studying a subject in detail if you had nothing else to do. It also became easier to see how much intellectual and emotional investment could get tied up with such activity, and how destabilising it was when threatened.

There were many things to do and contemplate if you were not planning and preparing an escape. Prison life was not all work, frantic pacing up and down the yard and lock-up. It had its lighter side too. There was sport, books to read, letters to write, visitors to see, and many other things. I would not like to give the impression that life was pleasant and that prison was fun, but to avoid insanity you had to find distractions to take your mind off your immediate predicament.

Each prisoner found solace in different things. I took up drawing, an old hobby but one that real life had never provided me with enough time to pursue. I was not allowed to buy my own pencils and paper because I was not "studying", but to get around this restriction I got Denis to order the equipment for his course work so that he could pass it on to me. There was nothing to inspire artistry so I took to copying pictures from magazines and memories of better times. Drawing was very therapeutic and it helped me overcome the boredom of the long evenings and take my mind off the details of the escape. So many ideas and plans had been rushing through the recesses of my brain for so long that it was not easy to stem their momentum.

The warders did not mind me drawing, even though it was not strictly permitted. A huge portrait of Robin I had copied from a photograph stood proudly atop my cupboard for a long time; a picture of a revolutionary hero I drew for Stephen remained pinned to the inside of his cupboard for months. But when they found a picture I had drawn of a guerrilla with AK-47 and all, they drew the line. All my pencils and drawing books were confiscated and I was put on the carpet. I tried to argue that there was nothing wrong with the picture, as it was only a drawing and not a real guerrilla. But they were not convinced and threatened the direst punishments if I drew anything more.

For a month or two I drew no more and took to reading instead. But a budding artist's urges can't be suppressed so I got Denis to order some more equipment and I carried on as before. The only difference was that I had to return the paper and pencils to his cell each morning and dispose of my works of art down the toilet before open-up.

Stephen took to writing poetry and prose, which like drawing were also tolerated "illegal" activities. The authorities believed that unauthorised writing was by definition subversive, and he had no cause to write anything apart from letters as he was not allowed to "study". Denis was a serious reader and writer but his studies took up most of his time. Tony was totally absorbed by his philosophy course and Dave K spent his time reading trash. Jeremy, Raymond and Dave R, involved themselves in deep "extra-curricular" studies. Jeremy was also a keen poet and produced some stunningly inspirational poems, considering the bleak environment in which he had to write them. Johnny was a reader but preferred more upmarket titles than Dave K. Alex was the dreamer. He would lie for hours on his bed looking up at the ceiling and dream of freedom. Before Steve and I arrived and introduced the theme of escaping, he would nearly smoke himself to death while mulling over his predicament. He gave up that foul habit, thank goodness, when getting out gave his life more meaning.

Books were an essential part of our lives, as nothing else removed our minds from our pickle as effectively as they did. But we had a problem: the supply of good books. Each prisoner was brought three per week from the prison's library at Central, meaning there were 30 to choose from. But most were rubbish and so were ignored by all except Dave K. He claimed to read over three hundred books a year, which is no great feat if you're locked up on your own for 15 hours each day.

To meet our insatiable demand, the warder in charge of library books tried to institute a system whereby we could order what we really wanted from the main Pretoria City Library. This never really worked, as there was no system of connecting our orders with the books that arrived at the prison library at Central. There was also no categorisation: the books were just arranged in alphabetical order. At one stage, the older comrades related, practically all the books were categorised under "T" because so many titles started with "The". A warder sometimes wrote out a list of the books on the shelves that *he* thought would be of interest to us. Needless to say, he was not very good at judging our preferences.

There were other sources of books: the University of South Africa library books mentioned earlier; the three books a month that the "A" groupers could buy; and our own library. In our own library were a couple of thousand titles bought by the comrades over the years. Departing prisoners were not allowed to take with them those they had paid for, so they became prison property. All were of a high quality – a fine collection by any standards – but long since read by those who had been inside for years. Although our prison censor had a list of books banned by the government, it appeared that he kept no record of what had been ordered in the past, for he never removed anything from our shelves that subsequently got banned.

We also had a vast range of magazines to read. Each prisoner could order several titles of his own choice, and in this way, we provided ourselves with a comprehensive selection. The magazines were circulated, and when read by all were meant to be returned to the censor. But like everything else, if there was anything worth keeping it was torn out and stored or the magazine just not returned. Magazines were important for keeping contact with the real world, for keeping up with it and for providing a feel of the times. It was no wonder that the authorities for so long denied the comrades permission to receive periodicals: they helped keep us alive spiritually.

The censor's main task was to watch out for anything "subversive" and sexually stimulating. "Subversive" meant anything about "communism", "socialism", "Marxism" or "revolution", anything critical of the South African "government" and, naturally, anything that could undermine security such as electronics, chemistry and locksmithing. Censors were not very sharp, so there was about a fifty per cent chance that a "subversive" book would get through if the title was innocuous enough – a chance we considered high enough to justify losing the book if it was not approved.

While we never went without something to read, it was a constant struggle to ensure that there were sufficient books of interest and value. Ours was political imprisonment so we had to keep fighting to keep our intellects alive, and to keep at bay the darkness our keepers wished to impose.

On the cultural front, apart from books, there was music. Our record collection must have been one of the finest anywhere and contained more than five hundred titles. Each prisoner was allowed to order one record every three months, adding to our collection about forty new records a year. Knowledge of new releases came from magazines and visitors, so we were pretty well informed of the latest trends in the music world.

Those comrades who were interested in music and familiar with our collection, chose the records that were played each evening. They wrote up lists of a week's records and gave a copy to each comrade. Every day the four or five chosen records were given to the night-warder who played them on the turntable in his office, in the order in which he was instructed.

Some of the comrades took the music very seriously and lay on their beds for hours savouring the sounds. Sometimes you could hear someone dancing or singing in his cell or tapping his feet to the beat. The loudspeakers were at first mounted in the passage, so if something was not to your taste it was just too bad. Later, after they were remounted inside our cells, you could turn yours off if you could not stand a particular number.

Music had never interested me very much, but as paradoxical as it might seem, prison was a cultural experience for me. Our music collection was of such a varied nature that the comrades could arrange an educational programme to run over several nights. For instance, by selecting jazz records from various periods it was possible to assemble a history of jazz from Lead Belly to the present day.

Denis was the only one who regularly made his own music. He taught himself to play the guitar and after a few years of practice grew quite proficient. One or two of the others tried their hands – or mouths to be more precise – at the mouth organ. On the whole, prison is not a good place to learn a musical instrument because you can never find a secluded spot where you can practise, and everyone is forced to hear your first discordant notes.

The music in our cells did serve certain vital functions as far as the escape was concerned: you could be sure that so long as it was playing no one could hear a prisoner filing a key or testing a lock, even if the cell was bugged. And the records, because we chose the order in which they were played, served as a clock for timing certain activities. More about this later.

The films we saw on Friday afternoons could not exactly be placed under the heading of "culture". They were all chosen from the catalogue of a film-hire shop in downtown Pretoria. The films were fetched by a warder, but invariably the ones we wanted to see were "out on loan" and we ended up seeing one chosen by the warder. Our choice was usually for films with some cultural value, but these were films that bored the warders. They preferred junk, American, car-chase films and would normally get their way by saying that the film they had brought was all that was left. Many of the comrades got so angry with this that they preferred to stay in their cells and read. There was nothing we could do about it as we were not in a position to question whether the film we had ordered was really out on loan or not.

Nevertheless, over the years some good films were shown and, curious as it may seem, most of us saw more movies in prison than we would have seen if we had been outside. But then there are more interesting things to do on the outside.

Weekends were set aside for sport. Although none of us were fanatical sportsmen, it was an activity valued by all because it provided an outlet for releasing pent-up emotions and frustrations. It also kept us fit in body and mind and provided a distraction from our cloistered little world. Tennis was the main sporting activity – not real tennis, for our court was only two-thirds full size and we only had wooden beach bats. Denis and Jeremy were the champions; I was the worst. Tony did not play because of his coordination problem, but Raymond was remarkably good considering he had only one good eye.

The tennis court also doubled as a volleyball court: the net posts were tall enough to support the net at the correct height for the game. Despite it being a popular game, we were seldom able to play volleyball because of the difficulty in mustering sufficient players to make up two equal-sized teams. Prior to Stephen's and my arrival, volleyball was played every weekend because the prison staff, including Captain Schnepel, joined in. But they must have received instruction from a higher authority to not play sport with the "communists", as they suddenly stopped participating. There was to be no fraternising with the prisoners – if friendships developed it could lead to a member of staff wanting to assist the prisoners in their seditious activities.

Everyone took to "jogging" in the prison yard. This may sound impossible to outsiders, as jogging usually conjures up images of leisurely runs through leafy parks. Our "track" must have been no more than a hundred metres per lap, and for most of the way around it was hard concrete. Every morning before breakfast most of us put on our running shoes, T-shirts and shorts and ran anything from five to a hundred laps. More than that was too much of a strain on the ankles. To prevent boredom, one week we ran clockwise and the next week counter-clockwise.

The monotony of running round and round the yard was countered by the knowledge that we were doing it to keep fit – an essential prerequisite for escapers. And certainly, it did keep us fit. It provided us with much of the stamina we needed to keep in sight our goal, the front door. It is surprising that our jailers saw nothing fishy in our keenness to run every morning, come rain, frost or burning sun.

Aside from the aspects of prison life that made it just bearable, there were two others that helped us maintain our sanity: letters and visits. Without these conduits to the outside world you could easily forget you were a human being with wishes, hopes and desires; you could become thoroughly institutionalised and see the world entirely in terms of the prison. This is why for some long-term prisoners without relatives, their saddest day is their day of release. Their whole world collapses: they lose their "family", they have nowhere to go, no one to receive them and everything they have built up is left behind.

Letters were a very important component of our lives as they were one of the few ways we could remain in contact with reality. Letters, university communications and library books were collected from the censor at suppertime by Dave K, while the rest of us waited in the dining room in anticipation of what he would bring. Every day you hoped for a letter, although you knew that you only got one, two or three per month depending on your grading. If nothing arrived when you expected something, it made you feel miserable and you'd swear they were deliberately withholding your mail.

Prisoners who had just arrived in prison, like Stephen and myself, were classified as "C" group prisoners and only permitted to send and receive one letter of 500 words per month. "B" group prisoners were allowed two letters per month and "A" groupers three. Denis was allowed four letters as a special dispensation for being a life prisoner. If more than your allotted number arrived, they would usually ask which one(s) you wanted.

Five hundred words a month sounds very little but when you have nothing to write about it seemed an awful lot. A 500-word letter written to you, on the other hand, seemed very short. People outside had so much to write about, did so much, led such exciting lives –

they didn't appreciate their freedom!

The censorship of incoming letters was not overly severe. Perhaps this was because our correspondents had become circumspect over time. They knew that all letters, in and out, were thoroughly perused by the security police and the prison's censor. This knowledge enforced a self-censorship on the writers in both directions.

If a prisoner wrote something "unacceptable" he was simply handed the letter back and told to rewrite it. This routine could be exploited if you wanted to pass a little message to the chiefs: you could write something directed at them, something you would like to say but could not do in any other way. I took advantage of this once, after a fly-past on "Republic Day" by a formation of jets spewing out vapour trails of the much-despised orange, white and blue colours of the apartheid flag. I wrote in a letter that the sight had made me vomit and that I hoped they would not come and pollute the clear blue sky above our prison again. The next day I was on the carpet to face the wrath of a red-faced captain. That I had provoked such indignation gave me great satisfaction.

It took them nine months to figure out that my correspondent "Makaira Herscheli", or "Molly" for short, was Robin. I concocted the name out of the scientific terms for the bird "robin" and the fish "marlin", which was her surname. It must have come as a shock to them to find out that my letters were, in effect, going directly to the ANC office in London, where Robin was still working. I was hauled up again and told discreetly that I could no longer write to this person. I did not argue the point and meekly accepted the instruction, knowing that I would still be able to write to her using another false name that I had previously established for her. At the next visit I wistfully reported to my mother that I was no longer allowed to write to "Margaret", whom she understood to be Robin, and asked her to get me the address of my other London friend, "Sally". A month or so later I had a new address and resumed the unbroken communication I'd had with Robin.

Prisoners were also allowed to receive photographs from their correspondents, and have photo albums to keep them in. These were not supposed to have more than 12 pages. What the authorities had in mind were albums with six leaves, with two or three photos neatly pasted on each side. When the album was full you were supposed to hand in surplus pictures so they could be held in safekeeping until your release. But everyone wanted all their pictures, not just the latest ones. Old ones carried memories. To get around this restriction, the comrades, instead of ordering normal photo-albums, ordered loose, clear-plastic pockets that could be put into ring binders. A sheet of white paper was inserted in each and the pocket literally stuffed with pictures on each side of the sheet. In this way you could keep dozens of pictures. Whenever the warders demanded that we hand in some of our pictures, we pointed out that our albums were the regulation 12 pages and that it was not specified how many pictures you could have on each page. Their pettiness knew no bounds (neither did our deviousness, they would have said).

For your birthday and at Christmas you were allowed to receive 12 cards. Twelve cards were more than any of us had ever received for our birthdays, but at Christmas it had long been a tradition for sympathisers both in South Africa and abroad to send cards to political prisoners. The officers were never quite sure how to cope with this annual flood of greetings and salutations. They tried various ruses to prevent us knowing of their arrival and of how many had arrived. With monotonous predictability, each year they tried at first to deny that there were any cards at all, and then let us have them very slowly to give the impression that they were very few and far between. Some years they kept them all until Christmas day or after, and then give us eight or so and said there were no more. But we knew that hundreds of cards arrived for us because one year the censor, after receiving a complaint about being tardy with our letters, forgot himself by complaining about the sacks of envelopes he had to go through.

Another year the censor, who had resigned and was about to leave, decided to allow us to choose our own cards from the bundles that had arrived. He called each of us to his office window in turn, and read out the name of the sender of each card from the pile he held, and then asked if we wanted it. Of course, each prisoner said "not that one" until he had read out every name. In this way we were able to find out who had sent the cards and get some idea of the numbers that had arrived.

Visits, like letters, were regulated according to your grading. "C" group prisoners were allowed one visit by one person per month, lasting 45 minutes. "B" groupers one visit per month by two people at a time and "A" groupers two visits by two people. There were some exceptions to this rule: those who had no family in South Africa, such as Dave R, Dave K and Alex, could receive several special visits over a week or couple of weeks if they had relatives visit them from abroad. Visits were strictly non-contact except for those who had small children (such as Alex and Dave R during our time). They were allowed short contact sessions with their children, under close scrutiny in one of the administration offices. This applied until the child reached the age of six. After that – *verbode* (forbidden).

I placed visits below letters in order of preference because I found them rather intimidating. The visiting room was very small: the same size as a cell but split down the middle by a chest-high counter and thick glass panes. There were three positions in the room with stools on each side. For us politicals only one visit took place at a time; for the *stokkies* three at a time. A warder sat on each side to make sure nothing "illegal" was said and visitors were pre-warned that they were only allowed to discuss "family matters".

Your voice carried through to the other side via holes in the pegboard panels on each side of the window. Inside the panels were hidden microphones that recorded every word spoken. We weren't supposed to know about this, but became aware of it when Denis was once taken into the main office while the door to the small office next to the visiting room had inadvertently been left open. In it he saw tapes turning while a prisoner was having his visit. When they saw him looking at the tapes the door was not very discreetly slammed in his face. The cryptic language used by the comrades in trying to extract news from their visitors must have confounded the warders in attendance and Big Brother who listened to the tapes afterwards. They must have thought they were unearthing all sorts of "terrorist" plots and conspiracies.

This was the setting in which we had to conduct our conversations. What could you say when you knew that your every word was being listened to and then sent to security police headquarters for detailed analysis? I also found it embarrassing to sit in front of my family in my prison uniform, with my cropped hair and in such an uncongenial environment. Others did not feel as intimidated and looked forward to their visits with great anticipation and excitement.

I said everything there was to say about the place at my very first visit; after that I didn't know what else to say. Most times I put in a few good words about the prison – to give the impression that I was quite happy and the last person who would harbour thoughts of escaping. Occasionally I even "bragged" about the impenetrability of the place to make my watchers think that I was totally intimidated by the security measures. After saying my bit I got my visitors to do the talking. Most of us made a point of saying things to confuse the warders, as it was agreed that we should always take advantage of every opportunity to present ourselves in a light other than the correct one.

All visits had to be conducted in one of the two official languages – Afrikaans or English. The only person affected by this ruling was Alex, whose mother – who visited him twice a year from France – spoke Greek and French but very little English. Boris, his son – who came with her – spoke only French. The captain didn't mind this too much as he reckoned that Alex couldn't say too much to a young kid that would be a security risk. Little did they know.

Marie-José, Alex's wife, was permitted by the prison authorities to visit him but she could never get a visa to enter the country as she had been deported to France shortly after their detention in 1972. Every year she applied for a visa and every time the application was turned down. This perverse prohibition drove Alex to desperation and at the end of February 1978 he went on a hunger strike to try to force the authorities to change their minds. The prison authorities claimed to be in sympathy with him, but said they could do nothing about the visa as it was out of their hands. Alex soon realised the futility of the exercise and terminated his fast after 10 days.

Denis's wife Esmé, too, had problems obtaining a visa. She had visited him once or twice but for many years had been refused entry from Britain, where she had been living since shortly after his imprisonment. Dave R's wife, Sue, had also been deported and was likewise refused a visa to enter South Africa. Dave K's ex-wife, Norma, could get a visa but she considered it too risky to go to South Africa because of her anti-apartheid actions in London.

There were other visitors to our prison apart from our permitted one or two per month: priests, envoys, judges, big-shot prison officials, lawyers, doctors and government ministers. Apart from the priests and doctors, these visits were not frequent.

Although all of us were atheists, we all – apart from John and myself – saw priests, ministers or rabbis. This was not because we wanted to atone for our "sins" but because we became so desperate to see faces other than those of our captors that we were prepared to put up with all that was involved in being "religious".

The "Jews" – Denis, Dave R and Raymond – had it best. Their rabbi seemed to be an interesting chap but the chief benefit came from the organised way the Jewish community cared and catered for Jewish prisoners in general. Twice a year each of them received a huge food hamper containing cold meats, biscuits, dried and fresh fruit, tinned goods and the like. As with everything else, these were shared with everyone.

The "Catholics" – Tony, Jeremy and Steve – invariably returned from their visits swearing that it was the last one they would be attending. Monseigneur McGuinness was a musty old bore who insisted on reading passages from the Bible and engaging in long prayer sessions. As hard as they tried, the "Catholic" comrades were unable to persuade him to organise food hampers.

Dave K was the "Anglican". The minister visited him because the two were old friends who had known each other outside. For Dave, religious visits were like an extra visit. They started each session by discussing the Bible and ended by discussing ordinary lay matters.

John and I did not see religious practitioners because we could not decide which creed we belonged to, and did not feel the "benefits" were worth it. When I first arrived at Pretoria I tried to sign on as a Jew, after the others had advised me of the advantages. But they didn't fall for that one.

Then I thought I would be a Catholic because I didn't want to see a priest on my own. Finally, I decided against having a religion when I suspected that the Catholic priest was a bore. When the prison chaplain came around to sort out my "religious needs" he couldn't understand when I said that I had none. He could understand my not wanting to see a spiritual adviser but was incapable of understanding that anyone could not believe in God. He had a form to fill in and could not leave it blank. Eventually I was classified Anglican, I think, because I said my father was a member of that denomination at one stage.

The "foreigners" – Dave R, Alex and Steve – were from time to time granted the "privilege" of seeing envoys from their respective countries. The French envoy always told Alex that he was doing everything in his power to secure his release and obtain permission for his wife to visit him. Alex grew cynical about these claims since nothing ever happened, but he continued to see the envoy as it amounted to another visit from an outsider and he could ask questions about France.

Stephen and Dave R were visited by a British envoy who made similar claims of action. But no one expected much from their envoys as their respective governments had seldom shown much sympathy for the plight of political prisoners in South Africa. For a long time these governments had regularly made the misguided claim that political prisoners were legally sentenced by the courts for breaking the law and that judgments could be trusted because the South African legal system had always displayed a healthy measure of independence. They never questioned the so-called laws under which the accused were charged and sentenced and under which the judges made their judgments. They never said anything about the "security laws" that presumed guilt or about the illegitimate racist "parliament" that passed those laws in the first place.

Judges were supposed to visit the prisons to see for themselves the implications of their judgments and the sentences they handed out. In all the time I was there only one judge came around. His visit was so brief and cursory that the impression he got of the prison and its prisoners must have confirmed his prejudices. The ones who didn't come must have had implicit faith in the system for which they worked.

Visits by big-shot prison officers were more frequent but were clearly just acts of duty. Probably many of the heavies from head office had never been near a prison or had not visited one for many years. Some of them were prepared to receive representations from the prisoners, but as their visits were impromptu the prisoners were not given time to formulate a list of demands, although there were always the standing demands for less censorship and for permission to receive newspapers. It is difficult to know if these regularly presented demands fell on deaf ears or if over the years they had a compounding effect. On occasion we felt that they had an impact but, unlike the Red Cross, they never produced any immediate response.

Representatives of the International Committee of the Red Cross visited all South African political prisoners once a year. They were allowed to do this provided they did not make their reports public. The Red Cross contributed significantly to the well-being of all political prisoners and were responsible for some of the greatest improvements in conditions over the years.

The authorities never let us know when the Red Cross was coming, but we could always sense their imminent arrival by a change in the behaviour of the warders. Demands that we had made to the Red Cross the previous year were suddenly fulfilled or we were required to make the prison look clean and orderly for no apparent reason. In 1979, for instance, after many years of complaining to the Red Cross that our tennis court was cracking up and that it was becoming impossible to play on, it was suddenly dug up and a new surface laid down. A few days later the Red Cross arrived.

All the prisoners looked forward to Red Cross visits. The team arrived early in the morning and spent the day with us. They ate our food – you could be sure we would be served something exceptional that day – and questioned each prisoner in turn to find out if they had any personal problems. The visitors told us about the conditions of other political prisoners in South Africa and around the world. In all ways, they told us, we were better off than our black compatriots and, in some ways, better off than many political prisoners in other parts of the world. In one respect we were worse off: in the provision of news, the denial of which they considered to be very serious. Without a doubt their pressure helped persuade the authorities to give in on this matter and from 1980 allow political prisoners to receive newspapers.

The only member of "government" who visited our prison during Stephen's and my short stay was the new Minister of Police and Prisons (later the Minister of Law and Order), Louis le Grange. His visit was just a familiarisation exercise. The 10 of us were made to stand to attention on the tennis court as this tall, close-eyed butcher with swept-back grey hair made his whirlwind inspection. The sight of the chief figure behind all the police massacres, detentions, torture and imprisonment of South African patriots was enough to make us throw up. Perhaps the radiations of our hostility were the cause of his scurrying off so quickly.

Chapter Twelve

Stage One

The plan for the attempt we had just abandoned after the scare over the new sentry post became the basis of our new escape plan. We were now determined to get out without having to accost the night-warder, and without leaving a trace. But before we could proceed with the plan, we had to be absolutely certain that we could open door six using our own resources.

Going out via door six and without the warder's knowledge meant a total re-conceptualisation of our escape plans. All of our plans to tackle the warder were discarded, as well as the need to rely on the complicated contingency route through the visiting room. While this meant abandoning all notions of taking the warder's car, the advantages of getting out secretly were so much greater that it did not matter.

In any case, as our intelligence improved, it became obvious that it would not be so easy to simply hop into the warder's car and drive off into the sunset. And after Jeremy's withdrawal, the warder's car had no particular advantages for us as there was no point in driving it somewhere to hire another car as we would have no driver's licence. To get away from Pretoria we could just as easily, and probably more safely, use our money to hire a taxi; less favourably catch a bus or train. It was these observations that led us to the conclusion that if we wanted to proceed we had to find a way of getting to door six to see if we could open it.

It had long been suspected that door six used the same key as door two. We arrived at this conclusion by a complex process of deduction. As we had never seen any keys on a bunch carried by a warder that could not be linked to a particular lock, key six had to be one of those that were in regular use. It could not be one of those on the night-warder's bunch as he was locked into the prison by door six. He only had two keys: one that opened the section doors (our door three) and one for door four (the grille out of the admin section). His section-door key was different to the number ones we had used to open three, but this was because his could not master them. If he had been able to do so he would have had access to half the cells, and we knew that he could not open the cells with the keys he carried. If a cell had to be opened at night in an emergency, someone from outside had to bring the day-keys (i.e. the ones and twos) or a key to unlock a locker containing them in the office. This meant that the departing day-staff had to leave with at least one bunch of the day-keys to lock the doors on their way out, including six. From this it was reasonable to deduce that six used a number one or number two key. It seemed less likely that it would be a number one, as key one was related to the section key used by the night-warder. Door six – being solid – looked very much like our door twos.

Our experiences with the number two locks had taught us that it was not good enough to know that a particular lock used a particular key – it had to be tried out. But to test six was altogether a different matter to testing our ones and twos, or even three and four. The only time we could get down to test it was during the 8 pm inspection round, when we had a small window period of about fifteen minutes. This meant that we had to be pretty certain that our keys would work, because there would be no time to modify them on the spot.

The project to go down to test door six became known as "stage one" because it was to be the first part of a two-stage project to test our keys in all the doors on the way to the front door. "Stage two" would be the testing of the doors beyond six to the front door. "Stage three" would be the actual breakout.

Stage one, or at least the first stage-one attempt, was carried out around the beginning of August 1979. The general plan was the same as the one we had previously worked out but it contained certain refinements to make it workable. As with all our plans, it relied on Sergeant Vermeulen being on duty.

We had decided against using the dining room as our hiding place while Vermeulen passed to go upstairs, in favour of the film equipment cupboard under the stairs to our section. The dining room had the disadvantage that its door was visible from the end of the passage at door four. We could not take the chance of exposing ourselves to view while entering it. The film cupboard, on the other hand, was set well back from view.

It was easy enough to obtain the shape of the key for the film cupboard: I simply measured it one Friday when Dave K was given the key to get the film equipment out. When the equipment was repacked in the cupboard after the film show, it was arranged in such a way that it allowed two people to crouch inside not too uncomfortably. The key was a typical wardrobe key, simple in construction, and I easily made a replica out of a piece of flat metal that I found in the workshop.

A number of other details also had to be worked out. As we had no watches there was no way of knowing when it was 8 pm or when we should go downstairs. We couldn't just go down and sit in the cupboard for hours on end – that would be far too uncomfortable. This is where we took advantage of our music records.

Vermeulen never carried out his inspection at exactly eight, but only after he had finished playing the records that had been selected for the night or when he came to the end of a record at around inspection time. As he was required to play them in the exact order given to him, it was possible to tell pretty accurately how near we were to inspection time. A certain record placed in the list could signal the moment for us to go downstairs; the last record when it was eight. The record chosen as the signal record was *Parallel Lines* by Blondie, an album popular at the time.

Vermeulen was so reliable and predictable that he never left his office if a record was coming to the end, even if he had been called upstairs by a *stokkie* who had pressed his bell. It was thus quite safe to move downstairs during the last cut of a record because Vermeulen wanted to be in his office to turn it over or put on the next one.

Without any opposition, Alex and I were chosen to carry out the mission. We had the most experience in practical matters and had worked out the plan; we were also the only ones who would do it. This is not to say that we were not dead scared about doing it. We had been messing around with locks for months and both of us had been out of our cells while our doors were supposed to be locked, but the thought of having to remain out of our cells for probably more than an hour, violate the sanctity of the admin section and expose ourselves to the possibility of bumping into Vermeulen was terrifying in the extreme. The thought of it caused us to break into shivers of cold fear; our bellies locked solid and we felt weak in the knees.

This then is how the first stage one was carried out: At around 6 pm, that is, an hour and a half after lock-up, we placed dummies in our beds. These were created by placing our prison overalls on the bottom sheets of our beds and stuffing them with clothes, books, towels etc. to make them look like authentic bodies under the blankets. There was no need to worry about the head because this was towards the wall below the passage window and out of sight from the passage. (The authorities realised this fatal error after our departure: one of the first things they did was to turn the prisoners around so they could see their heads from the window.) In the unlikely event of Vermeulen looking through our windows, we arranged our cells to appear as if we had eaten our sandwiches, undressed and gone to sleep.

At around 7 pm we both unlocked our inner doors with the number one keys we had earlier concealed in our cells. Alex unlocked his outer door using the crank mechanism, after I had signalled to him with a towel that I could hear no sounds coming from Vermeulen's direction. After emerging from his cell, Alex relocked his number two, turning it once only, and tiptoed down to my cell to unlock my outer door. While Alex made his way to the shower, I emerged from my cell and relocked my number two with the key he had passed through my window. I then made my way to the shower too.

Alex had opened the geyser door and removed from the cache the keys we needed, the pea and our balaclavas. After readying ourselves, we crouched – one in each cubicle – behind the low walls separating the showers to wait for the signal record to end. Here we were out of view of Vermeulen if he had looked into the showers from the passage. If he had come right into the shower room he would obviously have seen us but we reckoned that if this were to happen, his sudden discovery of two masked "terrorists" with a "gun" would give him such a fright that he would probably drop down with a heart attack. Then we would have had the prison to ourselves.

We were dressed in our prison overalls but had decided that if we got caught, we would threaten Vermeulen with the pea, tie him up, release Stephen, get dressed in our proper escape clothing and make our way out as best we could. Around our necks we carried our running shoes tied together by their laces.

When the Blondie record came near to the end, we rose from our hiding places and poked our heads out of the shower to watch for the all-clear signal from Stephen – a wave of a towel – before proceeding to door three.

On the signal, we crept down the passage towards the section door (door three). I peeked through the keyhole to make sure no one was standing on the other side and then slowly unlocked the door. We went through, and after listening for any movements from downstairs, I relocked the door and we cautiously made our way down the stairs to the cupboard. Alex unlocked the cupboard door and the two of us squeezed inside. Once inside, we realised that there was one small detail we had not thought about: how to hold the door closed from the inside. The small lock jutting out on the inside did not afford a proper grip – a minor detail, but an important one.

From inside the cupboard we could still hear the music coming from our section. It was an eerie sound and much louder than expected, but reassuring in that it indicated that everything was in order. Silence would have been much more frightening as we would have had no idea how long it was to the eight o'clock inspection round. Our thoughts in the pitch darkness, the agony of our contorted limbs and our pounding hearts flooded our senses.

As soon as the music stopped we heard Vermeulen picking up his keys and making his way towards door four. The sound of him opening the grille so close by made us shudder with fright. Alex tensed and as he did so his sweating fingers lost grip of the lock by which he was holding the door closed. The door swung open a little and a bright shaft of light entered the cupboard. He's seen us, we both thought, but Alex managed to regain his grip and pulled the door closed just as Vermeulen came into view of it. I swore quietly in Alex's ear.

As Vermeulen walked over our heads and up the stairs Alex's hand was shaking so much the door rattled as if there was an earth tremor. "Oh God! He must've heard it," I cried out aloud, forgetting myself in that moment of terror. But no, he continued on his customary way up the stairs and into the *stokkies'* section. He must have been in a trance.

As soon as we heard the clang of the *stokkies'* section door closing we leapt out of the cupboard and made our way through door four, which Vermeulen had conveniently left open. As we turned the corner after door four, door six – the last major obstacle in our path to freedom – came into view. We stared at the solid blue barrier in awe like two archaeologists finding the entrance to some long-concealed tomb. It was closed across the passage as we had suspected.

I unlocked door five, a grille a few inches in front of six, with the number four key. The key glided around with no resistance and we swung it open so that I could get to six. I inserted a number two key into six and tried to turn it, but it wouldn't turn – not even a little bit. My heart sank. Another long battle ahead, I thought. I tried several of the other number twos but none of them turned. I also tried a number one key, just in case, but it also refused to turn.

I remembered how long it had taken us to get our number twos to work, and then we'd had hours to test them each night. How often will we be able to get down here to test this door? How long is it going to take to get this one right? Is this really the end? Alex prodded me back to reality as I contemplated the problem: "Take it out. There's no more time. We'll have to try again." I relocked five and we made our way back to the cupboard, baffled and dismayed. The wait for Vermeulen to return seemed to take an eternity. We had arranged for Denis to detain him for as long as possible by asking him the latest on the rugby front, and obviously Denis was carrying out his task with relish. In fact, Vermeulen took so long to return that we wondered if something had gone wrong. Has he discovered us missing from our cells? Has he radioed for reinforcements?

Eventually we heard him coming out of our section and his casual footsteps descending the steps above our heads. The release of tension as he locked door four turned our fear into defiance and we congratulated each other by telepathy. As soon as we heard him throw his keys onto the table in his office and turn on his radio, we came out of our hiding place, scurried up the stairs and made our way back to the shower. We returned to the cache everything we had taken out of it, apart from a number one and a number two key. After Stephen had given another all-clear, I relocked Alex in his cell, returned to my own and relocked my number two with the crank.

After I had relocked my cell doors and cleaned up all evidence of the "misdemeanour", I expected to come down from the agitated state, as one normally does after a stressful event. But there was so much adrenaline pumping through my veins that night that I couldn't calm down and wasn't able to get a wink of sleep. I lay awake all night wondering if I would be able to face another stage one. My nerves could only take so much. The keys hadn't worked and it seemed we might have to go down many times. I wasn't sure if I had the guts to do it again.

The whole episode, including the days preceding the actual operation, was one of the most agonisingly stressful, self-inflicted experiences of our lives. It took us both a few days to come down from that high and when eventually we did, we tried to reassess the situation. Although none of our keys had worked in door six, we were not convinced that the door did not use a number two key. Close examination of the keys the next day revealed that some of them had almost turned and that the problem had been caused by the ward cutaways not matching the wards exactly. Why they did not jam in our number twos we could only ascribe to the fact that our cell doors were opened and closed much more frequently than number six, causing the wards to be more worn. One thing was for sure: door six did not use a number one key.

Very shortly after our first stage-one attempt a series of disasters and near-disasters occurred. The first happened one Friday morning while we were supposed to be cleaning our section. Alex and I had completed our chore of cleaning the showers and for some reason had taken out of the cache one of the sacks of clothing and the pea. As we were going through the sack we heard the section door open. I peered out of the shower and saw that it was *Bewaarder* Moreby, the most hated of all the warders, who had just entered. I shouted to Alex. He instinctively slung the bag into the closet and closed the door without locking it, and tucked the pea into his belt under his shirt.

Moreby must have seen my worried look and made his way

directly to the shower to see what was going on. Alex grabbed a rag and pretended to be cleaning the wall. I went to the entrance again to see what Moreby was doing. As I turned to look out, Moreby stepped into the shower and the two of us collided head on. "What's going on here?" he demanded. "Nothing, Mister Moreby. We're just cleaning the shower as we're supposed to. What's the problem?" Alex glanced casually over his shoulder but said nothing. Moreby stood with his hands on his hips for a few seconds scanning the scene, hoping to find something wrong. Satisfied that he could find nothing, he warned, "You just watch out," and left the shower. I guess he must have thought that Alex and I were having it off, for what else could explain our red faces?

After that incident, Moreby kept a closer watch on the two of us than he had previously done. He was a totally insecure character always out to ingratiate himself to his superiors, and he desperately wanted to uncover some dirty business and bring it to the attention of the captain.

A second misadventure involving Warder Moreby occurred shortly after the shower incident. It was on a day when our usual workshop attendant, Loggie, was off duty and Moreby had taken his place. Alex, foolishly, started making a spanner for dismantling door seven's lock out of the handle of an old can opener. Moreby spotted him doing something that wasn't required for the particular job in hand and started to walk towards Alex's bench to see what he was doing. If Alex had thought quickly enough, he could have invented some explanation for the unfinished and unrecognisable object, such as saying it was intended to be a butter knife or something for the garden. But when you feel guilty your first reaction is to conceal what you are doing, and that's what Alex did. He placed the piece of metal on the shaft of his vice that extended under his bench. Unfortunately, it did not balance properly and fell to the floor with a loud clang just as Moreby approached. Moreby picked up the suspicious object and immediately headed for the captain's office with his little prize.

Nothing actually came of this incident as far as Alex was concerned and we even managed to turn it to our advantage by getting Moreby transferred to another prison very shortly after it happened. This was achieved by complaining bitterly to the captain the next day about Moreby's attitude toward us, which had always been one of bossiness and aggression. We did not find his rapid transfer unusual because our complaint was clearly the pretext the captain had for a long time been waiting for. Prisoners and staff alike despised Moreby. He was a twisted character who took out his frustrations on others by being extremely arrogant and rude. He was the only English-speaking warder in the prison and hated us intensely because we could tease and taunt him more easily than the others.

At the time we did think that the discovery of the spanner-in-the-making was being taken seriously because the very next evening the warder on *pos* duty remained on the catwalk after lock-up at four thirty. Until that day, the catwalk had been unoccupied during the period from lock-up until ten at night. Everyone interpreted this change as a sign that the authorities suspected what we were up to and had closed the major loophole in their security.

It was sometime later that we found out from Sergeant Vermeulen that this change in the *pos* duty shifts just happened to coincide with a genuine change in routine. Apparently, the warders had for a long time been asking for a three-shift day – for some reason that was of interest only to the warders themselves. The opportunity to introduce the new routine was taken when an important awaiting-trial prisoner was brought to the prison. He was Eschel Rhoodie.

Eschel Rhoodie was one of the main characters in the notorious Information Scandal, a major occurrence in white politics at that time. He was alleged to have been one of the villains who spent vast sums of public money on propaganda exercises overseas. He later fled South Africa and from exile began to spill the beans on the other crooks in the "government", which included Prime Minister Vorster. He was arrested in France in August 1979 and immediately extradited to South Africa. At his trial he was convicted on five counts of fraud and sentenced to 12 years' imprisonment, some of which were to run concurrently, making the sentence an effective six years. However, he was subsequently acquitted on appeal and allowed off scot-free. Illegally spending millions of rands of public money was evidently not a crime, unlike the act of distributing some ANC leaflets.

We did not at first know of Rhoodie's presence in the prison because our newspaper delivery system had broken down at that time, and of course it was cut out of our radio news broadcasts. But somehow the news filtered through and then we were able to see him through cracks in the fence surrounding the *stokkies'* yard. It was peculiar to see a prominent regime figure mixing with the ordinary *stokkies*, most of whom were petty criminals and only in prison because they could not afford decent lawyers to get them out on bail.

The interpretation that the 24-hour *pos*-guard was a response to suspicions of an escape attempt prompted a major gathering of the escape group to discuss the issue and the strategy to be adopted in light of the change. The meeting proved to be a major turning point. Denis expressed his apprehension and declared that he could not contemplate going while a guard remained on the *pos* over the crucial four thirty to ten period. He and Dave K were of the opinion that the guard would eventually be withdrawn, citing as evidence a similar incident in the past that had reverted to normal when the crisis passed. Dave K considered the guard on *pos* duty to be a setback but not an insurmountable problem. Dave R adopted Denis's position and recommended that all escape-related activity should cease until the guard disappeared. He proposed that all of us should rather concentrate on other projects that would promote our interests, such as pressurising the authorities to bring all political prisoners, black and white, together in one prison such as Robben Island.

Alex, Steve and I saw no reason for all this gloom. We wanted to proceed with the escape preparations whatever the situation. The problem of the warder could be tackled when we reached that bridge, as had been done with all previous bridges. To halt preparations at this stage might mean halting them forever. The extension of *pos* duty would not affect our immediate objective: the testing of the doors down to the front door.

As we were split down the middle on the issue, the other three had to submit to our proposal that we be allowed to go ahead with the project to test the doors down to the front door – that is, carrying out stage two. The others were insistent, however, that we should not go beyond stage two, which in practice meant escaping, until the four thirty to ten period was free of the *pos*-guard.

It was decided too that it would be too risky to ask for outside help while there was a guard on the *pos* during the escape. It would neither be possible to park an escape vehicle outside the prison nor be correct to expose other parties to the very real possibility of being shot. A decision was made immediately to advise our comrades outside that all plans of assistance should be held in abeyance until further notice.

Another near-disaster followed closely in the train of the previous ones. One evening as I was getting something out of our cache in one of the geyser closets during shower time, I noticed that the sack was wet on top. How was this possible in a warm environment? There was only one explanation: a leaking tank. But that was impossible because it was an insulated tank and any leaks would only show at the bottom, not at the side. As I pulled the sack up to save the easily damaged wooden keys, a drop of water dripped onto my hand from the roof of the closet. I knew it then – another leaking pipe!

Pretoria Prison was built by prison labour, which was a large part of the explanation why from time to time leaks appeared in someone's cell or in one of the downstairs rooms. It had been found that the prisoners who had installed the plumbing had deliberately sabotaged the system by tightening all the pipe couplings only one thread before they were encased in concrete. It was not possible to repair all the joints in one go, as no one knew where they were. To replace the whole system would have meant virtually knocking down the entire prison. Leaks just had to be repaired when and where they appeared. But we couldn't report this leakage because we weren't supposed to know what happened inside the locked geyser closets.

The sack of contraband in the closet with the leak was huge – too large to be placed with the rest of the stuff in the other closet. We could leave it on the floor of the other closet but if the warders opened it for any reason they would see it and then search the closet for more. That way we would lose everything. It was better to take it out and leave it somewhere else until we could find a better place. In the absence of any better places just then, there was nothing else we could do but hide it in the nearest cell – Alex's – until the next morning, which fortunately was a Friday.

The next day we assessed the situation. The leak appeared to have worsened overnight; we knew from past experiences that leaks had a habit of spreading – meaning that if it was leaking above the one geyser it would probably soon leak above the other. Both caches had to be cleared out. But where could we move all the stuff? It was a mountain. There was no other safe basket for our eggs.

As we were contemplating what to do with our gear while cleaning the section, a warder burst in to announce an inspection by the big brass from prison headquarters. We couldn't believe our ears and our bad luck. The bastards were bound to look under the beds, and then everything would be exposed. More than exposed, there would be pandemonium. How would the captain explain to his chief a huge bag of keys and civilian clothing simply lying under one of the prisoners' beds? Did they never have shake-ups?

There was one chance. Raymond was ill in bed and if we put the sack under his bed it was unlikely they would disturb him by going over his cell. Alex appealed to Raymond, but Raymond, quite rightly, would have none of it. He was not involved in the escape and not prepared to take unnecessary chances – not unreasonably I thought. Alex in his usual uncompromising way swore profusely at all concerned. There was nothing we could do but cross our fingers and hope they would not look under the beds.

Each prisoner was expected to stand in his cell while the inspection took place. As my cell was first, I tried to be as friendly as possible to set the tone for a casual, chatty inspection. It appeared to work. The big shot responded favourably: he asked a few questions about how I was getting on and then after a cursory glance around the cell passed on to the next. Alex's heart must have been punching the inside of his chest by the time the big one got to him. Fortunately, when he reached Alex's cell he had grown bored looking into the cells, which all looked equally clean and tidy, and disinterestedly passed on to the next.

As soon as the officers and retinue had cleared out we set about finding another hiding place for our sacks of goodies. There was one place that might be suitable – the sealed off stairway at the far end of our section. We could tie the sacks together and hide them around the corner on the first step of the stairway. By sitting on the floor and stretching a hand through the bars, it was possible to reach far enough to place the sacks out of sight.

The sack in the other geyser was taken out and the one under Alex's bed brought into the shower. The two were tied together and while someone stood at door three to listen for warders, they were carried to the end of the passage, pushed through the bars and out of sight around the corner. It was a reasonably good place, but without much effort anyone could have stuck a hand around the corner and felt them. We just hoped the warders were not in the habit of doing that.

The leak grew a lot worse and the water started to pour down a hole into the downstairs toilet. This was gleefully pointed out to the captain and a few days later the leak was repaired. It was a major job. Both geysers had to be removed and the wall containing the pipe had to be chiselled open to expose the leaking joint. Fortunately, we'd had the foresight to clear both hiding places.

The real scare occurred while we were attempting to retrieve the sacks the following Friday. Alex put his hand around the corner to grab our precious hoard, but instead of grasping the sacks his hand bumped them and both went tumbling down the stairs to the first landing. I sent up a howl of despair. How were we going to get them up now? All that work and irreplaceable clothing gone down into a black hole. A mirror revealed nothing: it was too dark and dusty. Even those who were not participating in the escape commiserated with us, for they knew what efforts had gone into creating and collecting it all.

Someone hit on the brilliant idea of making a grapnel out of wire, which on the end of a piece of string could be thrown in the direction of the sacks. Hopefully it would catch onto one of them so they could be pulled up. From somewhere suitable pieces of wire and a long piece of string appeared.

Alex spent more than an hour throwing the grapnel in the direction of where he guessed the sacks to be lying. I stood behind him chewing my nails while Stephen stood guard at the section door listening for warders. What we would have told them had they come in, I don't know. There would have been no use in making up a story, since any commotion at the end of the passage would have drawn attention to the sealed-off stairway.

After many, many throws, Alex pulled on the string and felt resistance. Like a fisherman he wondered if he had hooked some debris or, finally, the big one. It was the sacks! He slowly pulled up his catch until he was able to lay a hand on it. In no time the sacks were back in their holes behind the geysers and Alex was being applauded for his miraculous retrieval. I felt like throwing him down the dark abyss from which he had just reeled in our precious bags!

Despite the previous terrifying experience, the disused stairway was retained as an alternative storage place. A month after the leak saga one of the geysers burnt out and had to have its element replaced. This happened on a Tuesday but the problem could not be reported until the Friday when the sacks could again be placed around the corner at the top of the stairway. The comrades in the cells on the side which drew their hot water from the failed geyser suffered most, but they understood the problem and bore with us.

To avoid losing our sacks down the stairway a second time, we tied a long, strong cord to them and a piece of black cotton to the other end of the cord. The other end of the cotton was tied to the bottom of one of the bars sealing off the stairs and covered in dust to conceal it. Instead of placing the sacks on the top step as we had done the first time, they were pushed down until they came to rest in a stable position. If they had fallen any further it would not have mattered as the cord was long enough to allow us to pull them up from as far away as the landing. Disasters can be useful.

In early September we attempted a second stage one. The tactics adopted were somewhat different to those we had used during the first attempt. Since there was now a full-time guard on the *pos* who looked directly into our cells, we had to open our doors in daylight when it was difficult for him to see into the cells, which were relatively dark compared to the outside. To further obscure the guard's view Alex and I opened our windows halfway and placed tall objects in front of them and on top of our cupboards. Several other refinements were added: to prevent our grilles clanging when we closed them, we taped pads of tissue paper to our door frames; to prevent my number two springing open when I unlocked it, I fixed a hook under it and from this tied a bootlace to my grille.

We exited from our cells as soon after lock-up as possible. As before, we left dummies in our beds and arranged our cells to look as if we had undressed and gone to bed. Alex came out first because his cell was in a better position relative to the guard on the *pos* (most of the time the guards sat in the sheltered alcove at the end of the catwalk opposite my cell, from which position they were unable to see into Alex's). Alex then unlocked my number two as before, handed me the key and hid in the shower. Instead of coming out immediately I had to wait for the guard to move towards the other end of the *pos*. When he eventually moved, I untied the bootlace holding my door closed, came out of my cell and locked my number two behind me. I joined Alex in the shower, where he had already taken out of the cache all that we needed for the expedition. We put on our balaclavas, dressed in our escape clothes and finally pulled our overalls over the top. We then took up positions, one in each shower, to wait for the signal record (Blondie again).

Since we had planned to go down to the cupboard at about 7 pm, the two-hour wait in the shower presented a problem we had not thought of: where to relieve ourselves. The obvious place was down the shower drain holes above which we were crouched. But trying to pee down a small hole on a flat surface while dressed in escape clothing with overalls over the top, proved to be almost impossible. Standing up didn't help because it was then impossible to hit the target, and if we missed the target the warders would smell it the next day and ask questions. If there was a next time, we agreed, we would bring along a watertight bottle that could be stored overnight and emptied in the morning.

When the signal record came near to the end, Stephen signalled with a towel that he could hear no movements from downstairs. We tiptoed in our socks down the passage to door three, opened it cautiously and moved silently down the stairs to the film cupboard as before. But, oh no! The cupboard key wouldn't turn. I felt sick at the thought of all the nervous energy wasted. Both of us felt like kicking it in but realised it would be wiser to return to the shower and our cells. Fortunately we had given ourselves an hour so there was plenty of time to get back before the eight o'clock inspection.

Getting back into our cells was the reverse process of coming out. When Stephen signalled to us in the shower that the *pos*-guard was in his corner, I locked Alex back into his cell and returned to the shower to wait for Alex to signal that the guard had moved along the catwalk towards his end. As soon as I heard a bang on the wall I rushed back to my cell and relocked my number two using the crank method as usual. No sleep again that night as I lay feeling the unstoppable pounding of my heart.

The next morning, we tried out the cupboard key to find out why it hadn't turned. Of course, it worked perfectly – old Murphy playing his tricks again! The dimensions of the key must have been slightly out, we concluded. That Friday I checked the key against the original and found it to be a fraction of a millimetre too high. I filed off the surplus metal and tested it over and over to make sure there would be no repetition of the problem.

A third stage one was attempted about a week later. Several other improvements had been made since the first time: we had made a "handle" consisting of a drawing pin and a bootlace to hold the film cupboard door closed while inside and we had modified all the number two keys so that the wards would not jam in number six.

Using the same procedure as before, we made our way down to the film cupboard at about 7 pm. At eight o'clock, after Vermeulen had passed overhead, we came out of the cupboard and made our way into the administrative section. Instead of coming with me to door six as he had done the first time, Alex kept watch at the end of the passage opposite door four while I tested the keys. The plan was that if he heard Vermeulen coming back to his office prematurely (he could have been called on his walkie-talkie, for instance) we would nip into the warders' toilet next to the office until it was safe to come out again.

I tried the modified keys in door six. All of them turned through 180 degrees but none unlocked the door. I couldn't understand it. The fact that they had turned inside the lock proved that the lock definitely used a number two key. But why wouldn't our keys turn the bolt? Surely they were correct. After all, they'd worked in all the number twos in our section. As I was contemplating these problems, I heard a whispered but impatient shout from behind me. Our respective estimates of the time used up were different: I wanted to go on and solve the problem; Alex wanted to get back. I looked around and could see that he was beginning to lose his normally cool demeanour, so I relocked five and turned back.

As I ran back towards Alex, I gave a thumbs-down sign. The disappointed look that drew across his face was the saddest sight I had ever seen. He just stood there spellbound with his hands hanging in a questioning position. He had thought I was taking so long because I had been successful. I almost had to drag him back into the cupboard.

Although none of our number twos had worked, we were still not convinced that door six did not use a number two key. The fact that the keys had turned part of the way indicated that the ward cutaways were correct, and since the wards were of a complicated pattern, key six had to be very similar if not identical to key two. We were forced to assume that the reason our keys had not unlocked the door was because they had been cut to work in our cell doors, which were opened and closed far more frequently than number six and were consequently more worn. Our number two keys must have been lifting the levers of the number six lock fractionally too high and were thus not able to turn the bolt. As it turned out, our assumptions were correct.

To overcome this problem, I decided to make a special shaftless key that had the same cut depths as door two's key. By having no shaft, the absolute dimensions were rendered irrelevant. The key could be jiggled up and down until all the levers were aligned to allow the bolt to slide through the gateways in the levers. This idea was borrowed from our picking device that worked on the same principle.

The new key was made from two pieces of sturdy wire that Dave K had found in the garden. I drew a template to which the wires had to be bent and then Alex hammered and twisted them to shape in the workshop. The pieces of wire were then soldered together on top of the template. (The soldering iron belonged to us prisoners but was kept in the office for the odd electrical job.) The "bit" of the key was made out of wood and then glued with epoxy to the shaped ends of the wires. Finally, the cuts were filed to the same depths as number two.

We tested the key in all the number two locks in our section and it appeared to work well. It was metal, meaning that it could be turned with much greater force than the wooden keys, which relied on the dimensions being absolutely correct because no force could be applied.

About mid-October we made our final stage-one attempt. Following the same procedure as the previous time, Alex and I made our way down to the administrative section at 8 pm to test door six. As on the previous occasion, Alex stood guard at the end of the passage near door four while I tested the new key. This time I had more confidence – I knew for sure that six was going to give up its unreasonable resistance.

I opened five and as I took key six from my pocket my heart sped up – they were beats of expectation and excitement, not fear. I pushed the special key in, located it between the inner faces of the lock and turned it slowly. It turned with such ease I thought I had missed the levers altogether. I turned it back to check what had happened and as I did so I heard a loud "clonk" as the bolt shot back out. It had worked! What had all the fuss been about? I turned the bolt in and out several times to make sure that it really had worked, and then one and a half times to see if it would work on the second revolution. No problem! The key turned so easily there was no need even to jiggle it up and down to make it work.

I withdrew the key and relocked five. When I turned to run back towards Alex I could see that this time he had not allowed his ever-overflowing optimism to get the better of him: he had expected the worst and had a pre-set disappointed look on his face. But when I gave the thumbs-up instead of the expected thumbs-down, the look instantly changed from dark gloom to one of excited elation. He leapt for joy and shouted, far too loudly I thought, "We've beaten the fascists!" Inside the cupboard again we forgot our normal anxiety and shook hands and hugged each other in congratulation and with excitement at the prospects. We now knew that we were as good as out.

Chapter Thirteen

Stage Two

Having completed stage one successfully, Alex, Steve and I were keen to get on with stage two. Before proceeding, a meeting of the escape group was held to discuss the strategy to be adopted. Denis was unhappy with the plans as they stood but said he would not stand in our way. He was still worried about the guard on the *pos* and felt that our current plans might lead to disaster. He was still of the opinion that the guard would eventually be withdrawn, despite the fact that there was no evidence of a crisis situation, which he believed had been the cause of the guard being put there in the first place. Dave K was for proceeding but Dave R only agreed in principle that we should proceed: he preferred deferment.

Stage two was to be different from stage one in that its object was not to test one door but all the doors beyond number six. This meant that we needed much longer than the few minutes afforded by the 8 pm inspection round. If we went down immediately after lock-up, we could give ourselves about three hours to work on the doors. But how could we get past the warder in his office without being seen?

The plan that finally emerged was for Alex and me to go down to the film cupboard as soon after lock-up as possible. Someone would open their lamp cover (with the lamp spanner made from a bent nail), break the bulb or replace it with a burnt out one, and call Vermeulen to bring up his lamp spanner and help change the bulb. Vermeulen would have to wait in the section while the bulb was being replaced because he had to turn the light off and on from the outside, get a new bulb from Dave K – who kept a supply in his cell – and finally collect the spanner and old bulb. While he was doing this, the two of us would come out of the cupboard, pass through door four, press the button for door eight in the warder's office, open five and six and then close them behind us. Beyond door six we were cut off from view and would have until the 8 pm inspection to attempt to open the remaining doors on the way to the front door.

Stage two would also involve attempting to find out if there was a way of seeing out into the street to ascertain what time the sentries came on duty at the gate, where they stood and how they operated. It was also agreed that if there was time we should attempt to enter the captain's office, which was the first office in the administrative section after coming through the front door. This would be useful for seeing the position of the *pos*-guard.

Shortly before eight o'clock we would relock the doors beyond six and wait next to door six for Vermeulen to go upstairs on his round. Door six would then be opened and we would proceed back to the cupboard, closing all doors behind us. After Sergeant Vermeulen had returned to his office we would return to our cells in the same manner as we had done in stage one.

Theoretically, after completing stage two we would have all the keys needed to get to and open the front door and be in a position to leave, provided the existing security arrangements prevailed.

The planning for stage two was, in fact, the planning for the actual breakout and the action was in effect a practice escape run. The plan had come a long way from the first one and even from the last one that was current before stage one took place. Knowing that it was now possible to penetrate beyond door six without having to have the contingency route through the visiting room, there was no longer a need to accost the night-warder. It was also now entirely feasible to make our way out of the prison right under the warder's nose and without leaving a trace. This offered a tremendous advantage in that it would give us thirteen and a half hours to get away before our absence was discovered, assuming they would only discover that we were missing at open-up the next morning. Not only that, if for any reason we had to abandon the attempt, we could have a contingency plan to return to our cells at 8 pm.

All those remaining in the escape group accepted in principle the plan for stage two. But when it came to the crucial question of who would break their light bulb, questions of security and incrimination were raised. Objectively speaking, Dave R was in the best position because his cell was at the far end of our section and thus furthest from door three, which Vermeulen would leave open when he came in with the lamp key. It would take Vermeulen some time to walk the length of the passage and back, giving us more time to get through door six and place him in a better position should we happen to make any noise while going about our business downstairs.

Stephen, who had offered to break his bulb in lieu of Dave, was in the worst position because his cell was nearest to door three and opposite the *pos*-warder's alcove. The *pos*-warder would easily see Stephen standing on top of his cupboard, fiddling with his lamp and the light going out, but when in his alcove Dave's cell was out of his line of sight. But Dave R refused to be included in this plan because he believed that if we got caught, he would automatically be implicated. To reduce suspicion being pinned on him it could be arranged that he replace his bulb with a burnt-out one from a downstairs room. Afterwards he could smash the good one and flush it down his toilet, together with our lamp spanner. If we were caught, his burnt-out bulb could in no way be linked to the fact that we were wandering around the prison. But Dave found this too problematic.

The following weekend a long and heated meeting of the escape group took place. Stephen expressed the view that all should share the risks, but this was not accepted. Although he had not contributed much in a material sense to the escape preparations, he had always been firmly behind Alex and me in all our thinking and actions, had voted with us on practically every occasion and had never hesitated to assist in whatever way he could. He was prepared to break or replace his bulb if no one else would do it, but he was in the worst position to do so. He felt that if he could do it so could others, because the risks were the same for all.

After hearing our views Dave replied that he had given the matter his most intense thought and believed that the plan would only end in disaster. He saw no reason why everyone should share risks because in any organisation those best at performing certain tasks should specialise in those tasks. He then launched a bitter attack on the three of us, accusing us of forming a secret clique and of having motives other than those publicly expressed. He claimed that we had acted against the decisions of the group, that we had ignored moratoria placed on escape activities and had made secret contingency plans. Jeremy and Raymond had dropped out of the group for the same reasons, he declared.

The allegations stunned even Denis and Dave K. Alex, Steve and I listened silently to all this, for we knew that what he was saying was the collective statement of all those who had withdrawn from the escape project. When he had finished, we did not counter his allegations but asked him again whether he was prepared to assist in the carrying out of stage two. He replied that he was not and that he was withdrawing himself from the escape group so long as the existing strategy and conditions prevailed. He made it plain that he was not opposed to the idea of escaping but wanted outside assistance, the guard on the *pos* to disappear in the evening and the plan of execution changed so that there would be no unnecessary risks. Since these were impossible conditions to meet and matters over which we had no control, the three of us considered him to be expressing his resignation from the escape group. This entailed him losing the vote and no longer being informed of developments. He accepted this and withdrew from the group.

Denis had never formally refused to assist in the stage-two attempt, but it was obvious that there was not much advantage in him breaking his bulb instead of Stephen. Dave K, when we put pressure on him, agreed to assist by replacing his bulb with a burnt-out one. Finally, a plan was worked out that involved both Stephen and Dave – one that eliminated any risk for Dave. This required Stephen breaking his bulb but Dave being responsible for delaying Vermeulen.

Immediately after lock-up Alex and I would make our way down to the film cupboard. Denis would call Vermeulen to tell him to bring up the lamp spanner. (This was normal practice as Denis was responsible for calling the warder for whatever reason while we were locked in our cells. Dave K was permitted to keep a supply of new bulbs in his cell because in the past when bulbs had burnt out after hours, the night-warders had not had access to the spare ones locked in the store.) When Vermeulen came upstairs with the spanner Denis would direct him to Stephen's cell. Stephen would unscrew his lamp cover as slowly as possible and perhaps drop the spanner a few times to cause a delay. He would extract the broken glass with great care so as "not to cut his hands". Then he would tell Vermeulen to go to Dave K to fetch the new bulb, thereby moving him further down the passage. Dave K would be "unable to find" the bulbs in the box under his bed, so as to delay him even further. Stephen would find it difficult to install the new bulb and "lose" the screws for the lamp cover by dropping them under his bed while trying to replace the lamp cover. In that time Alex and I would hopefully have advanced from the film cupboard to a position beyond door six.

Stage two was finally carried out in early November. The tension that Alex and I experienced before the event was even greater than what we had endured before the stage ones. This was because stage two was a much more involved expedition, amounting in effect to a dress rehearsal for the actual breakout. We had been out of our cells for almost as long before, but somehow the thought of placing ourselves on the freedom side of the warder's office was far more terrifying. The stage ones had been hit-and-run guerrilla operations; this time we were placing ourselves right in the middle of enemy territory – over the enemy's lines as it were.

We had no idea what went on beyond door six. No one had ever seen a light on in any of the windows beyond the warder's office so we assumed the area was sealed off and dark at night. But we did not know for certain: maybe someone popped in every now and then to shout to Vermeulen through door six; maybe the front door was left open for the sentries on gate duty to use the toilet; maybe the lights would be on in the passage. Would we be able to turn them on if they weren't? Would turning them on alert the guards in the street or the guard on the *pos*?

In much the same way as before, Alex and I placed dummies in our beds, released ourselves from our cells, took from the cache all that we needed for the adventure, and made our way down to the film cupboard. The major difference this time was that we went down immediately after lock-up. This in itself was a much riskier venture as we could not tell what Vermeulen would be doing so soon after lock-up. We knew though that he was alone because when the day-warders left they did so with much loud banging of doors.

Stephen broke his bulb by loosening his lamp cover with the spanner we had made for the purpose and by squirting water inside with a syringe (bulbs would often burst when moisture condensed inside the lamp cover and dripped onto them, so this wasn't such a strange happening). Denis shouted for Vermeulen and as the sleepy old screw entered our section, the two of us leapt out of the cupboard and made our way beyond door six, after first pressing the button for door eight in the office. If door six had not yielded to our forward thrust, our contingency plan was to duck into the warders' toilet to wait until Vermeulen had returned.

Once through six, we found ourselves in the "cage" between doors six and seven. Unexpectedly the passage light was on, allowing us to see all the way to door nine across the far end of the passage. We had expected the light to be off and had brought along a piece of cloth to place along the bottom of door six to prevent it shining through when we turned it on. The light being on was a great relief, not only because it allowed us to see what we were doing but because we had worried that if it had been off and we had to turn it on, it would have lit up the door-less visitors' toilet and been seen by the *pos*-warder.

Before getting to work on door seven we waited for Vermeulen to return. We wanted to be sure that he had not smelt a rat and that he was going to settle down in his office and get on with what he usually did in there. To prevent him from seeing anything in case he had a habit of opening five and peeping through six's keyhole, we taped a little flap over it on our side. After waiting about ten minutes, we could hear him closing the section door and door four. Watching him through the keyhole as he walked down the passage towards us was a peculiar sensation that was both frightening and exciting. He appeared to be looking directly at me but at the last moment he swung into his office and banged his keys down on the table.

I had made several roughly cut keys for door seven based on the very infrequent glimpses we had had of its key. As expected, none of them worked. This did not worry us in the slightest as we had expected to have to dismantle the lock to open the door. For that purpose, we had made two special spanners to loosen the bolts holding it together. One of them was a kind of ring-spanner that Alex had made from an old can opener (he never gave up!) and the other a sort of box spanner

I had made from wood. Yes wood, or "arborium" as we preferred to call it. The idea was that the metal spanner would be used to do the initial loosening and then the wooden spanner the final loosening. The wooden spanner was really a piece of dowelling tightly jammed into a metal pipe with the shape of the nut chiselled in one end. Although we had brought along a shifting spanner from the workshop in case ours were not the right size, we made our own spanners because we thought the shifting spanner would be too noisy to use.

The lock was bolted to the bars by four bolts that had to be very quietly and carefully loosened. Fortunately, the ends of the bolts had not been hammered over as they were in our cells, but just in case we had brought along a triangular file to clean the threads. Vermeulen was sitting a mere three or four metres away so the nuts had to be turned very slowly to make sure the spanner did not slip and bang against the lock or drop on the floor.

After what seemed like an eternity, we were able to extract the bolts and loosen the screws holding the face of the lock with a screwdriver we had also brought from the workshop. Once the face was removed, the levers and bolt were exposed. I carefully removed the levers and stacked them on the floor so that they could be replaced in the correct order. Then we pushed the bolt back and opened the door. Door eight was already off its bolt and only had to be swung back and hooked against the wall.

While Alex attempted to open the captain's office door with a piece of plastic card (it had a Yale-type latch) I tried out our various small keys on door nine. As luck had it, the key for the visiting room worked and I opened the door. We both crawled through on hands and knees into the small vestibule between doors nine and ten and surveyed the last door between us and freedom. From the ground it appeared tall and robust but because of the kind of lock we knew it had, we did not expect it to be much of a problem to breach.

It had taken us longer than expected to reach the front door and when we looked up at the windows it was already quite dark. We could hear voices coming from close by in the street. The window panes in the vestibule were of frosted glass but we dared not stand up for fear that our shadows would fall on them, allowing those outside to see our movements. I was dying to try out our keys on door ten but Alex would not allow it. He was right; it was too risky.

We retreated into the passage and relocked nine. I felt annoyed and frustrated at not having a chance to get my keys and picks into ten's lock. For me it was an admission of defeat and forebode another stage-two attempt if we were going to get it to give up its secrets. We had also not figured out the nature of the security outside.

We took the parts of lock seven into the visitor's toilet, which was halfway between doors seven and eight and out of Vermeulen's earshot, so that I could examine them and take measurements. I took all the usual measurements to get the shape and size of the key and then made careful tracings of the levers onto a piece of paper so that I could later cut a key to the correct dimensions without having to test it in the actual lock. This is where my earlier experiments with paper "levers" came in useful. To make absolutely certain that the key seven I would be making would definitely work the next time we needed it, I rounded and widened the gates in the levers with a file so that virtually any key would have worked in the lock. We knew enough about the prison's keys and locks to know that sabotaging the lock in this way would not impair its functioning when the correct key was used. I carried out this little task with great delight because I knew that I was rendering the lock almost ineffectual as a security device.

Suddenly it struck us that the whole operation had taken a long time and that we had been too lax about the time. Hurriedly I pushed the levers back into position, replaced the cover, tightened the screws and began to fasten the bolts. It was a slow and tedious process so we took turns to do the tightening. On one of my turns, the spanner slipped and made a loud clang against the grille. "What the hell are you doing?" Alex shouted, "Vermeulen must have heard that." In a state of panic, I went to door six, lifted the flap and peeked through the keyhole. There was Vermeulen, standing directly in front of the door with his hands on his hips and looking directly at it. My heart stopped cold and in an irrational fit of panic I took one of the number two keys out of my pocket, pushed it into the keyhole and turned the lock its second turn (we had left it un-mastered). Why I did this I can't explain. Perhaps I imagined Vermeulen would test the lock. A guilty conscience makes one do strange things. As I withdrew the key, I realised that I had exposed the end of it through the keyhole and made a noise turning the lock.

Both of us thought this was the end of the road and dived into the visiting room, closing the door behind us. We huddled together in fear, waiting for the inevitable. Alex cursed in my ear: "You stupid bastard. What did you do that for?" I had no reply. We both agreed: "When he comes, we'll use the pea. We'll tie him up. We'll get out somehow." We waited for a siren, for frantic shouts, for voices on his walkie-talkie, for Vermeulen to unlock six to find out what was going on. But after a few excruciating minutes, we realised that nothing was happening. Vermeulen had not shouted "Who's there?" or "What's going on?" He had not attempted to open the door to find out what had caused the noise; no sirens were blaring. The silence was terrifying.

We emerged gingerly from our hiding place and took another peek through the keyhole. There was no one there. "Perhaps he's radioed or phoned for help," Alex suggested. The only sound we could hear was the plaintive wail of music coming from his radio.

Suddenly realising that eight o'clock was very close, we continued to reassemble the lock. While Alex tightened the bolts, I removed all traces of our activities and wiped down the bars with my handkerchief to remove fingerprints. Almost as Alex tightened the last nut its last turn, the eight o'clock bell rang.

Through the keyhole I watched Vermeulen come out of his office and turn the corner at the end of the passage. Door four clanged as he went through it and we could hear him making his way up the stairs to the *stokkies'* section. As soon as we heard the clang of their section door, we opened doors six and five, relocked them behind us, and dashed back to the film cupboard. Alex pulled the cupboard door closed, and in the darkness I suddenly thought: had we, in the rush, replaced the levers of door seven in the correct order? I couldn't remember taking any special note of doing so and they had been truly mixed up while I was filing them. Alex tried to reassure me that we had not mixed them up and that all was in order. Only the next day would tell.

No sleep again that night. On top of the nervous tension of the build-up to and the carrying out of the operation was the thought that the prison staff would not be able to get into the prison in the morning: What if they can't open door seven? Their forensics guys will check the lock and suspect the obvious. Levers don't just swap themselves over on their own!

My fears were allayed the next morning when the cells were

unlocked. Everything seemed normal: the same dozy old turnkeys; no angry-looking captain or big shots. Later in the day Denis was taken out to the dentist and reported on his return that lock seven had operated quite normally. Perhaps our filing job had been so good that it really didn't matter in which order the levers had been replaced, or perhaps we had replaced them in the correct order after all.

* * *

There was a belief among some of the comrades that being a political prisoner was not a complete waste of time. Political imprisonment served a purpose: it inspired others and kept alive the notion that there were fighters against apartheid who had sacrificed their personal freedom for the greater freedom of the oppressed.

I never subscribed to this theory. I was not proud of being in prison; it was a most undignified condition. In fact, I was downright ashamed that I had failed in our mission and allowed the enemy to score one over us. While there were people like Nelson Mandela who had been turned into martyrs and symbols of freedom, and whose imprisonment had ultimately served a political purpose, your average activist could not champion the cause better by being inside than out.

To maintain that being in prison served a purpose seemed to me like an excuse for the fact that you were doing nothing or believed you could do nothing about it. If you weren't bent on escaping what else could you say? Giving purpose to imprisonment was, I rationalised at the time, a simple justification for the fact that the enemy had stopped you fighting against their evil rule and that they were wasting your time and making a mess of your life. In the fight against apartheid it was not good enough merely to be doing *something* against the system – you had to be doing your *utmost*. By being in prison you certainly could not say you were doing that.

It was legitimate to argue that if you had made up your mind not to challenge your immurement then you should make sure that the time was not wasted. Every opportunity had to be used to advance your knowledge as best you could: an educated ex-prisoner would be of more use to the movement than an uneducated one.

Our motivations to escape were manifold. It would be impossible to rank them in order of importance, although we liked to believe that our primary motivation was political. We had to free ourselves so that we could throw ourselves back into the struggle, so that we could achieve a victory over the apartheid regime.

We had a duty to escape, a duty to our organisation and to the oppressed in whose name we had gone to prison. We viewed ourselves not as "common criminals sentenced for serious crimes against the security of the state" but as prisoners of war. As members of a liberation movement we had been captured while participating in a war of liberation. To escape was to continue waging that struggle; to reconcile ourselves to our fate was to surrender.

Despite claiming that we were in prison for ordinary criminal activities, the enemy viewed our confinement as a victory over the ANC, as an action aimed at thwarting the struggle to overturn their political rule. So long as we remained in prison, they were reinforcing that victory and depleting the forces of the resistance. An escape would turn their victory into a defeat, undermine their supporters' belief that the apartheid state was invincible and had security under control, and boost the morale of all political prisoners and opponents of apartheid.

Certainly, being in prison was not a pleasant experience and among our strongest motivations to get out was the desire for individual freedom. To live with the thought that for the next 12 or so years you are not going to be able to decide what to do with your life is pretty daunting. But we had got into prison through being inspired by political motives so no one could claim that our motives to get out were entirely personal.

To emphasise some of the personal motivations that drove us to the front door, I wish to say a little more about the unpleasant aspects of life in prison, and correct the impression, if it has been given, that our prison was a three-star hotel without egress. This was most definitely not the case; although compared with the conditions faced by our black comrades on Robben Island and elsewhere, ours were five-star.

The worst aspect of prison life, as any prisoner will confirm, is the almost complete loss of freedom to decide what you will be doing with your life for the duration of your sentence. As white South Africans this was for us a particularly acute loss; for our black comrades less so as life outside was in many respects the same as life inside. It is no exaggeration to say that for black South Africans the country was one giant prison where they had virtually no freedom to decide what to do with their entire lives.

In prison you developed a better understanding of the meaning of personal freedom, not because the experience gave you some unique insight into its essence but by learning what it means to be utterly un-free. There are degrees of un-freedom but so far imprisonment is the most extreme form yet devised by humankind. Even in imprisonment there are degrees of un-freedom, solitary confinement being the most extreme.

The thought that you will be un-free for the length of your sentence is terrifying and demoralising, especially if it is a long one. My 12 years seemed to me a meaningless, interminable period. I tried various ways to give it content: I compared it to the previous 12 years of my life but that only made matters worse, for time seems to go much slower when you are younger. I tried reminding myself that my release date, 1990, was a mere decade and a bit away, and decades were not a long time. None of these ploys had the desired effect because I could not visualise myself out of the world for the whole of the 1980s. When I was released, I would be 41 years old; my entire thirties would have been spent inside and my remaining youth would have been wasted. How poor Denis must have felt with his life sentences, I could never comprehend.

The reverse side of losing your freedom is that other people decide what you will be doing with your life. You lose your dignity as a sovereign being. You become a thing, a piece of property with a number, like a farm animal with a label stapled to its ear. If you damage yourself you can be charged with damaging prison property in the same way as if you had smashed a window. To your number becomes attached your surname, but this is just another label to make it easier for the warders to distinguish you from other objects of prison property.

Imprisonment is a thoroughly degrading experience. It reduces you from being a self-respecting, proud, motivated individual to a piece of trash. You are cast into what society views as its rubbish bin, or, to be more precise in our case, apartheid's rubbish bin. As prisoners of apartheid we began to understand what it must have felt like to be one of the countless victims of apartheid's grand plan, such as those who were uprooted and removed to some remote, rural dumping ground. Fortunately, for anti-apartheid prisoners, the degradation did not stick and taint you for the rest of your life. On the contrary, having spent a period in jail for opposition to the apartheid state raised your status in the eyes of the majority of the population. There was no need to feel any shame at being imprisoned for political reasons. The only shame came from letting down your side and allowing the enemy to get the better of you.

Imprisonment is also an intensely lonely experience, made worse by the fact that there is no relief from it. You can expect no commiseration from your fellow prisoners as they are in the same boat, and people outside can do little to help. Although in our case we were held in the same section and were together in the yard during the day, for nearly 15 hours a day we were locked in our individual cells with only ourselves for company. In that time, we were left to stew in our own thoughts, which were not always the most rational or comforting.

Because prison life is so routine and ritualistic, because every day is so much like the previous ones, because nothing new ever happens, your thoughts tend to become repetitive and part of the routine too. The same boring images return to you day after day, night after night. There is nothing to trigger new chains of thought. They seem to take on a life of their own; they separate from your body and your life.

In the university psychology class, they taught us about the unity of mind and body and the fallacy of Cartesian mind/body dualism. In prison you come to think that perhaps Descartes was right. Your thoughts rise above your existence. They fly out through the bars, out over the walls and away to freedom. You're back in Cape Town visiting your friends, driving around the streets, going shopping, climbing mountains and going spearfishing. You're also placing leaflet bombs on every street corner, blowing up police stations and courts and wreaking your vengeance on the security cops. Your thoughts are so free yet your body remains trapped in that little cage that is your world. You look out of your window and can see, over the top of the wall, the buildings and trees that are out there. They are so near. You look at the size of your body and think how small it is, while the hole above the prison skywards is so large. Why can't I just lift my little body over that wall and place it on the other side? If my thoughts can be out there, all I've got to do is move my body a short distance and they'll be reunited. Perhaps we can make a giant balloon to lift us out of the yard. Perhaps a huge kite, a glider, a rocket. There must be some way?

You miss your family and friends terribly. How you wish you could be with them so they could cheer you up, so you could explain everything. You visualise your mother sitting at home grieving for you. How you wish you could put her at ease. The suffering you've caused is worse than your own. How could you do this to others? You've embarrassed your family. How do they feel every time they have to say they have a son or brother in prison? What do people think? Visits are no compensation because the glass between you only reinforces your separation. The frustration caused by your powerlessness is torture.

You realise how important women are in making you a complete human being, not in some sexual sense that you can't survive without them, but what an important component they are in making society human. Contact only with men makes you begin to notice that relationships are rough and lack a certain perspective that you would not normally notice. You can't describe it because you wish to avoid the sexist clichés of feminine softness, kindness, caring, submissiveness and so on. But you notice it particularly when for some reason you suddenly have contact with a woman, such as when you are taken to a doctor or dentist. You immediately become strongly aware of the difference in the way you have been spoken to, of the way the person has responded to you, of the way you have responded to the person. It fills you with a strange sense of warmth and satisfaction, as if in that fleeting moment you have made real contact with a human being.

Sexual drive never disappears but after a few years, they told me, it is reduced to manageable levels. The palm of your hand is more frustrating than relieving, as you know there is nothing to give you relief from that reliever. The comrades had found that eliminating reminders that women exist was worse than not doing so, as frustrating as it was. If you did so you had to rely on your memory and that could lead to uncontrollable fantasising. To prevent this, the comrades had for years been ordering a range of women's magazines in which they would normally not have had the slightest interest. The thought of a bunch of activists reading *Vogue* or *Woman's Own* might seem somewhat incongruous, but the magazines served a purpose: they kept alive the visual image of the opposite sex which was as important as keeping alive the skill in relating to them.

Boring is the word for life in clink. Every day is a repetition of the previous one. Even the efforts you make to overcome your boredom are boring. Reading, drawing, listening to music, thinking and sleeping are not in themselves boring; it's when you do them at the same time and in the same order day in and day out. There are no highlights, nothing to look forward to, nothing to look back to. Time shoots by but paradoxically also feels static. There are no reference points, nothing to give time meaning and motion. Nothing moves; nothing changes. It's a movie of a still life.

As for our material conditions, let's just say they were not intolerable. However, we could not help comparing our conditions to what we knew were the lot of our black comrades. The authorities claimed that one set of regulations applied to all political prisoners and hence conditions were the same for all. Such claims were irrelevant, for in the last instance it was the unwritten regulations that made the difference: black prisoners were subjected to all the indignities and injustices inherent in the apartheid control of the prisons; we were not. It cannot be denied that over the years, conditions on Robben Island, and for political prisoners generally, improved.

For many years the prison chiefs did not deny that conditions for black prisoners were inferior: special regulations applied to them covering diets, clothing, bedding, work, numbers of prisoners per cell – everything. Only in 1977, for instance, was it decided that black political prisoners should be given beds to sleep on. Many books have been written describing the appalling conditions experienced by Robben Island prisoners in those years. Read for example *Island in Chains* as told by Indres Naidoo to Albie Sachs, which describes life on the island from 1963 to 1973. The conditions you will read there bear no relation to anything described in this book.

Conditions refer to different things. First of all, there were the things that the prison authorities were obliged to provide, what they referred to as our "rights": food, clothing, shelter, protection. Then there was the regimen imposed on the prisoners – work, inspections, chores – the daily routine.

The very notion of a prison conjures up thoughts of bad food. Ours was uniformly poor but it would be wrong to say that it was bad. Occasionally, very occasionally, we were served something that was better than poor. Never though did anything remind us of home cooking. Most times the food was edible, often not.

Dieticians from the regime's Department of Health allegedly formulated our diets scientifically. Where they got their training, you could not help wondering for there was something profoundly "unscientific" about our diet. It consisted largely of carbohydrates to make you feel filled but little of what contributed to general health. Even if the basic ingredients of a healthy diet were there, the cooking process leached out of the food any goodness that it might have contained.

The main characteristic of our food was monotony. Breakfast and supper at the beginning and end of the day were almost identical; lunch at midday varied slightly from day to day. The latter usually consisted of a helping of meat of some sort, stamped *mielies* (maize) or *mielie*-rice and an overcooked vegetable or two. The meat would be chicken legs, bony fish, gristly stew or "plastic meat".

"Plastic meat" was a sort of imitation meat made from soya beans and served at least twice a week. We had no objection to that; it was just the way they cooked it – in tons of pork fat. Its taste was so vile and its effects so violent that most of us refused to touch the stuff. We tried a boycott but without success as there was nothing with which the cooks could replace it.

In protest, we regularly left the pot standing in the middle of the tennis court where it had been dumped by the black prisoner-porters. At every opportunity we complained about the muck, but the more we objected the more determined they became to keep it on the menu. We did not feel inclined to pursue the matter too far though, as it wasn't really an important issue.

Breakfast consisted of porridge – either *mielie pap* or oats – bread and "coffee" or "tea" made from substances bearing no relation to real coffee or tea. The evening meal, supper, consisted of soup, coffee or tea and more bread. Included in our daily rations were a white powder for making "milk", sugar, a sort of pink or orange sticky substance euphemistically called jam, and over-salted, prison-farm butter, but only enough for a very thin scraping if you saved some for your morning bread. Once a week at suppertime, on separate days, there was crumbly cheese, a blue hard-boiled egg, bruised fruit, runny peanut butter or some other semi-edible extra.

Most of our food came from prison farms but occasionally farmers would dump surpluses or imperfect crops on the prisons. At different times of the year there were sudden gluts of one thing or another: sacks of oranges with spotted skins, boxes of dented avocadoes, bags of bruised apples. It never rained but it poured.

Poor food over which you have no control is very demoralising. To add a little spice to our diets we took turns on Saturday afternoons to prepare for each other small savoury or sweet snacks from the meagre grocery purchases the A groupers were allowed to make. A tin of spaghetti and tomato sauce or a packet of pudding, which under normal circumstances would be considered junk food, were devoured with great relish. Culinary standards sink to a low level in clink.

Prison clothing doesn't fit; everyone knows that. It is either too large or too small. Most of the comrades didn't care, for it was not as if we were expected at the opera. I found it degrading to be kitted out in the prison's vestments and the poor fit reminded me all the time of where I was. To lessen the sense of shame I dismantled all my shirts and trousers and refashioned them to look and feel more like civilian clothing and less like bin liners. I enjoyed sewing and sat for hours at night refashioning my clothes while listening to the music.

There were two uniforms: one for summer and one for winter. The summer one consisted of a green safari suit with short trousers; the winter one of light brown longs, a similarly coloured long-sleeve shirt, a brown jersey with red rings around the neck and bottom, and a brown corduroy jacket. Of course, there were shoes and socks, but they didn't seem to mind if we went barefoot in summer. Other items provided were green overalls, grey pyjamas, baggy underpants, hanging vests and red handkerchiefs. All of it was made by prison labour and like all products of alienated labour they were shoddy and ill-conceived. From an escapers' point of view none of it was of much use apart from the handkerchiefs, underpants and vests, which could be turned into other things.

Each prisoner was expected to wash and iron his own clothing, but with only two pairs of each item you wore everything for as long as possible and covered the smell with deodorant. The older comrades were more institutionalised and the product of earlier, more severe prison regimens. They washed and ironed regularly; the rest of us as infrequently as we could get away with. Trousers under the mattress kept them permanently pressed; shoes unworn meant less polishing.

Our health provisions, too, were not scandalous. But as with all aspects of our condition, we could not help comparing them with those of the black prisoners. We found it astonishing that the prisoners with whom we smuggled newspapers asked us for the most basic things like aspirin, plasters and soap. It was claimed that all prisoners were granted the same health rights, but again black prisoners were faced with the prejudices of the apartheid jailers. If they asked for medicaments, they would be accused of being malingerers or shirkers; we would be given virtually anything without question.

A warder disguised as a medical orderly appeared each morning with a tray of medicines to dispense to the prisoners. The medicine queue was generally longer than it would have been in ordinary life. The great range of ailments the prisoners complained of was a function of the poor diet and most of them would undoubtedly have been avoided had our food been more wholesome. Colds and flu were common, upset stomachs the order of the day, piles everyone's blight and headaches the normal condition.

A doctor visited the prison once every two weeks but he brought with him the attitudes he had picked up at other prisons: when a prisoner complains about a medical problem there is usually an ulterior motive, such as a desire to get off work or be taken for a joyride to see a specialist in town.

This was understandable but it took a lot to persuade him when you had a genuine complaint. Specialists, too, cast aside their Hippocratic oaths when dealing with prisoners. In their eyes a prisoner was not a real patient worthy of dignity and respect: consultations were abrupt and perfunctory; they would tell you what was wrong with you before you had a chance to explain your problem; everything you complained of was an "exaggeration".

We feared to think what sort of treatment black prisoners received from outside doctors, if ever they saw them. One dentist who treated me displayed his vicious racism when I was taken out to have a tooth-nerve removed (the prison dentist only did extractions). On the counter in his waiting room were displayed a number of large bullets.

One of my accompanying warders made some comment in connection with these, prompting the dentist to produce the associated weapon. He brought out the largest revolver I had ever seen, so huge that he needed two hands to hold it up. To explain its power he said that if he stood 10 "kaffirs" one behind the other the bullet would pass clean through all of them.

The warders' attitude to the *stokkies* was quite different from that shown to us. This was because they knew that the *stokkies* would not kick up a stink like we would if anything went wrong or was not found to be satisfactory. Very frequently alcoholic *stokkies* were brought in and given no assistance to get over their *delirium tremens*. They screamed and shouted for hours and quite often we heard them smashing their cells to pieces. Sometimes they pulled down their bookshelves, smashed their toilet bowls, ripped out their sinks, broke the pipes and caused a flood. Sometimes they damaged themselves too. More than once we saw bodies being carried out with a blanket pulled over the face.

This is not to imply that the warders' attitude towards us was impeccable. On many occasions they paid scant regard to the rules. Prisoners who complained of serious problems after lock-up were left until the next morning instead of a doctor being called immediately. One comrade, it was reported to me, who had a stroke during the night was only visited by a physician the next morning, with serious consequences. It twice happened during my term, once to me, that prisoners were brought back to the prison far too soon after having an operation. In my case I had barely woken up from my nasal procedure, and while still in an anaesthetised and bleeding state, I was slung into the back of a prison van and carted back to the prison. A shortage of staff, they explained.

Work is another concept normally associated with prison life. But there was no chipping of rocks or sewing of mailbags for us; that was "kaffirs' work". Prison was a microcosm of life outside: whites did the more skilled work; blacks the backbreaking manual labour.

Most of the comrades, especially the academic types among us, welcomed any respite from work so that they could get back to their studies. John and I, and to a lesser extent Dave K and Denis, were the only ones who liked to work with our hands as well as our brains. This is not to say that we preferred prison work to reading: we felt there was sufficient time to read and study, and grew more bored than normal if there was nothing else to do but read. We had creative energies to be dissipated, even if on prison work.

The carpentry work was dusty and boring but there was little pressure on us to increase productivity. Alex deliberately did everything incorrectly and as slowly as possible, as a kind of running sabotage. I couldn't bring myself to do this as I have an innate perfectionist streak that had to find an outlet. I treated my work not as something for the prisons but as something on which I released my pent-up drives and obsessions. Raymond was a scream: he regularly fell into a trance while sanding his pieces of wood and would wake up half an hour later to find that he had sanded a huge dent into an otherwise perfectly smoothed surface. Johnny was the expert, who showed us how to cut dovetails, sharpen our tools and disguise our mistakes.

There were other forms of work as well: the garden had to be tended, the dishes washed, the dining room kept clean, the dog shit collected each morning, the prison cleaned each week and sundry other little chores. Occasionally one of us was required to assist in tidying up or repairing a cell that an enraged or delirious *stokkie* had torn apart.

Inspections were central to prison life. Every day at opening and lock-up there were inspections. These were mechanical affairs and seldom was a prisoner brought up for bad appearance or for having an untidy cell. At around eleven each day there was a more formal inspection, or rather, a tour of the prison by the captain to inquire if there were any "complaints and requests". It was important to know the difference between a complaint and a request: a complaint could not be acknowledged unless there was an accompanying request; a request could not be granted unless there was a preceding complaint.

The main inspection was on Fridays when the captain inspected the section on his morning tour. Beds had to be clean and properly made, floors shiny, ledges and grilles dust-free and windows spotless. He always made his longest stop in Alex's cell because Alex refused to recognise the official standards of cleanliness and neatness. This was why it took Alex so long to reach A group.

At weekends we had to stand to attention on the tennis court while the captain walked slowly along the rank as if he were inspecting a guard of honour. He checked our uniforms and haircuts and recommend a trim before the end of the day if your hair was longer than the stipulated half thumb's length. Haircuts were a routine carried out by our in-house barber, Johnny, every two weeks. Alex and I attempted to set new standards by having our hair cut only once a month. It appeared to work, for by the time we said goodbye our hair had reached a respectable length. The captain's instructions were just ignored; Brylcreem also helped.

Such were our conditions. Not an abysmal state of affairs, but even if we had been served haute cuisine, had been given Paris fashions, had a swimming pool at the bottom of our yard and had personal videos in our cells, it was the spiritual conditions that mattered. Prison is prison and that means you've lost your liberty. No quantity of "privileges" can compensate for that. Nevertheless, the struggle for better conditions continued, both outside and in, until inside became part of outside, until all our comrades were freed. Then the prisons would become ours and the real criminals would fill the cells.

Chapter Fourteen

Another Stage Two – or Out?

Although stage two was completed without incident, it had not been an entirely successful operation. We had not figured out how to open door ten and had not established the nature of the security arrangements outside the prison. The voices we had heard in the street could have belonged to anybody and might not have been those of guards.

Nevertheless, we had demonstrated to the sceptical that our plan was a viable one and that we would not just disappear into the dusk without our fellow escapees. All were welcome to join us.

The earlier decision that no progress should be made beyond stage two as long as there was a guard on the *pos* from four thirty to ten, was now felt to be due for review. As it was, three in the group of five were for proceeding. Decisions could now be made rapidly without the over-cautious slowing progress.

A series of meetings were held to discuss the next moves. Dave and Denis wanted another stage two to be carried out to clear up the two main unknowns: whether door ten could be opened and what sort of security arrangements existed on the gate outside. Alex was determined that the next step should be to get out, but with the reservation that it be called "stage two/three". This meant that all those who wanted to get out should come along on the attempt, and if it was not possible to make the final break we could return at 8 pm.

Stephen agreed with Alex that the next step should be a stage two/ three but I was more in favour of another straightforward stage two. I felt that it was vital first to establish that the keys I had made for door seven, based on the tracings of its levers we had taken on stage two, actually worked; whether it was possible to open door ten without too much bother, and what the nature of the security arrangements outside the prison were.

Denis wanted outside assistance and felt that it was too dangerous to even contemplate going so long as there was a guard on the *pos* when he was expected to emerge from the front door. He was in effect withdrawing his active participation but stressed that he was prepared to assist in any way that he could.

Dave K's attitude was non-committal and ambivalent. He also wanted another stage two to take place to eliminate the major unknowns. He did not consider the guard on the *pos* to be a very significant obstacle and felt that if we looked enough like civilians as we emerged from the front door and kept out of his view by walking close to the base of the *pos* wall, we would not arouse too much suspicion. He preferred outside assistance but was prepared to go without it if another stage two took place. Then he would be able to make up his mind. For those of us who actually had to do the stage twos this position was intolerable. After all, who would face the stick if something went wrong and we got caught?

At one of the meetings, a decision was taken to contact the escape assistance group and inform them that any preparations that had been made to assist us and were being held in abeyance, should be scrapped entirely. In other words, the matter was closed and we no longer wanted assistance.

During the final month before the escape, there was an almost permanent state of discussion between the five of us who still constituted the escape group. It is impossible to relate all the changes of attitude, position and conflicts that took place, so what follows is a summary of the general situation.

As pointed out from the start, there was a fundamental difference in attitude between Alex, Stephen and myself, and the others. The three of us always felt that the longer we took to get out, the greater were our chances of being caught. Every day that plans were discussed, the likelihood of our being overheard increased; every day the cache remained in existence, the greater were the chances that it would be discovered; every time contact was made with the outside, the chances were increased that the secret would be revealed.

The others accused us of being impatient but our view was that the participants in an escape bid should as far as possible be in control of their situation. In other words, we had to tackle obstacles directly or plan around them rather than wait for them to disappear of their own accord. More than likely the obstacles would not disappear and new ones would appear. The reality was dynamic, even if it felt static in prison. To wait for the ideal conditions was to wait forever.

Dave's and Denis's hesitancy was motivated by an underlying belief that everything might end in disaster. We had not tied up all the loose ends and there were too many unknowns. They had fought for years to have their conditions improved and feared that if the attempt failed, all the privileges they had won would be lost and it would be back to square one. This fear was well founded and quite understandable, but the pursuit of freedom is an investment that has its risks.

The fears of the others were more difficult to understand. At first we believed they arose out of a lack of guts, but it was unfair to regard our comrades that way. It was not your average, law-abiding citizen who ended up in Pretoria Prison for actively challenging the apartheid state – and they would probably go on to do things that the three of us would never have the guts to do.

The whole exercise taught us much about human nature. It was wrong to expect from our comrades the same enthusiasm to get out that we displayed. Stephen and I had arrived determined to escape, we had come prepared to escape, we believed all along that we could escape, we did not have to have faith in anyone but ourselves and we had very long sentences ahead of us; Alex took to the escape idea because he had always had escaping on his mind and had considered "settling in" as a sign of capitulation to his captors.

The situation for the others was quite different. When they found themselves in prison they probably looked at the security arrangements and thought no further about escaping than the instinctive thoughts that all prisoners have when they first end up behind bars. Seeing no obvious ways out and not having the practical abilities to facilitate an escape, they reconciled themselves to their fate and did everything they could to make their stay as comfortable and meaningful as possible. When we came along, we stirred up the peace and created a stressful and dangerous situation.

They suspected us of operating secretly, saw that we did practically everything on our own, thought that we mistrusted them and went ahead with our plans willy-nilly, ignoring everyone's fears and needs. Inevitably our over-determination was interpreted as recklessness, and that frightened them. Some even believed that we had a death wish.

There were a number of factors at this juncture that provoked us to force the issue and press for an immediate speeding up of activity to get out. For the first time the three of us were in a position of absolute majority in the escape group; only Dave K served as a barrier to our immediate departure.

Planning for the escape had begun in July 1978 and by then (November 1979) had been going on for almost 17 months. Since February 1979 we had been in a position to go ahead with the escape and several attempts had been put off at the last moment. Objective conditions had progressively worsened – there was a sentry post in the street, the gate outside had been moved closer to the front door, there was a guard on the *pos* during the crucial four thirty to ten period – and there was no reason to assume these conditions would revert to the *status quo ante*. In times of political tension, security arrangements become tighter, not more relaxed.

The money that Steve and I had brought in with us was rapidly going out of circulation and we were uncertain if it would still be accepted as legal tender. It was nearly a year and a half since the currency had been recalled and from what we could ascertain from the warders, it appeared that there were none of the old notes left in circulation. We were worried that if we got out and had to hire a taxi or buy food and clothing, the money would not be accepted and it would arouse suspicion. This was possibly the main factor behind our belief that there was no more time for delay.

Our clothing was of summer weight and thus only suitable for summer use. Later in the year it would not provide adequate protection and look out of place. There were also the associated problems of storage and discovery.

One other major factor looming over us towards the end of 1979 was the imminent release of John Matthews. His sentence was due to terminate on 15 December and so it was imperative that the escape took place before that date. If it took place shortly after his release, he would be suspected of assisting the escapees. It would seem obvious to the authorities that he was somehow involved in the planning of the escape.

Material preparations for the escape had long been completed, including the manufacture of keys for door seven. The workshop was closed for the month of December so it was not really possible to make anything else, although we could still enter it with our own keys if we needed to.

The presence of Vermeulen on duty during the early evening shift was of vital importance. He had always preferred this shift and refused to work any other. Our main worry with him was that he would go off sick or drop dead, as he suffered from high blood pressure and had already had a few minor heart attacks. He was in his final year in the Prisons Service before his retirement and it worried us that he might be moved to some more leisurely post for his final months. Whatever the case, we would be taking a chance if we did not make immediate use of the fact that he and his heart were still on the beat.

Since our request for outside assistance had been cancelled, another factor that had been a cause of delay in the past was removed. Although it would have been good to have someone waiting outside the prison to whisk us away to safety, we had grown used to the idea of doing things for ourselves. We had learned through bitter experience that it was impossible for people who were not intimately involved in the escape to understand the multitude of problems we faced. We had put so much effort into the attempt – practical, mental, nervous and persuasive – that we wanted to complete the job by ourselves. We could not contemplate the thought that it might end in disaster through others' mistakes or misunderstandings.

A final factor was the knowledge that sometime during December there would be a new intake of warders. It was usually new warders who were put on *pos* duty, so if we could time our escape to coincide with their arrival, we could use this fact to our advantage. The new warders would not know us well by sight and they would probably not know how to respond if they saw a group of "civilians" walking out of the front door of the prison. The new intake in fact arrived four days before our departure, much to our delight.

All these factors together were the arguments that Alex, Steve and I used to persuade the others that the time had come for us to make our departure. There was little they could say to counter the arguments, although most of them expressed their apprehension and stated that they were not entirely happy with our decision.

Dave K still needed to be convinced. He insisted that we carry out another stage two before he would commit himself to saying if he would come out or not. Alex and I, as the ones who would have to carry out the stage two he wanted, were worried that he might in the end, after we had put ourselves through all the risks and stress involved, still refuse to join us. To get around this I offered to do a stage two on my own, since Alex refused to go again. For a short while Alex agreed to this but then refused to allow it to happen because he felt it weakened our position.

There seemed no way out of the impasse. In a rare fit of compromise Alex then offered to do a stage two on his own provided that Dave would state beforehand that he would come out if all proved clear. But Dave remained firm in his resolve that a stage two had to be carried out before he could make up his mind.

My own position during this period changed from wanting to do a stage two to a final position of supporting Alex and Steve in going for a stage two/three. I realised that my demand for a stage two was only delaying progress. Alex subsequently refused to allow a stage two to take place and insisted that, come what may, the next step was to try to get clean out.

Although I was prepared to change my position on this matter, I was not as confident as Alex about the success of a stage two/three because I did not believe that we would be able to get to the front door quickly enough. We had to assume the worst: that the keys for door seven would not work; that we would have to disassemble lock seven; and that lock ten (the front door) would not succumb to lock-picking. If things turned out otherwise, well and good, but it would be wrong to plan on the best possible outcome.

I was further worried that to take four people along on what I believed would more than likely not turn into a stage three, was too risky. In practical terms it meant that we would not be able to use the film cupboard as a hiding place as it was too small to accommodate four people and that we would have to use the dining room instead. To get four people out of their cells, and possibly back into them if the attempt was aborted, was far too dangerous.

Alex, Steve and I then held a meeting to discuss how we could get past the Dave barrier, which was proving to be more of an obstacle than some of the prison's doors. No one was going to do another stage two, so to wait for his decision was to delay the escape forever. We decided to put it to Dave that since he could not make up his mind about coming, we had to assume that he did not want to come and that the three of us were going ahead with the escape without him.

Since I was now the only member of the "hard core" on the WC (Alex had resigned) it became my task to approach Dave with our resolution. This I did and to my surprise he accepted it without argument. He seemed to accept the decision with a sigh of relief, as if a giant burden had been lifted from his shoulders.

The three of us could now proceed rapidly to make the final preparations for the actual escape. With Dave's exclusion I no longer felt any need for a stage two because if it was not possible to go out, the stage two/three could more easily be reverted to a stage two. The only remaining problems were to find a way of distracting Vermeulen so that we could get past him and beyond door six as we had done on stage two, and to choose a suitable date for departure.

There were three ways we could distract Vermeulen. The first involved someone replacing their bulb *a la* stage two. The second involved switching off the prison's lights to get Vermeulen upstairs to investigate. This meant coming out of our cells as on stage two and, on the way downstairs to the film cupboard, switching off all the lights at the switchboard on the first floor. Denis would, as official warder-caller, shout to Vermeulen that the lights had gone out and Vermeulen would then, we hoped, go upstairs to investigate. This would give us our chance to make for door six. The third possibility was a contingency plan thought up by Alex, which could have been used if everyone had refused to help on the other two. This involved Stephen and me going downstairs first and waiting in the film cupboard. Alex would then break his bulb and call Vermeulen. When Vermeulen went upstairs Steve and I would pass through door four and while I was opening doors five and six Stephen would in some way damage the record player (by bending the needle for instance) and then join me beyond door six. I would leave door five un-mastered and door six closed but unlocked. We would then proceed down the passage and attempt to make our way out. All the rest of the doors would be closed but left unlocked. Alex meanwhile would replace his bulb and immediately after Vermeulen had returned downstairs also go downstairs and hide in the film cupboard. Vermeulen would spend some time checking the record player and then, not being able to find the fault, return upstairs to report the problem to Denis. Alex would then be able to come out of the cupboard, unlock door five and make his way out.

Naturally, Stephen and I were unhappy with this plan because we wished to go out as a team and there was the possibility that Vermeulen would not do as we expected and Alex would be left behind. However, we realised that if the worst came to the worst this was the only viable option.

When the first of these two plans was explained to Denis and Dave K, we were surprised to find no hostility towards them. Perhaps they were only too glad that the plans signalled in one way or another the end of the escape saga. At one stage Dave K was even willing to replace his bulb with a burnt-out one, but later he felt that switching off the lights was a safer bet as it could not lead to a finger being pointed at him. This meant pushing the task of helping us onto Denis.

Our preference was for the bulb method because it gave more positive control over Vermeulen and the assurance that he would enter our section where he would be out of earshot of our activities below. Also, it was a tried and tested method of distraction.

The switchboard method gave no certainty that he would enter the section first to find out the cause of the problem. It worried us that he might notice the light out on the stair landing and go straight to the switchboard, reset the tripped switch and return immediately downstairs. Whatever the case, he would, while rectifying the problem, be outside our section and in a better position to hear any noises we might make.

We explained our preference for the bulb method to Denis and at first he agreed to replace his bulb with a burnt-out one, but later also felt that the switchboard method would be safer.

The next and final problem was the choice of date. The time was the end of November and we were keen to leave immediately, but there were a number of considerations. The question of whether it would be better to go on a weekend or weekday no longer existed, or rather, had been turned around to exclude weekends. Since the gates had been moved closer to the front door we were able to hear them opening and closing more clearly than before. During the preceding weekends we had heard the gates operating from about three in the afternoon; during the week only from about six.

Denis was of the opinion that since so many discussions had been held during the preceding weeks (we had tramped the grass flat on the far side of the yard) it would be best if we waited about two weeks and had no meetings during that time – he was worried that our captors might have suspected something was up. We could see his point, but at this stage we were not amenable to yet another delay of the escape.

Everyone knew that a new batch of warders was coming to the prison, that John Matthews was due to be released on 15 December and that Captain Venter was due to go on leave in the second week of December. We felt this latter point to be relevant because we were worried that another officer might take over and introduce some strange or more rigorous routines or security procedures. By suggesting that we wait, Denis was hoping to have the escape postponed until after Johnny's release, which in reality meant making us wait some months so that Johnny would not be implicated.

Perhaps it was just impatience, but we were annoyed most of all that we were being kept in prison not by our jailers but by our comrades.

When the two weeks were up, the three of us announced on the weekend of 8 and 9 December that we were going to attempt an escape during the coming week, with the first date being Tuesday the 11th, and if that day did not prove suitable then on each successive day. Denis and Dave K felt that it would be unfair to go in Johnny's last week as his release date might be deferred if he had to undergo questioning or if the authorities wanted to take revenge.

In earlier discussions, Johnny had displayed no hostility so we were sure he would not disapprove. We did not believe the authorities could or would prevent his release on the 15th because they would make themselves look stupid if they thought he was involved in escape plans in the last week of a 15-year sentence.

Denis reluctantly agreed to our plans in the end, although he repeatedly expressed his unhappiness with our decision. Dave K refrained from commenting but clearly, he too was apprehensive.

Having sorted out this last problem we made our final preparations that weekend. The money was divided three ways and put in the pockets of our escape trousers. The clothing we were going to use was removed from the general sack of goods, placed in another sack and arranged in such a way that it could be easily retrieved. The rest of the clothing was tightly wrapped in another sack and pushed to the bottom of the space behind the geyser where it was irretrievable by hand. The surplus keys were bottled and given to Dave K to bury in the garden for the comrades' future use.

Our prison clothing that we would not be using before the escape, our spare sheets and blankets were all washed to remove odours so that they could not be given to sniffer dogs to get our scents. Our cells were carefully cleaned of all suspicious objects: notes, addresses, letters and all else that might give something away. All books and objects of value were transferred to the others' cells.

I dyed my running shoes – which were bright yellow with blue speed stripes – with the blue drawing ink I had specially ordered for the purpose. The others brought up their running shorts and shoes from the storeroom and placed them in their cells. We also put other paraphernalia at the ready: escape spectacles, cloth bags (made for holding keys and tools but used in our cells for holding boot polish), T-shirts, deodorant and pepper for disguising odours, etc.

The last task of the WC was to work out with the remaining comrades what they should say when questioned after the escape, as they undoubtedly would be.

The rookie warders arrived on the Friday before the weekend, as expected. Alex, Steve and I made every effort to remain out of their sight so they would not get to know our faces. Captain Venter had been away for a few days and our fears that someone else would replace him were unfounded. His absence in fact seemed to lead to a loosening of discipline among the officers and warders. When the cat's away...

Chapter Fifteen

Escape!

Preparations for the escape had been going on for so long that it was hard to believe that we were actually going to escape. We had invested so much emotional, mental and physical energy in the preparations that in a way we were, like someone about to spend their life's savings, apprehensive about taking the big step. If our plans and equipment did not work (i.e. if we got caught) the thought of all that effort going down the drain was more daunting than the thought of the extra years that would undoubtedly be added to our sentences. However, we were sufficiently confident that we would make it and did not feel that we were taking a blind gamble with our future and our lives.

We were sorry that our comrades were not coming with us because we knew that if we could clean out the prison it would be a political victory of gigantic proportions. If we made it by ourselves it would be victory enough, and we knew the escape would be more likely to succeed with just three people. The whole business had taught us many things: above all that people's needs are different and that we should not have expected from others what we expected from ourselves. We learned too that people in a prison situation needed a routine of certainties and that uncertainties were destabilising and threatening.

Strangely, as Tuesday 11 December drew nearer, Alex and I

experienced less apprehension than we had during the stage ones and twos. But then getting out was not going to be much different to the stages, and we had got used to doing those. The confidence we felt was much like the feeling you get if you've studied hard for an exam or trained hard for a strenuous sports event. Stephen too displayed no apparent fear and his faith in us added to our general feeling of confidence.

There was little to do by way of preparations on the preceding days – we were totally prepared and had been for some time. There was just some tidying up to do: cleaning up our cells to eliminate clues, preparing our clothing to streamline our exit and washing everything that could be given to dogs to pick up our scents. Since the prison authorities and the police would undoubtedly go over our cells with a fine-toothed comb after the escape, we flushed our treasured letters down our toilets and destroyed notes and documents that we had kept among our belongings. It was not easy to do this as we knew that if we didn't succeed, our lives would be bleak without the precious sentimental things we had clung onto for so long.

On the big day, as had been agreed, everyone attempted to act as naturally and casually as possible. The warders did not appear to suspect anything, but it was hard to believe that they knew nothing of our plans. Deep down we could not help thinking that they were playing the same game with us as we were playing with them and that they would be waiting outside the front door to nab us as we emerged from it, to cause us maximum embarrassment.

As there was no work that day – the workshop had been closed since the beginning of the month – we had to enter the workshop to get the few tools we needed for the task ahead: two screwdrivers (one large and one small – for dismantling seven's lock and to force any other recalcitrant doors), a chisel (in case ten would not yield to our more gentle persuasions) and a file (in case we had to modify any keys). The tools were hidden in the storeroom, as usual, to be taken up at a convenient time. Apart from this, there was nothing else to do downstairs.

The three of us tried to keep out of sight of the new warders by keeping indoors as far as possible. The temptation to go out was strong as it was a bright, warm summer's day. We wanted to gloat at our captors and take a last look at the walls that had immured us for so long. The walls had lost their solid, impenetrable look – they were now paper, transparent and no longer aroused that sickening, deadening, hopeless feeling that made us sigh in despair and caused our guts to sink every time we looked at them. They were only there surrounding us because we had chosen to leave them there until that day. The thought that we could just walk through them with minimal effort whenever we wanted to, made a mockery of all the misdirected security measures that were kept in place against us.

We spent the day trying to read, but it was not easy to concentrate as our minds were already outside, and reading was an in-prison activity. We did not discuss the escape because there was nothing more to discuss; we spoke to nobody because there was nothing more to say.

Lunch tasted awful as we had been preparing our palates for more savoury fare. We only ate it to make sure we wouldn't have to eat another like it again, and we weren't sure when our next full meal would be. Certainly, we weren't going to do something as foolish as treating ourselves to a lavish restaurant meal once we got out, although we had enough money to buy all the food we would need.

At shower-time, we extracted the bag holding our escape equipment from behind the geyser and arranged our civilian clothing in three neat piles on the floor of the geyser closet so that we could retrieve it with minimal fuss later. The workshop tools we had brought up in a Thermos were placed, together with the pea, in the key-bag and left on top of the geyser (we secretly hoped that a leak wouldn't develop above it all – that would have been the supreme irony!). We each brought to the shower our running shoes and left them with our balaclavas, gloves and caps on top of our respective piles of clothing. I removed one number two key and three number one keys from the key-bag and each of us hid one of the number ones in tins of sugar in our cells, and Alex the number two as well.

The geyser door was locked and we enjoyed our last shower: we had an appointment with the public and did not want to smell like a bunch of musty old convicts. At supper we stuffed ourselves with several plates of vile prison soup and ate all our bread, barring a slice or two to take up to our cells for leaving on our tables to give the impression that we had eaten our supper and gone to bed. Tuesday was also book day, when the large box of library books was brought into the dining room. The three of us selected our books as usual and tucked them under our arms to take up to our cells for a good night's read.

The three of us were on our own now; in spirit, we had already departed. As there was still a little time before lock-up, we walked up and down the tennis court as we normally did. To our surprise Raymond came up to us, wished us luck and said goodbye. We had not been expecting any goodbyes, so his well-wishes were heartily accepted. That one small gesture instantly changed our attitude towards him. He had no idea how much encouragement his acknowledgement of our technical triumph and agonising months of planning gave us. His good wishes were tantamount to a collective farewell.

Then a warder shouted "time". We smiled as we heard for the last time that hated and oft-repeated word, which constantly reminds prisoners of their predicament and summarises the essence of it.

Lock-up took place at half past four as usual. The warder in control of the keys locked the doors in the usual mindless way and the sergeant in charge of inspecting the prisoners trod the length of the passage and back like an impatient yo-yo. No one appeared to suspect anything and as our hated jailers trooped out of the section and locked the section door, we silently bade them farewell and good riddance.

As soon as we heard the clang of the section door we set to work. In a scene repeated simultaneously in three cells: bedclothes were pulled back and prison overalls were placed on beds, overalls were stuffed with clothing, books, towels and other items to make dummies as had been done several times before. At the bottom of the "legs", shoes were propped up vertically to simulate feet and then bedding was pulled over and the lump pummelled into the shape of a sleeping body.

We undressed ourselves and placed our day's prison clothes in hot, soapy water in our basins so that they could not later be given to dogs to get our scents. We dressed ourselves in our blue sports shorts, our escape socks and white T-shirts. I put on the hideous pair of spectacles I had put aside for escape day and hooked my normal pair under the elastic of my shorts. To further confuse the dogs, we sprayed our beds and clean prison clothing with deodorant and filled our prison shoes with pepper. To confuse the night-warders we arranged our cells to look as if we had put our things away for the night and gone to bed. I left a book open on my table with my reading glasses on top of it, and a half-eaten sandwich on a plate. Alex and Steve arranged their cells in a similar fashion, and Steve and I fixed hooks under our number two doors and tied them to our grilles with bootlaces.

This all took just a matter of minutes, as we knew exactly what to do – we had practised it every night the previous week. We had rehearsed the procedure often and knew precisely how long it would take us to get our cells and ourselves ready – less time than it took for the *stokkies* to be locked up, the staff to have their end of day inspection in the administrative section and to lock up the prison and clear out. I stood at my window to listen for the inspection (you could hear them shouting orders and stamping their feet to attention), for the clang of the metal doors in the administrative section and for them to roar off in their cars.

As soon as I heard these familiar sounds, I banged on the wall to signal to Stephen to unlock his grille and waved a towel out of my passage window for Alex to do the same (he was watching with his shaving mirror). Each of us unlocked our grilles with the keys we had hidden in our cells at shower-time, and to prevent our grilles clanging as we went out we taped toilet paper to the door frames where they made contact when closed. (This little touch was later to confuse the authorities, as one of their theories of how we had escaped was by stuffing tissue paper in the holes into which our bolts protruded to prevent them coming out – quite impossible actually.)

Alex was the only one with a number two key. The plan was for him to come out first and open my number two with it, and then Stephen's number two with his number one key. I listened again for movements, this time to hear if Vermeulen was moving around. Hearing nothing, I gave Alex the all-clear by signalling again with a towel out of my passage window.

After making sure that the *pos*-warder was in his alcove opposite my cell, Alex stuck the crank mechanism out of his passage window and opened his number two while I watched with my mirror. There was a slight delay before he emerged but I knew that he was dismantling the crank and replacing the brush on his broomstick. His door eventually swung open and he stepped out into the passage. He relocked his number one and two properly – two turns – before running down to our cells in his socks to unlock our number twos. He passed to me through my window the number two he had used, and then disappeared into the shower to get out the equipment.

Stephen and I could not release ourselves immediately as we had to wait for the *pos*-warder to move to the far end of the catwalk. Fortunately, being a new warder and still keen to obey the rules, he soon moved across to the other end out of view of the inside of our cells. I banged on the wall again to signal the all-go to Stephen. We loosened the bootlaces holding our doors closed, removed the hooks and put them in our pockets (they were no more than little metal brackets). We swung our doors open, locked them both properly and then joined Alex in the shower.

Alex had already removed our gear from the closet and dressed himself in his civilian clothing – as any prisoner would do who is about to leave prison! He had placed our clothing and shoes in two neat piles on the floor of one of the shower cubicles. Steve and I pulled on our "civvies" over the shorts and T-shirts that we were already wearing and, unconventionally for departing prisoners, donned gloves and balaclavas. We wanted to be sure of leaving the authorities completely mystified how three prisoners had spirited themselves out of the prison without a trace. And in case we bumped into Vermeulen, we did not want to be recognised.

I collected the keys Alex and Steve had used to release themselves and placed them in the key-bag. I took out of the bag the pea and the key for the film cupboard and gave them to Alex, and placed in my pockets all the keys we would need to get beyond door six. I then gave Steve the bag to carry.

This had all taken just a few minutes. We had rehearsed the procedure so often in our discussions and minds that it was as if we were doing something quite routine. Up to that point we had not had a chance to feel any apprehension; we were doing exactly what we knew had to be done. Besides, there was no need to worry that we were not doing things right: our actions were meticulously coordinated like those of well-trained dancers. Every minute detail had been worked out; every action was highly purposed. The only unknown was the precise movements of Vermeulen. We just hoped that this creature of habit would not do something unexpected on our big day. In any case, this was not the first time we had come out of our cages; we had done so many times before.

After pushing the empty sack that had held our clothing to the bottom of the space behind the geyser, I relocked the door and we got ready to go downstairs. We slung our running shoes around our necks by their laces and edged towards the entrance of the shower to listen for any warder movements. Hearing nothing, we tiptoed in a crouched position down the passage to door three. Our thoughts as we passed our comrades' cells were for what they must have been thinking: surely they can't just be sitting there getting on with their studies and ignoring our momentous actions?

I peered through the keyhole of door three to see if there was anyone standing on the other side. Assured that all was safe, I quietly unlocked and opened it. Steve and Alex scurried down the stairs to the film cupboard while I went to the switchboard and turned off the lights for the first floor. By chance we had discovered beforehand that the face panel of the switchboard was loose and that if it was pulled forward it could be jammed into the rim of the switchboard door to prevent it opening – just a small move to delay Vermeulen. I relocked door three and made my way downstairs to join the others in the cupboard.

The space inside the cupboard was very limited and only just big enough to accommodate the three of us. By carefully repacking the film equipment we had increased the space considerably, but it was still a tight squeeze. Because I was the smallest, I crouched low on the floor between the legs of the others, who stood in an uncomfortable semi-crouched position. Stephen stood deepest in the cupboard while Alex held onto the bootlace to pull the door closed. We had practised this the Friday before, and so knew exactly our respective positions and duties.

After two or three minutes we heard Denis's shouts, as he called Vermeulen to come and investigate the sudden power failure. The *stokkies* also started making a commotion and probably a number of them had pressed their emergency bells in complaint at the sudden darkness. It struck us at that moment that if we needed to do another stage two/three, we could rely on the *stokkies* alone to call Vermeulen out of his office.

We heard an unperturbed Vermeulen acknowledge Denis's call. He picked up his keys and wearily made his way down the passage to door four. He unlocked the gate and, without relocking it, made his way up the stairs. As he walked over our heads our silent laughter and excitement almost made us burst out. We were really enjoying ourselves and not half as scared as we thought we would be. Fortunately, Vermeulen went directly into our section without checking the switchboard first. We dashed out of the cupboard, closed the door without relocking it – in case we had to make a hasty retreat – passed through door four, and ran down the passage to doors five and six.

Alex was in such a hurry to get out that he forgot to press the button for door eight in the office. I shouted angrily at him, but he immediately realised what he hadn't done, spun around and sprang into the office to press the button. We heard a loud buzz and clang as the electric bolt released the door. It was much louder than we had remembered, but then our senses were in such a state of arousal that every slight noise sounded greatly amplified.

I opened doors five and six, and after we were through them, I relocked both completely by turning their keys twice. We had done it; we were now out of sight of the warder and ready to tackle the remaining three barriers across our path to freedom.

I had made three keys for door seven. The first one I tried almost turned the lock but jammed just as it began to move the bolt. The cuts were obviously too high. The second one glided around as smoothly as a perfectly machined cog – the sabotaging of the levers on stage two had obviously done the trick. The door swung open and the three of us burst through into the last section of the passage. The door was left unlocked, as we did not know at that stage if we would have to pass back through it. Door eight was swung back and hooked against the wall. Door nine was opened with the visiting room key that had been found to work on stage two.

All of this had taken only a few minutes. It was just past five, according to our calculations, and there we were standing in front of the last fetter on our freedom, door ten.

We strained our ears to listen for noises of the street gate opening and the voices of guards. There was nothing, just total silence. Although it was what our surveillance told us we should expect, we could hardly believe it. It meant that if we opened the front door we could just walk out, totally unseen and unheard and no one would ever know how we had got out. Could our luck be so good?

As we surveyed our last barrier, we spotted something on the door that no one had ever noticed before: at eye level was a small flap that opened to give a view of the street outside the prison. Alex lifted it up and drew in the view from outside. With a gasp of disbelief, he reported that there was nobody outside and that the gate of this maximum-security prison was standing wide open. He invited us to have a look. Sure enough, the gates in the street were hooked back against the walls on both sides of the street and the sentry box was totally empty.

Without wasting a moment, I pulled out of the key-bag a smaller bag containing the little keys we had made for the wooden doors. I tested each one expectantly but not one of them turned in the lock. I cursed in disappointment: we had been relying on one of them to work. Although we had our picks, the thought of having to struggle with this last door had not entered our planning. Alex impatiently grabbed the keys from me and tried each one, but had no better luck.

I took out our set of picks and started to jab the levers while Alex attempted once again to open the captain's office. We had more or less given up the idea of using his office as a vantage point to determine the position of the *pos*-warder, but still wanted to get into the office so that we could leave Captain Venter a little memento or liberate his bottle of brandy. But the captain's lock was also playing stubborn that evening. Stephen urged him to give up and reminded him that we would soon be able to get more brandy than we could possibly drink!

I tried all our various picking devices but the accursed bolt refused to turn in. It seemed absurd to be fiddling with this last lock when all the other 16 or so we had opened to get to it, had done so without the slightest fuss. Our impatience to get out was building up to an explosive pitch and at any moment the sentry was expected to come on duty outside. If the picks did not work there was only one other way of opening the door: violence.

Alex tried the picks but he also made no headway. In anger he flung the fiddly bits of wire on the floor and announced aloud what we had all been silently contemplating – bust the goddamn door open! He pointed to the wooden doorpost and indicated that he was going to dig away the wood behind the locking plate so that it could be bent back sufficiently to allow the bolt to pass. The only other option was to turn the attempt into a stage two and go back to our cells, but I dared not mention it at that moment.

It was not an easy choice to make because if the sentry came on duty while we were chiselling, going back would mean the end of the escape attempt – forever. The damaged doorpost would be investigated and what other conclusion would they come to than that an escape attempt had been made. No one breaks into prisons. It also meant leaving evidence of our route of escape and turning what had been a perfectly clean attempt into something messy.

At this point I melted into a state of sheer terror. Alex, as usual, remained as calm as if he was performing a routine operation. Making snap decisions had never been one of my strong points so I just opted out and let Alex and Steve decide what was best. Both were in agreement that strong-arm tactics were needed. We had tried gentle persuasion and that had failed. And to hell with leaving evidence of our breakout; the main thing was to get out. We should grab the chance while it still existed; there was no question of going back.

Like a surgeon Alex asked for the chisel, and Stephen acting the dutiful nurse accordingly handed him the requested instrument. I winced as he dug the point into the well-varnished door frame and a large chip of wood fell onto the doormat. Such methods were not my style and drove home the point that we had broken one of the main "rules" of escaping: each step has to be reversible so that you can abort your action to try again another day. I knew then that there was no going back. It was now or never.

Alex seemed to be enjoying himself as he chiselled into the doorframe. I swallowed a handful of sweets that we had brought along, as someone had told us they were an antidote for the effects of too much adrenaline. I doubted it, but the sweetness helped to distract my attention from the situation. Every now and then Alex tested the locking plate with the large screwdriver to see if he had removed enough wood, and several times it slipped and made a frightful noise that I was sure Vermeulen or the *pos*-warder had heard. I went to door six to see and hear if there was any response, but all was calm. Vermeulen was listening to his radio, and in the distance I could hear the muffled sounds of music coming from our section. Assured that all was in order, I locked door seven in case we had to dash out quickly;

if we couldn't get out there would be plenty of time to reopen it. Door eight I left hooked back against the wall; if I closed it we would not be able to get back in if we had to retreat.

After what seemed like half an hour, but was probably less, Alex had gouged out enough wood from behind the locking plate to allow him to bend it back sufficiently. Steve and I had prepared ourselves to leave: masks and gloves off, caps on and all the tools and keys packed into their respective bags. In my obsessive meticulousness, I brushed the wood chippings under the doormat.

There was still no sentry on street duty, so with a strong heave Alex pulled the door handle. The bolt made a loud noise as it scraped past the locking plate, and the door swung open. He poked his head out and cautiously looked up towards the end of the catwalk to see if the *pos*-guard was in view. There was nobody – the guard had conveniently taken a walk down to the far end. Alex boldly stepped out onto the small roofless porch between the front door and the yard wall, and beckoned us to follow. I stepped out next and then Stephen followed, pulling the door closed behind him. We were out! The door didn't close properly as the bolt was still sticking out, but there was no time to worry about minor details just then.

We glanced quickly up and down the street. As far as we could see it was totally deserted. As casually as possible we stepped out into the bright summer sunshine, turned right, and keeping as close to the base of the *pos* wall as possible, made our way towards Potgieter Street, the main road from Pretoria to Johannesburg that runs past the prison complex.

We were out. Not yet away, but out.

Part Three

Getting Away

Chapter Sixteen

The Long Walk

The feeling of freedom after escaping from a political prison is almost impossible to describe in terms of the experiences of everyday life. It is a feeling known only by an exclusive club of people who have released themselves from custody with the knowledge that their action was not a flight from justice but a political act. The sudden relief from the constraints of captivity, the sudden expansion into the wall-less world outside released an explosion of emotions and triggered feelings of the most sublime elation. It was as if we were walking on air, floating, flying, and invisible to the world. Stephen recalled later that he felt like flapping his arms and flying off like a bird.

The distance to the traffic lights at Potgieter Street was only about a hundred metres but the sudden ability to see that far, and further, was a most curious sensation. For nearly two years Stephen and I, and Alex for nearly seven, had not been able to see further than the end of the prison yard. Now suddenly the world seemed so big. It stretched so far into the distance that it felt like it would swallow us up and prevent anyone from finding us.

Alex crossed the road and walked down the left side of Soetdoring Street, the street in front of the prison, while Steve and I continued on the prison side. Near the lights a car was parked in which a warder sat talking to another who was standing outside and leaning on his elbow against the car. The warders paid no attention to the three characters walking past, as they looked no different from any of the other pedestrians making their way home that evening. At the lights another warder was standing waiting for a lift. He also did not bat an eyelid. Their lack of response confirmed that we were indeed invisible and gave a tremendous boost to our confidence and sense of defiance.

Alex had trouble crossing Potgieter Street as the rush-hour traffic frightened him. Steve and I assisted him over, and once across we made our way down a side street that we knew led in the direction of Pretoria's main railway station. We had studied maps of the area cut out of the smuggled newspapers, so had a reasonably good idea of where we were heading. To our left were marshalling yards, goods sheds and many railway tracks. Our maps had not shown us how to get across to the station on the far side. We imagined that we would have to scramble over the tracks and climb a few fences, but to our surprise, we came to a footbridge leading over the tracks. A sign indicated that it led to Pretoria Station. We pulled our caps lower and walked across in single file a few metres apart, not daring to look up for we were still in hot prison territory. There were many people crossing the bridge in both directions, as it was coming up for 6 pm. With each person who passed the more confident we became, so that by the time we reached the other end we were walking proudly with our heads held high.

The bridge terminated at the top of some stairs and from there it was as if we were looking down at the Promised Land. In front of us was the station forecourt and at the bottom of the steps were rows of taxis waiting to carry us away. Alex scrambled down the steps and approached the first taxi driver he came to, and asked how much he would charge to take us to Kempton Park (we were still too scared to ask to be taken to the exact place we wanted to go to – Jan Smuts Airport). He quoted a fee of R28, which we accepted without question as it was not too large a chunk out of our money supply. The driver, who was black, was very friendly and suspected nothing odd about his prospective passengers. And why should he have been suspicious of three cheerful guys who looked as if they wanted to get out of town for a good night out?

We drove through the outskirts of the city that had been our stern host since the time we started our respective terms, and were not unhappy to see the last of that unfriendly citadel of apartheid. Soon we came out onto a motorway and were travelling well over the speed limit in the direction of Kempton Park. The countryside was green and beautiful, as it was the middle of the rainy season. Alex could not refrain from repeatedly commenting so, but after seven years of concrete corridors and yards anything would have looked beautiful to him.

About half way to Kempton Park we informed the driver that we had changed our minds about going there and asked him to take us on to Jan Smuts Airport instead (now O. R. Tambo International Airport). Since Jan Smuts was only a short distance beyond Kempton Park, he had no objection and cheerfully carried on in the same direction. He probably found himself discussing subjects not usually broached by his usual customers but we could not restrain ourselves from talking. The sudden ability to converse without smelling the foul breath of a warder over our shoulders, released with a gush our suppressed desire for uncensored verbal intercourse.

At the airport we paid the driver R36 with our outdated money. He accepted it without comment, confirming that the notes were still legal tender. Just to be absolutely certain, Steve and I made Alex go inside the airport terminal to ask at a forex desk if the money was still in circulation. The task fell on his shoulders because he was less likely to bump into someone he knew and he looked and sounded more like a "foreigner" than either of us. As such it was more excusable for him to ask a question that could have been a stupid one for us South Africans. He returned to confirm that the money was still in use. We then sent him back inside to find out if it would be possible to hire a car with a driver from one of the car-hire firms at the airport. Unfortunately, that service was not available so we sent him off once again to purchase tickets for the airport bus to Johannesburg.

On the road to Johannesburg we were in high spirits. The other two accused me of looking like an escaped convict. I removed my cap and couldn't help agreeing that it did look a bit out of place in the midst of the *haute couture* of the rest of the passengers. The passengers pretended to ignore our joyful remarks and looked down their noses at us as if we were just a bunch of scruffy drunkards taking a joy ride.

It must have been about 8 pm when the bus arrived at the terminus at Johannesburg central station, as it was already dark. Vermeulen would be doing his inspection round and if our absence had not already been discovered, some of the comrades would be wondering if we were going to return to our cells in a short while. As we stood in the centre of the big city with neon lights flashing all around us, we laughed to ourselves that they were soon going to be kicking themselves for not joining us.

Our planning did not extend as far as covering the situation in which we found ourselves, so we held a gathering in the station car park to decide our next moves. Alex was still keen to make directly for the Swaziland border and wanted to do so immediately. Stephen, finding himself in Johannesburg and in what he considered home territory, thought he would be better off trying to make contact with some of his friends. In the light of this I felt it would be better if I accompanied Alex because we could not all throw ourselves on Steve's friends, and Alex would be at a disadvantage if he went off on his own. He spoke no Afrikaans and was not as familiar as Steve and I with place names and routes. There was not much else to discuss so we shook hands, wished each other luck and agreed to meet again in London.

Having reached the end of the planned part of our escape, we turned our thoughts to absorbing some of the benefits of freedom. The first thing that came to mind was food – food of our own choice. I fancied a juicy grilled steak but Alex was more concerned with making our newly gained freedom more secure – he would allow no more than the purchase of a steak and kidney pie and a Coke from a station kiosk in the huge "whites only" concourse. Although in normal times one would only buy such food in desperation, the fact that we had chosen to buy it ourselves and were able to eat it in our own time, made it one of the most memorable meals we could both remember. I also bought from the kiosk a pocket-sized road map of South Africa (*see picture*).

Alex wanted to head east in the direction of Swaziland but the furthest any train was going in that direction that night was to the city of Springs on the East Rand. Although Springs was only 60 kilometres away, going there was better than standing looking at the departures board so we bought two tickets in the hope that once we got there, we would be able to get a bus to take us further. I felt somewhat uneasy about this plan as I could envisage a situation where we would find ourselves stuck out in the night with no transport to take us further. But the alternative of spending the whole night wandering aimlessly around Johannesburg was even less attractive.

The train was almost empty so we sat down in a section that was unoccupied, and proceeded to dismantle and discard out of the window our escape equipment and keys. Why we had thought at one stage that wooden keys would not be strong enough to open the prison's locks I don't know, because when we tried to break them apart with our hands it was almost impossible to do so. Each one had to be split open with the chisel and then painfully chipped into unrecognisable pieces. It was sad to have to destroy our precious keys like that. They embodied so many hours of painstaking labour and had been hidden and tended so carefully for so long. It was also hard to believe that after a few minutes' use they had given up their designated function and would never be needed again. After arriving at Springs, we buried the remaining tools in a churchyard, apart from our trusty chisel that we retained as a weapon to supplement the pea.

The bus station at Springs was totally deserted. There was no sign of any buses, nor were there any people waiting for them. Our hearts sank as we surveyed the empty, oily ranks. We had visualised ourselves being over or near the Swaziland border before daybreak. Now the vision of being on safe territory for breakfast faded and the prospect of having to get to the border under cover of the darkness of several nights loomed. Freedom was not going to be as easy as we had thought; we were going to have to struggle for it. But one thing was for sure: we were not going to allow ourselves to get caught – we would crawl on hands and knees to the border if we had to.

If you have no wheels the only way to get somewhere is on foot. So, we set off eastwards. To sustain us on our journey we stopped at a shop and bought some sweets, a large slice of cheese and two cartons of milk. After the skimmed, powdered "milk" ration we had received in prison, the fresh, creamy milk glided down our throats like nectar.

We discovered a signpost pointing the way to Ermelo, a town our map indicated we would have to pass through, so we set off in that direction. For about an hour and a half as we walked through and out of Springs, we held out our thumbs in the hope that someone would stop and give us a lift. But at night, motorists in South Africa (most of whom at that time were white) grew paranoid and were loath to stop on dark roads to offer assistance to stranded hitchhikers.

Outside Springs at a place called Largo, the road crossed over a railway line and from the bridge we could see flashing lights in the distance. A roadblock was our immediate, simultaneous thought. If that's what it was then it meant that our absence had already been discovered and we would have to face the full might of the "security forces" all the way to the border. Standing on top of a bridge while the cops were looking for us was dangerous, so we ran to the bottom and turned into and made our way down a rough farm track leading off the road at right angles. We climbed through a fence and walked across a ploughed field. There was no moon or stars that night, and as we stumbled in the furrows it suddenly occurred to us how absurd it was to be scrambling blindly across the countryside after our meticulously conceived plans had got us out of the prison and to that point so effortlessly. My morale dropped to a low ebb and I suggested turning back to spend the night in Springs. Alex angrily rejected that suggestion and urged me onward. There's no doubt that without his irrepressible determination we would have remained in Pretoria Prison for very much longer.

When we finally reached the road again, a short distance beyond where the suspected danger had appeared to be, there were no flashing lights and no signs of cars being stopped. Puzzled but relieved, we shrugged our shoulders and proceeded along the road in the direction of the next town on our map, a place called Devon.

The night was warm and calm, and walking through the fresh air was invigorating after years of breathing stale, wall-bound prison air. The sense of freedom was intoxicating and we felt like singing. For several hours we joked and laughed about incidents leading up to the escape, and tried to imagine how the warders would respond in the morning when they opened our cells and found dummies in our beds. We could see them going berserk and crowds of security police descending on the place to figure out how we had managed to get out. The escape had been a catharsis for us and suddenly all our pent-up emotions were flooding out.

At about two o'clock in the morning we suddenly noticed the flashing lights again, but this time coming from behind us. We couldn't understand it as we had just come down that road. Could it be a roving roadblock, we thought? To avoid whatever it was, we dived into the nearest bush. The flashing light was very slow moving and took about twenty minutes to reach us. It was also very noisy, making a sort of rumbling, puffing noise like a steam engine. The "roadblock" eventually reached us: it turned out to be a line-painting machine that was repainting sections of the white lines down the centre of the road. It went past us and stopped about a hundred metres further on. The flashing light went off and the workers climbed down from their monster machine and started to pull out their flasks and sandwiches. It was a coffee break. We waited another 10 minutes and then decided it was safe to carry on. There were several smallholdings behind us, so we reasoned that it would not seem too strange for a couple of white men to be walking about at that time of night. The workers ignored us as we trudged past – we must still have been invisible.

At about five, when the sun was just beginning to light the distant horizon, we reached Devon. The walk from Springs had been more than 40 kilometres so we were beginning to feel the strain on our feet. Strangely though, we did not feel tired. The excitement of the night had kept the pangs of sleep at bay.

At the town we made our way to the railway station to find out if there were any trains or buses to Ermelo. The lone guard in attendance informed us, much to our dismay, that there were no buses out of the town and only one train a day – at midnight. He suggested that we try hitching, but after our experience the previous night we were not inspired by the suggestion. On the other hand, the thought of walking the more than 200 kilometres to the Swaziland border was not inviting, so we thought we would at least give hitching another try. It was daylight now and people would probably be more willing to pick us up. After only a few minutes of thumbs-out, someone stopped and offered us a lift. It was a different matter now that they could see our white faces.

On the way, our driver stopped at a café to buy his breakfast. We took the opportunity to replenish our supplies and buy a newspaper to see if there was any mention of the escape. But there was nothing, which made us feel much easier. It was a curious sensation to hold and possess a whole newspaper, but because it didn't arrive in an envelope under a cell door the news seemed flat and boring. As soon as we set off again, I commented to Alex that there was nothing in the news "as usual", in the hope of provoking our driver into mentioning the escape of three dangerous "terrorists" if he had heard anything about it on radio or TV. But he had obviously heard nothing.

Our driver took us a distance of about forty kilometres to the turn-off for the town of Secunda, where he worked as a technician at the SASOL oil-from-coal plant. From the point where he dropped us we could clearly see the refinery in the distance. Six months later it was attacked by ANC guerrillas with limpet mines, causing millions of rands of damage to one of the most strategic installations in the country and maximum embarrassment to the apartheid regime.

Beyond the drop-off point there was little traffic and most of it large trucks, the drivers of which at the best of times were reluctant to stop for hitchhikers. The time was about 6 am and approaching the time when our absence would be discovered if it had not already been discovered. The countryside was flat and open, so it was imperative for us to make some rapid headway. Alex suddenly hit upon the bright idea of holding up a R10 note alongside his thumb when a truck or car passed. The trick worked a wonder. The very first truck that came along pulled up to a rapid halt, its trailer almost skidding off the road. Alex climbed up to the driver's window and asked where he was going. The driver explained that he was going in the direction of Piet Retief to deliver some mining equipment to a mine outside the town, and was going there via Ermelo. Alex shouted the details down to me but as soon as I heard the word "Ermelo" I told him to accept. We climbed aboard and handed the driver his ten rand.

The driver's mate climbed over the seat and sat on the bunk at the back of the cab; Alex and I sat in the passenger's seat and watched through the large windscreen as the truck swallowed up the miles below us. In half an hour we had covered a greater distance than we had walked all night. The rapid progress we were suddenly making made us think that we could probably get right to the border before the authorities realised what had happened and mobilised roadblocks that distance away. Between the two of us we still had a considerable amount of money and wondered if we could use it to persuade the driver to take us all the way to Amsterdam, a small town we had planned to pass through on the way to the Swazi border. Piet Retief was south of Amsterdam and to get to both places entailed passing through Ermelo. At Ermelo the road branched south-east to Piet

Retief or carried straight on to Amsterdam. It was possible to reach Piet Retief via Amsterdam as a road connected the two towns. In other words, to get to Piet Retief from Ermelo via Amsterdam meant travelling two sides of a triangle as opposed to the one side if travelling directly there.

From our map-book we calculated that the direct route from Ermelo to Piet Retief was a distance of 97 kilometres and via Amsterdam 132 kilometres. But as the mine where the equipment had to be delivered was a short way up the road towards Amsterdam from Piet Retief, the difference would be less than 30 km.

Observing this fact, we told the driver that we needed to get to Amsterdam very urgently to attend to a sick relative and offered him a further R50 if he would take us there. The driver spoke over his shoulder to his mate. We could not understand what they were saying because they spoke in an African language, but guessed that they knew the sick relative story was bullshit as the conversation went on for a long time. Eventually the driver nodded his head and said that it would be okay to take us to Amsterdam.

We passed through Ermelo and followed the signs to Amsterdam. As we did so, Alex and I were quietly laughing inside. It was about the time the warders would be discovering that three prisoners had not woken for the morning inspection. The thought of them throwing back the bedspreads to find dummies concocted of clothing and books was thrilling to contemplate. Soon we would be in Amsterdam, where we could wait for nightfall to make our crossing into Swaziland. Up to that point we had seen no signs of roadblocks or police activity, meaning that our absence had not been discovered during the night.

Our visions of an early arrival at Amsterdam were soon deflated. About forty kilometres out of Ermelo one of the tyres of the trailer burst. The trailer began to slew about but the driver managed to bring the truck to a halt without incident. Fortunately, the wheels of the trailer were double-tyred so it was able to keep on a more or less even keel. The driver got out to inspect the damage and then reported that it would take some time to replace the wheel. Not having time to spare, we paid him the R50 and set off on foot in the same direction, again with our thumbs sticking out.

There was very little traffic on the road at that time of the morning (about seven thirty) and most of it private transport – not easily brought to a halt by our money method. After about an hour's walking, we decided that it was too risky to continue on foot in broad daylight. By that time the word would be getting out on the radio for the public to be on the lookout for escaped white prisoners. Further on we spotted a clump of bushes and trees just off the road beyond a fence, and headed for it. We entered the bushes and found it to be an ideal hiding place as they were sheltering a sort of gully around which the road skirted.

It was going to be a long wait for sunset so we cleared some ground and lay down to rest our weary bodies. Despite having spent the entire night on foot, neither of us could sleep: our thoughts and the excitement of the day would not let us relax. Huge, buzzing, mosquito-like creatures also gave us no peace.

At about midday, the sky began to cloud over and the temperature plummeted. Our clothing was totally inadequate and we grew progressively colder. Two hours later the skies opened up and within a few minutes we were drenched to the skin. The trees became so waterlogged that they offered no shelter at all. We moved into a deeper part of the gully in the hope that its steep sides would afford some shelter, but the rain was coming down so heavily that the sides began to slide down on us. The elements decided for us that we had to move on.

Shortly before we had left the road and hidden in the bushes, we had noticed a sign indicating a petrol station a kilometre further on. From our hiding place we had been able to hear voices and cars and trucks stopping and starting, but our reluctance to proceed to the petrol station to seek a lift was suddenly changed by the circumstances.

To our good fortune, the petrol station turned out to be a country store as well. A number of people were sheltering under the verandah in front of it. They did not seem to find it too strange to see two white men soaked to the core come striding out of the dense rain. Inside the store we asked one of the attendants, who were all black, to sell us some cheese. Instead of immediately responding to our request, one of them eyed us up and down and asked us to hold on while she went to call her "madam". Momentarily, both of us thought that we had just exposed ourselves and that she was going to the back to call her "master", who would soon appear with a shotgun and perform the noble duty of arresting us.

Our fears were allayed when a friendly white woman appeared through the door behind the counter and asked us with a genuinely worried look on her face what had happened. Thinking quickly, we explained that our car had broken down some distance back and that we had left it at a farm and were trying to hitch to Amsterdam to meet my brother who had all our luggage there. We had not been able to hitch a ride and had got caught in the rain when it started – hence our sodden state.

If we had been black we would probably have been booted out for dripping water all over the floor, but since we were white and apparently in distress she felt sorry for us and brought us two towels to dry our soaked bodies, as well as two steaming mugs of coffee to warm us up. It's a shame to think that such a kind person could have been prosecuted for assisting escaped prisoners.

Between us we still had a fair sum of money left, so we each bought ourselves an anorak to keep out the cold and Alex bought himself a pair of long socks to change into. To keep our bellies full on the journey ahead, we bought a stock of cheese, sweets and fruit. If we were to continue hitching in the rain, we realised that we would need raincoats too, so we asked to be shown the range in stock. All they were able to produce were two plastic raincoats, one light blue and the other bright yellow – the worst possible colours. But having no choice we bought the pair.

Having dried and warmed our bodies, we donned our raincoats, thanked the "madam" and her helper gratefully, and marched out onto the road looking like two ghostly apparitions. Fortunately, the very first car that came along stopped and the driver, obviously feeling sorry for us, apologised that he could only give us a lift for 20 km. As this was better than standing in the rain until sunset, we gratefully accepted and climbed into the already-full car. The occupants were Afrikaans-speaking so Alex was not able to converse with them, but I managed to keep a conversation going and tried subtly to direct the talk in the direction of the day's news. But like our first driver, they too appeared not to have heard anything about escaped convicts on the run.

The road passed through dense forest area and at a turn-off to a dam the driver stopped to let us out. He wished us luck in finding another lift and drove off in a cloud of mist. As we stood in the cold and rain contemplating our situation, we decided that we had pushed our luck far enough and should not try to solicit any more lifts. We hid in the forest until nightfall and then, because the border was only about forty kilometres away, proceeded on foot. We climbed through a fence and moved into the forest out of view of the road. Not finding any shelter under the trees, we decided there was no point in waiting for dark and carried on walking in the same direction as the road, the position of which we were able to determine by the sound of the occasional passing car.

Eventually we came to a path that seemed too well trodden to be a foresters' path, so we followed it for some distance until it came out to a small African village. The villagers and even their dogs stared in silence as the two phantoms approached and walked past without saying a word. From the village we followed a track that led back to the main road. As we approached the road it was already dusk, but before coming out onto it we waited in the tall grass for darkness to set in properly. As soon as we judged it to be dark enough (it must have been about seven thirty) we set off along the road in the direction of Amsterdam, a distance of about twenty kilometres.

Our map told us that it was another 20 kilometres from Amsterdam to the Swazi border gate at Nerston, where we planned to make our crossing. Since we had walked 40 kilometres the previous night, we knew that we were capable of covering the same distance by daybreak if we walked through the night. Our morale was still high, although we were more apprehensive than we had been the previous night and our limbs were beginning to ache. We had been through a lot in our short period of freedom, and as it got longer, we became more and more determined to hang onto it. For the first time we turned our thoughts to wondering what would happen if we were recaptured. The prison authorities would surely not take too kindly to the disruption the escape had caused. Both of us knew that our sentences would be infinitely extended, and for at least six months after recapture we would be forced to wear chains and be held in solitary confinement.

There were very few cars on the road that night but we could not allow ourselves to be seen at all. Our guess was that there would be full-scale searches mounted throughout the country and especially near border areas. Every time a car passed, the two of us dived off the road and hid in bushes or grass near the verge. There was plenty of time to look for hiding places because, as it was pitch dark and still drizzling, we could see the lights of cars lighting the horizon a great distance off. On a number of occasions, we could not find suitable hiding so we just had to lie flat in the grass and hope for the best. When this happened, we had to remove our technicolour raincoats, place them on the ground as groundsheets and I had to lie on top of Alex to conceal his white shoes and light-coloured socks and shorts. On two occasions we were certain that the passing vehicles were police vans.

At around midnight the lights of Amsterdam made a welcome sight in the distance. Our feet were by this time beginning to suffer the consequences of all the walking, but there was no question of stopping. As we approached the town, we considered skirting around it for fear that there would be a roadblock or that police would be positioned in the streets to be on the lookout for fugitives. But the distance around appeared to be great and we did not know if we would end up on the road to the border on the other side. Also, the road into the town was wide and well lit. It dipped down into the centre and up a hill on the far side, and from the approach appeared to be completely deserted. To reduce the chances of being seen, we walked apart – one on each side of the road – and met at the far side of town where a sign indicated the direction to the border gate. There was a slight scare as we sat down to rest our weary feet: a small car came up the hill towards us but then turned off just before reaching us.

Under the road sign we removed our shoes and massaged our blistered feet, and ate the last of our food. My left foot had developed a disabling cramp and I was beginning to doubt if I would be able to walk the remaining 20 kilometres to the border. But the rest and the fresh air on my soles worked wonders. The walk to the border, we knew, would be uneventful as the border gate was closed at night and the road led nowhere else.

* * *

We weren't there to witness it, but our fellow prisoners reported to us some years later what happened on the morning after the escape.

The escape had not been detected by the night-warders so there was nothing in the logbook. It was only at open-up at 7 am that the discovery was made. This meant that we had achieved our goal of obtaining a full 14 hours before the escape was discovered.

The warder who opened the cells that morning only discovered that something was wrong when he got to Denis's cell, the third cell along. He suddenly realised that he had opened two cells and there had not been prisoners standing to attention at both of them. This happening at one cell was not usually taken too seriously, as occasionally a prisoner would oversleep and have to be prodded into life. But when it happened at two consecutive cells there had to be something amiss. The warder went back to Stephen's cell and shouted at him to wake up. When there was no stirring, he opened the grille and pulled the bedspread back...

The warder ran out of the section and screamed for the sergeant in charge. He rushed back in and hurriedly opened my cell. Another prisoner gone! The blood drained from his face as he realised what was going on.

Complete pandemonium then broke out. A troop of warders came charging into the section and the remaining cell doors were hurriedly flung open to see how many more prisoners had turned into lifeless dummies. They got to Alex's cell, and finding another "sleeping prisoner", realised that three had flown. The remaining prisoners expressed utter surprise at the revelation that some of their fellow prisoners had gone missing in the night.

In no time the prison was invaded by a horde of security police, and the remaining prisoners were placed under close and permanent observation. The prison and entire terrain were overrun and surrounded by police, and the call went out to prevent the flight of three dangerous "terrorists".

Within a few days the prison yard was dug up in the search for clues. Every tree, bush, blade of grass and weed was uprooted. Sure enough, a bottle containing keys for every grille and door was soon unearthed from under the spinach patch...

Chapter Seventeen
Swaziland and Mozambique

O ur feet were killing us but we pressed on towards the Swaziland border. The rain had stopped and it became a bit warm-
er, but it was still overcast and pitch dark. It was so dark,
in fact, that we could not even see the white line down the centre of
the road and several times walked off the edge of the tarmac. Our
imaginations began to play games with us: the road seemed to be
running along the edge of a cliff, then over the top of a mountain,
then through a forest – we couldn't tell. Probably most of the time it
was winding through forest area, as that was how it was when it grew
lighter in the morning.

We talked very little and kept close to each other for comfort. Both
of us felt desperately tired. Several times I actually fell asleep while
walking, and bumped into Alex. Our food was all eaten and we began
to feel progressively weaker, but the thought of friendly territory close
by gave us succour. Strangely, we felt little apprehension even though
our common sense told us that we were reaching what could possibly
be the most dangerous part of our journey.

As the first taint of dawn pierced through the misty sky, we
came to a T-junction where a signboard indicated 2 kilometres to
the border gate. We turned right towards the gate and Alex paced
out 1,500 metres, from which point we could see the orange glow
of the lights at the border gate in the distance. From there we cut

left into the forest and walked at right angles to the road for about half a kilometre, then a right turn towards the border. Both of us had visualised the border as two, high, barbed-wire fences with a strip of no-man's-land in between. Maybe there would be dogs, landmines, alarms: who knew? We had decided that when we reached the fence, we would walk along it away from the border gate until we came to a suitable place to cross, perhaps where it went across a stream or over a rocky patch.

After walking some distance, a small, muddy stream crossed our path at the edge of the forest. At a point where the trees ran up to the stream, we stepped over it and scrambled up a steep bank on the other side that was cleared of vegetation. At the top of the bank was a rough track and along the other side of it dense bush that appeared to have been cropped so that it looked vaguely like a hedge. These signs of habitation made us think that perhaps we had not walked along far enough and were in imminent danger of being seen by border guards. Alex suggested taking shelter in the bush but after penetrating it some distance we came to a small African stone hut.

As we stared at it, we simultaneously came to the realisation that we might actually be in Swaziland. The area up to the border was not a bantustan and seemed to be entirely given over to forestry. Now suddenly there was habitation. It could be the only explanation. But where was the border fence we had expected? Where were the dogs, the guards?

The thought that we could be on safe territory (relatively speaking) gave us sudden courage. We turned back on our footsteps, re-emerged from the bush and followed the track in the direction of the border gate and main road. The bush thinned out and through it a small settlement came into view, with some houses being more substantial than mere huts. Alex suddenly noticed a woman washing clothes in a tub in her yard.

He ran up to her, leaving me standing on the track. I could see him speaking to her and then suddenly embracing her. He pulled a R10 note out of his pocket and thrust it into her hand. The woman stood bewildered as he shouted to me that, indeed, we were in Swaziland. I ran up to the woman and shook her hand, asking her to confirm to me that I really was in Swaziland.

What that woman must have thought when two dishevelled white men appeared out of the grey of dawn and started asking her which country they were in, must be left to the imagination. Whatever she thought, it is more than likely that her guess was not too far off the mark. To add to her puzzlement, we asked her how we could get from the village to Mbabane, the capital of Swaziland. She pointed to a house further up the hill that had a car parked outside, and told us that the person who owned it was a relative of hers, who might take us to Mbabane if we asked him.

The time could not have been later than five thirty, but having been up the entire night made us lose all sense of the meaning of the hour. Without thinking that we would probably be waking up an entire household, we knocked on the door of the relative's house for a good 10 minutes before it occurred to us that the lack of response could be accounted for by the fact that it was still very early in the morning. As we were walking away and planning to come back later, a drowsy-looking woman in a dressing gown appeared at the back door of the house and asked what we wanted.

Amazingly, when we explained that we were looking for a lift to Mbabane she did not display the slightest sign of annoyance at having been so inconsiderately aroused from her slumber at such an unreasonable hour. She explained that the car outside her house, to which we had pointed, belonged to her husband who was still sleeping. She invited us into the house to wait until he woke up.

Having lived all my life in a city, and coming straight from prison, I found it difficult to understand the friendliness of those people. Not only did the woman invite us in after we had woken her and probably her entire family, but after chatting to her for a while she offered us tea and ultimately breakfast. And the extended hand of hospitality did not end there. After breakfast we were offered use of the bathroom and even given a razor and towels for a shave. The thermal and personal warmth of that house revived our bodies and faith in humankind. We could not help thinking that they must have realised that we were on the run from something, but that it would have been more reasonable for them to think that we were fleeing bank robbers rather than escaped political prisoners.

When the head of the house finally appeared, it had already been decided what should become of us. The sister of the woman, who also stayed in the house, offered to take us up to the shop they owned on the main road, from where she would be able to arrange a lift for us. The shop had a petrol pump in front of it and, as they knew practically everyone who stopped to fill up, they could ask someone to give us a lift.

After eating breakfast, they escorted us to the shop where we waited for about an hour before a lift was arranged. An uncle had offered to give us a lift to a point on the main road halfway between Mbabane and Manzini. Unfortunately, the uncle turned out to be a businessman who owned half the booze shops in Swaziland, and that was the day he had to visit each of them before going on to complete his business in Manzini. But escaped convicts cannot be choosers so we had to be patient and content. Despite the frustration, we got to see some of the more unusual and beautiful parts of the country. As interesting as they were, we were not tourists and were impatient to get to Mbabane and out of the country as quickly as possible. Just as we were about to announce that we would prefer to try for another lift, he dropped us at the place he had promised to take us, about thirty kilometres from Mbabane. From the drop-off point the traffic was relatively heavy so we quickly got another lift into the centre of Mbabane.

In Mbabane, the first thing we did was to buy newspapers to see what sort of response there had been to the escape. It was headlined in all the South African papers: "Three Prisoners Escape: dummies left in their beds" read one; "Prison Official Held Over ANC Escape" read another. So they must have arrested poor old Vermeulen, was our immediate thought. An Afrikaans paper read: *"Polisie Jag Drie Wit Terroriste Landwyd"* – "Police Search Countrywide for Three White Terrorists".

Details were given of how the police had been mobilised throughout the country to make it impossible for the escapees to cross the borders into neighbouring countries. Obviously, their efforts hadn't been very successful! All the papers reported that we had escaped in shorts, white T-shirts and running shoes, the implication being that we had jogged our way to freedom. Most insulting of all was the offer of a R1,000 reward to anyone offering information leading to our recapture. Was that all we were worth?

What next? We had considered going to the Swazi police to ask them for protection and help but were not quite sure if that was a sensible thing to do as we had developed an innate aversion to police forces generally. I had heard somewhere, sometime (incorrectly) that the ANC had a bookshop in Mbabane and thought that maybe we could avoid the police by going directly there. We went back into the stationers where we had bought the newspapers, as it was also a bookstore, and asked one of the attendants if the ANC had a bookshop in Mbabane. The attendant hadn't even heard of the ANC, but when we explained what sort of organisation it was, he suggested that we contact the United Nations High Commission for Refugees (UNHCR) because they knew about people from South Africa. This sounded like a reasonable idea, and in the light of no other bright ideas we took a taxi to the United Nations building in town.

Alex went inside alone while I waited in the taxi. When the attendant at the enquiries desk asked what his business was, Alex abruptly demanded to see someone important. At first the attendant did not know how to respond to this unusual request, but when Alex said that he was from South Africa he was taken to see a worker concerned with refugee affairs, to whom he briefly explained his plight. At first the worker, a Swiss woman, was reluctant to believe the fantastic story that Alex was telling her, but when he threw the newspapers down on her desk, pointing to our mugshots emblazoned on their front pages, she hurriedly told him to summon me from outside so that she could hear more and decide what to do.

Together we explained to the startled woman how we happened to be where we were, using the newspapers to verify our story. On mentioning that we had thought of taking ourselves to the Swazi police she was horrified and said that if we had done that we would already be on our way back to South Africa. Thanks to our good fortune she was sympathetic to our plight and assured us that she could get us into safe hands, i.e., to the ANC. Most of all, she advised us, we should keep out of sight of the Swazi authorities as they were totally under the influence of the South Africans. Later we were to read in a newspaper report that a Swazi police spokesperson said: "If they are here, they will be arrested for illegally crossing our borders no matter what their motives are... Apart from breaking our law, they are criminals who have escaped from jail."

The Swiss woman made some hasty phone calls and then took us in her car to see the High Commissioner for Refugees himself, a man by the name of Godfrey Sibidi, a Ugandan citizen. While we explained again the circumstances of our escape, he made contact with the ANC over the phone. He found our tale fascinating and laughed his head off when we explained how we had done it. It was good to share our victory with someone in sympathy with what we had done. But he too was horrified that we had considered going to the Swazi police, and to ensure that none of his helpers saw us, some of whom were Swazis, he locked us in a small room. He sent one of his staff to buy us some food, which was our first proper meal since the last midday meal we had eaten in prison two days earlier. Food never tasted so good.

After waiting for a couple of hours in the room, the commissioner drove us some distance out of Mbabane to what appeared to be a seminary or church school of some kind. There we were introduced to, I think, the Bishop of Mbabane, and, at last, a representative of the ANC. The ANC comrade introduced himself as Stanley and shaking hands with him was like firmly grasping the hand of freedom. There was no going back to Pretoria now.

Having delivered us to the ANC, the commissioner bade farewell. Then Alex did something for which I have never forgiven him. The commissioner had shown great interest in the pea, which Alex still carried tucked into his belt under his shirt. As a token of gratitude, Alex handed him the pea as a souvenir. Since we possessed nothing else to offer as a gift, it would have seemed rude if I had objected too loudly. That was how we lost the pea, and it left me feeling quite sad!

The bishop took us to the dormitories where we were given soap and towels to have a wash. What luxury it was to just stand under those warm showers and let the water do the scrubbing. After two days' walking and after diving into muddy ditches the night before, our bodies had accumulated a great deal of sweat and grime. The warm water soothed our tired and aching limbs. Alex had trouble standing up, as his feet were massively swollen and his leg muscles so stiff that they were virtually incapable of flexing. Both of us collapsed on the beds that were offered to us after the shower.

A few hours later we were woken by some other ANC comrades and taken to a house in Mbabane, where we were given a first-class meal. Then on to another house where, finally, we were told to rest for a few hours because we were going to be taken across the border into Mozambique at dawn.

* * *

General – that was his name – picked us up at the crack of dawn. Our destination was the Mozambique border, he said. The drive to the border took about an hour, maybe longer. It was exciting to watch the sun rising above the hills to light the beautiful greenness of the countryside, a scene we should not, by rights, have been witnessing. It also made us realise how much we had taken such sights for granted in the past.

General's plan was that when we got near the border, the two of us would lie hidden on the floor of his car and then he would drive us through the border gate. Just like that. It seemed too easy to be true, but he assured us that he did it every day and had never had a problem. The Swazis, he explained, did not bother much about traffic going out of the country in the direction of Mozambique and the Mozambicans would not mind too much even if we were discovered – it was the sort of thing they expected.

A few kilometres from the border gate General drove off the road and stopped the car behind some bushes. He opened the car doors and we hid on the floor at the back. But when General pulled a tarpaulin over our heads Alex objected that it felt too much like a prison cell and made him feel unbearably claustrophobic. He wanted to walk across the border instead. If it had been so easy to walk across to Swaziland from South Africa then surely it would be no problem walking across here. General agreed that it could be done, but clearly, he was contemptuous of such a method of hopping borders and upset that we displayed so little faith in him.

To walk across safely meant taking a roundabout route that would involve a walk of two or three hours. Alex's feet were still in bad shape, swollen and stiff. He could not walk for 10 minutes, let alone a couple of hours through the bush. There was one more option, an extremely risky one, but if we were prepared to take the chance we could be over the border in a matter of minutes. Another chance? What the hell. We'd taken so many up to that point that one more didn't matter a damn. The proposal was accepted without further ado and we set off in the direction of the border gate.

Almost within view of the gate, General turned onto a rough track and drove towards the border fence. He stopped the car behind what appeared to be an abandoned shed and pointed to a sturdy two-metre high fence topped with barbed wire about thirty metres further on, and to another the same height about five metres beyond the first. The fences, he explained, ran along the borders of Swaziland and Mozambique respectively. The strip in between was no-man's-land but there were no mines or dogs in it, he assured us. All we needed to do was scale both fences and we would be in Mozambique.

On the other side of the fences we could see houses beyond a row of trees and bushes but there appeared to be no signs of life in that direction at all. What was the big deal? We would be over in thirty seconds and it was too early for anyone to be up to see us.

Our escort explained that we would have to wait for about an hour on the other side, as he would only be able to get through the border gate at seven o'clock. In case we encountered any problems, he gave us each a loaded pistol and told us to wait in a quiet back street of the town before moving on down to the gate shortly before seven. He explained briefly how the guns worked and then made us tuck them in our belts under our shirts.

At a corner post, all three of us climbed over the first (Swazi) fence and as Alex and I were mounting the second we noticed an old man in a long coat and wielding a knobkerrie charging towards us from the Swaziland side. General told us to get over the fence and run: he would deal with the man. The two of us leapt over the fence and started to run towards the houses on the Mozambique side. As we reached the bushes, we heard the sound of a scuffle as General engaged the old man in a fight. Alex turned around and with a loud battle cry ran back towards the scene with his pistol drawn. But all we could see was General running for his car and pulling away with the tyres skidding on the sandy road, with the old man in hot pursuit.

The part of the town in which we found ourselves must have been where the Portuguese colonialists once lived, as most of the houses were large and stately. To avoid being spoken to by the few people who were up and wandering about, we kept moving, slowly but purposefully, around two or three blocks of houses. Neither of us knew a single word of Portuguese so we did not even know how to greet the friendly but undoubtedly suspicious passers-by. Our first lesson in Portuguese was quickly learned: everyone bade us a courteous *bom dia*, quite obviously meaning "good day". We felt almost at home after that, casting smiling *bom dias* at everyone who appeared. There still seemed to be quite a number of white faces around so we could not have appeared too out of place that morning.

After about an hour of strolling around, we stopped to rest our still weary feet. There were more people about by then so we thought it would not look too strange for two of them to stop and sit on a low, stone wall for a rest. That was a big mistake, for as soon as we stopped, someone approached us and asked something in Portuguese. Not being able to answer, we replied clumsily that we were looking for someone from FRELIMO (the ruling party in Mozambique). Obviously, this answer, and coming in English, aroused the person's suspicion, for he quickly turned on his heels and walked back in the direction from which he had come. Approaching him from the opposite direction was a man dressed in uniform. The two met and stopped in the middle of the street. We could see the one who had spoken to us point over his shoulder and then both of them began to walk back in our direction. At that moment we thought of making a dash for it but realised that it would not have been the appropriate action.

As the official approached us, he asked in broken English what we were waiting for. At that very inconvenient moment the pistol tucked into the top of my trousers began to slip down my leg. I turned around to conceal what was happening but the official saw me suddenly groping myself. Stepping right up to me he asked brusquely what it was that I had hidden under my clothes. I had no choice but to reach into my trousers and haul out the gun and hand it to him. He turned to Alex and asked if he also had one. Realising that he could do nothing else, Alex withdrew his gun and handed it to him as a friendly gesture. Lucky he doesn't have the pea on him as well, I thought – almost forgiving him for giving it away earlier!

The official asked us to follow him and we set off down the street into the town. Neither of us knew what to say but did not want to appear as if we were feeling guilty. I asked casually if he was a member of FRELIMO and when he said that he was, we both shook hands and tried to be as friendly as possible. We explained who we were and where we were going but he seemed neither impressed nor convinced – but then who could blame him after discovering two suspicious-looking, English-speaking, armed, white men loitering in the streets of a small border town?

The official turned out to be a member of the border guard and took us to the offices at the border gate. There we were shut in a room with someone to watch over us. Once again we were in captivity and wondered what the outcome would be. Neither of us enjoyed the prospect of being locked up in a cell until the matter was sorted out. That could take days. We had explained to our "captor" that we were members of the ANC and were due to be met by the ANC (i.e. General) as soon as the gate opened and just hoped that the FRELIMO government's declared support for the ANC was the same in practice.

Fortunately, it was not long before the gates opened and General was one of the first to come through. Our official must have known who "the ANC" was because we could see him and General frantically discussing the matter in the road outside. Alex and I were not asked to join in the deliberations and had to be content just watching through the window of our room. After a while General joined us and appeared to be completely unperturbed by his altercation with the guard and with the fact that we had been "captured". All that worried him was the possible loss of his "irons" – the pistols he had given us. As for the old Swazi man who had given chase as we were mounting the border fence: General had "dealt" with him when he saw him again near the border gate. What that meant we weren't allowed to know.

After another long wait, several members of the local police or militia arrived as well as a vanload of ANC comrades, resulting in a gathering under the car shelter in front of the offices to discuss what should become of us. After an hour or so the gathering broke up and the two of us were taken into another room and subjected to a humiliatingly thorough strip search by a surly border guard.

The strip search signalled the end of our wait and was followed by a friendlier attitude from the official who had disarmed us. He led us to a small hut closer to the border gate where we were asked to fill in a form – an ordinary visitor's entry form. What had troubled them most was that we had tried to sidestep their administrative entry requirements and had avoided filling in the requisite forms. Climbing over the border fence with no papers and loaded pistols was okay, but not filling in the forms was unforgivable!

Having completed the forms, we were handed over to the ANC and driven to a house a short distance away in the town (a year later we learned that South Africans blew up this particular house). At the house were a number of ANC comrades, including Sue Rabkin, Dave's wife. She gave us a warm welcome and from somewhere produced a full bottle of brandy. On our empty stomachs the alcohol quickly worked its way to our heads, but it felt good after not having touched a drop of alcohol for so long.

The comrades served a delicious meal and then at about midday took us to the local police station to clear up a few more bureaucratic obstacles and attempt to retrieve the two weapons. Why Alex and I had to be present I'm not sure, as again we were entirely left out of the negotiations. The comrades disappeared into a room with the police and after an hour reappeared with smiles and handshakes all around. General was the most pleased of all: he had got his precious irons back.

After that it was back to the border gate where there was another long wait, this time for the arrival of a contingent of FRELIMO officials from Maputo. Following further lengthy discussions, we were asked to climb aboard the FRELIMO Land Rover that had brought the officials, and then were driven at high speed to Maputo with the ANC Kombi in pursuit.

In Maputo the Land Rover stopped outside an office where the uniformed front-seat passenger got out and another in civilian attire got in. The vehicle moved off and immediately we sensed a friendlier attitude. The new passenger offered us his hand and said that we were now safe and would be well looked after.

They drove us to a tall block of flats and took us up to a large apartment on about the ninth floor: our place of residence for the next few days, they informed us. The flat was well equipped and had an endless supply of alcohol. After settling in, a nurse arrived to attend to Alex's feet, which by this stage were so swollen and painful that he had difficulty in removing his shoes. She carefully rubbed in an ointment and then strapped bandages around his ankles.

After a few hours of adapting to our new status as "guests of the state", our mentor asked if there was anything special he could bring us to eat. In unison we explained that in prison our dream had been that as soon as we arrived in Mozambique, we would like our first meal to be giant prawns, for which the country is famous. Not believing for one moment that this fanciful wish would be fulfilled, that evening the most incredible meal of giant prawns arrived on silver platters from the famous Polana Hotel. Two bodyguards left in the flat with us were glad to join us in the meal, although obviously worried that someone would come in and catch them eating on the job. Thereafter three times every day until we left the flat, similar enormous meals arrived from the Polana Hotel.

Several times each day we were visited by a government official who appeared to have been placed in charge of us. He spoke no English but was fluent in French so Alex was able to converse with him. He was interested in details of South African prisons so I drew him a number of pictures of the layout and cells of Pretoria Prison and of the uniform worn by the warders. He gave his name as Antonio Paulo and came across to us as someone completely devoted to the Mozambican revolution. In long discussions with Alex, which Alex briefly translated to me every fifteen minutes or so, he talked about the struggle being waged by FRELIMO to overcome the superstitions of the peasantry, about South African aggression and subversion and other similar subjects.

Paulo contrasted with the character who had brought us to the flat and who also paid us several visits. Although friendly with us and apparently supportive of the FRELIMO government, we found out several years later that Paulo had defected to apartheid South Africa, where he provided the racists with a wealth of information about Mozambican security. Unless he was an agent from the start, it is difficult to understand the motivations of someone seemingly committed to the fight against racism to go and sell out to the racists.

A number of top ANC officials also visited us at the flat, including the legendary Joe Slovo. To each we had to repeat the tale of our escape from start to finish; from each we received equally hearty congratulations for having defeated the racists and for making them look like monkeys. Joe revealed that there had been a team of people mobilised to assist in the escape and that they were planning to use a furniture-removal van to carry us off. A safe house had been set up and other arrangements were at an advanced stage of preparation before they had received word calling it all off. They were surprised by the cancellation of the request for assistance and even more surprised when the escape actually took place shortly after that.

After four days in the flat, Antonio Paulo took us downtown to buy some new clothes and other items for travel. We were still wearing the clothes in which we had escaped, so greatly appreciated the opportunity to change into something clean and new. He bought us each a large suitcase, a shoulder bag, two suits, two pairs of trousers, five or six shirts, underpants, socks, a belt, a tie, handkerchiefs, shoes and sandals, deodorant, toothpaste, etc. In all, a complete kit to turn us into respectable people again. Later he brought us each a brand-new portable typewriter and between us a leather briefcase filled with sundry items of stationery and drawing equipment.

On the sixth day we were handed back to the ANC, who took us to a flat close to the beachfront. There we stayed with a foreign couple who were teaching at Maputo University. The couple took us on a number of sightseeing trips around Maputo Bay, which helped to make us feel well and truly free. Three days later we were taken to the airport in Maputo and driven right up to an aircraft waiting on the apron: clearance had been given for our departure without documents. From Maputo we flew to Luanda in Angola via Lusaka. Amazing what can happen if you are connected with the right people!

Chapter Eighteen
Angola, Zambia, Tanzania

Why they sent us to Angola we never quite discovered, but they must have had their reasons. Perhaps they felt that Mozambique was too close to home and suspected that apartheid agents would attempt to abduct us if they got wind of our location. It had happened in the past, so they were not taking any chances.

The ANC accommodated us in a flat in the centre of Luanda overlooking a large square. On the day of our arrival, a festival was taking place in the square and on display, amongst other things, was an exhibition of captured weapons from the 1975 South African invasion of Angola. It was a cheering sight to see other people celebrating a victory over our enemy, on top of the one we had just scored. What was most inspiring of all, was a sight we had dreamed of but not seen before – the black, green and gold flag of the ANC fluttering freely alongside other national flags. It reminded us that we were truly on friendly territory.

From the ANC office in Luanda, Alex and I were able to phone Marie-José and Robin respectively. The calls were not the first to let our families and friends know that we were safely out of the country: from Swaziland the ANC had contacted our families to let them know that we were safe. But the calls were the first we made ourselves, and the first time we were able to speak directly to our loved ones. Robin was over the moon. We were both so excited that we didn't know what to say, apart from asking each other, over and over, how we were feeling. Hearing her voice was the highlight of the short period I had been free. It was confirmation that I would soon be in a position to freely decide my own next moves.

A few days after arriving in Luanda, a message came that Stephen was about to join us. Alex and I were jubilant – Stephen was safe and the fact that we had all made it meant that we had well and truly beaten our enemy. We had grown increasingly apprehensive that something dreadful had happened to him because it was then about ten days since the escape and there had been no word of him. If he had been recaptured it would have meant that the escape project had been a failure: the effect that the escape had had in proving that the racist state's defences were not impregnable would have been lost, and the apartheid regime would have used a recapture as counter-propaganda that it was not so easy to evade their security apparatus.

Together with some comrades from the ANC office in Luanda, we arrived at the airport early. One of them had to be at passport control to explain why Stephen was arriving without papers. But no one matching Stephen's description arrived at the control. While those of us waiting near the arrivals gate were craning our necks to see over the heads of the awaiting crowd, someone from behind us shouted "Comrades!" It was Stephen! How the hell had he managed to get out without us seeing him? The answer was that he hadn't come through the regular entrance: he had grown impatient with the slow-moving passport queue and had casually walked through an open door and into the arrivals hall. The ANC comrades were horrified: this was taking hatred of bureaucracy too far. One of them hastily escorted Stephen back into the passport control, and fortunately for him, no one had noticed what he had done.

Back at the flat Stephen – with his hair now dyed dark-brown – told us how he had holed-up in Johannesburg for several days with friends, and how he had been escorted to and accompanied across the Swaziland and Mozambique borders by ANC members. From Mozambique his story was much the same as ours: he had also been kept in a flat and fattened on Polana prawns; he had also been bought a suitcase-full of new clothes and travel goods.

Our stay in the Luanda flat was broken by a number of visits to ANC residences in and around Luanda. On each occasion we addressed the comrades and told them a few brief details of our escapades – an experience which, for me, was more frightening than escaping from the prison itself. I had always had an excruciating fear of public speaking and these few addresses to the comrades were but the first of very many such talks to follow.

On one occasion, we were taken some distance out of Luanda to an ANC refugee camp to speak to the comrades there. The freedom songs they sang for us, in appreciation of our coming so far to tell them how we had defeated the enemy, were so beautiful and evocative that they brought tears to our eyes. Despite the clearly austere conditions under which they were living, their spirit and morale were inspirational.

Meeting the comrades in Angola gave us confidence that in the coming battles with apartheid they would be more than a match for the racists. Although the ANC did not have the resources of the apartheid regime and Umkhonto soldiers did not possess weapons as sophisticated as those used by apartheid soldiers, they had one weapon that no racist had: the conviction that they were fighting a just war of liberation against a universally condemned racist regime.

On 30 December, the three of us were flown to Lusaka where our official surfacing was to be announced early in the new year. Again, we were accommodated in an ANC residence, but this time under heavy armed guard. Our comrades were determined that the South Africans were not going to make a snatch-and-grab raid while we were in Zambia – a truly "front-line" country that had for a long time borne the brunt of racist and colonialist attacks because of its support for southern African liberation movements.

On New Year's Eve, we were taken to meet the leadership of the ANC. Ironically, the meeting took place in what appeared to be a carpentry workshop in a factory. Among those present were Oliver Tambo, the president of the ANC, and Alfred Nzo, the secretary-general. It was a great honour to meet these two friendly leadership figures, always portrayed by the South African media as demonic terrorists and enemies of freedom.

The gathering listened to our report with much interest and then discussed the press conference planned for 2 January. It was decided that we should prepare a press statement to deliver and distribute and that I should redraw the plans of the prison that I had drawn for the Mozambicans, which could be reproduced and handed out to the media representatives.

Someone also came up with the idea that it would make a strong statement if the three of us were photographed in Umkhonto military uniforms holding automatic rifles, and the pictures handed out to the press – demonstrating that we had been reintegrated into the ANC and were ready to continue the fight against apartheid.

Steve and Alex prepared the statement while I redrew the plan of the prison for duplication. The photos of us dressed in uniform were taken and developed in time for use on the 2nd, but someone high up decided at the last moment that it would not be a good idea to distribute them, so it never happened.

The press conference was taken very seriously by the ANC. The trio of fugitives was driven in a convoy to the centre of Lusaka. Near the centre, our car broke away from the convoy and drove into the grounds of a hotel where we were transferred, without being seen, to another car. In this car we were driven to a conference centre in a tall building, with the other cars keeping a safe distance behind. There we were ushered into the building, surrounded by a ring of bodyguards.

Gathered was a large contingent of the press corps, who had been given notice by the ANC that the president would be making an important announcement. President Tambo introduced the three of us, and Alex read out the statement:

> *We are certainly very glad to be in Lusaka. Our presence here is more eloquent than any statement. We have emerged from a maximum-security prison in the heart of the Pretoria regime, passed clear through the enemy's territory, and crossed heavily guarded borders. You see us now in a country whose commitment to the liberation of southern Africa is well known.*
>
> *A battle has been won whose significance goes beyond the number of prisoners that escaped. We have shown that for militants of the Liberation Movement, capture does not mean surrender. Although placed behind walls and bars, and closely observed by armed guards, for apartheid prisoners, the struggle continues.*
>
> *In the course of our escape we were reluctantly forced to damage the front door of the prison, and so leave*

evidence about how we got out. This damage, however, also constitutes important evidence about the mentality of our captors.

It should show that our captors did not supply us with keys and other help. In spite of this, a Prison Department official has been arrested. Characteristically the authorities have seized upon a scapegoat in order to conceal from the people the extent to which it is possible to overcome the security of the state.

The eleventh of December marked the last day of our captivity. In this bitter captivity remain our comrades: on Robben Island, in Pretoria and in Kroonstad. Tens of thousands remain imprisoned, for both direct and indirect political offences, throughout South Africa. Many of these face torture by the racist butchers.

Although for security reasons we are unable to give details, the underground machinery of the African National Congress, the South African Communist Party and our People's Army, Umkhonto we Sizwe, all of which we are part, played an essential role in getting us to where we are now. Once again, our Liberation Movement has successfully thrust its spear deep into the enemy's body.

The three of us now look forward with heightened enthusiasm to contribute with our full strength to the ongoing struggle to liberate South Africa from all forms of oppression.

While we join our voices to those of concerned humanity in the demand for immediate and unconditional release of all political prisoners in South Africa, our foremost concern is in the fate of our dear comrade James Mange to whom we bow our heads in respect for the heroism and self-sacrifice and whose murder the fascist oppressors intend to add to their sinister constellation of crimes. We shall not rest until James Mange and all other political prisoners of war in South Africa are liberated.

Amandla Ngawethu!

Maatla ke Arona!

All power to the people!

After the statement was read out, I described in some detail how we had done it, using the diagrams that had been handed out to simplify the explanation. The exposition ended with our emergence from the front door of the prison. We were, for "security reasons", not prepared to divulge any details of how we had got to Lusaka, apart from saying that it could not have been achieved without the assistance of the ANC.

After Stephen and Alex explained how the three of us happened to be in prison in the first place, the meeting was opened to the floor. The questions asked by the correspondents were the same ones that got asked at every subsequent press conference, namely: Why had only the three of us escaped? What were our conditions like? What did we plan to do in the future?

To the first we answered that for "technical reasons" it was not possible to get everyone out, but that we would have if we could have; to the second we explained that our conditions were not good but far better than those of our black comrades; and to the last we said that we wanted to get back into the struggle and that we were putting ourselves at the disposal of the ANC.

Most of the South African newspapers reported on the conference fairly dispassionately, quoting at length from the statement. Some were worried about plans of the prison being handed out in the presence of reporters from "communist countries". Despite our efforts to deny that we had disguised ourselves as joggers, most reports repeated that we had broken out of prison dressed in shorts, T-shirts and running shoes. This fictional story was presumably more appealing than the boring, correct one that we gave.

Knowing the truth behind the reports that we read about ourselves, we were given a unique opportunity to witness some of the downright lies that get published in newspapers. Some of the lies we read about ourselves were so preposterous that they could not simply have been sucked out of reporters' thumbs. They must have been concocted by the dirty tricks departments of intelligence agencies and then passed on to the gullible reporters.

One such report appeared in the Johannesburg *Sunday Express* of 6 January 1980. The headline read "Joe Slovo planned the Big Escape". The article in question began: "Former Johannesburg advocate Joe Slovo was the mastermind behind the spiriting away of three political prisoners who broke out of jail in Pretoria last month, according to informed sources in Pretoria." It was "Joe Slovo's network [that] spirited the fugitives safely through one of the most extensive police search operations in recent times. The three men were able to reach Swaziland within hours of escaping from jail." One can only guess who the "informed sources in Pretoria" were.

To the South African propagandists, Joe Slovo was the arch-villain and apartheid South Africa's Enemy Number One. Being a prominent member of the ANC and SACP, and being white, Joe Slovo was the mastermind behind everything that happened with regard to these organisations. He planned every armed action that occurred inside the country, instructed every "terrorist" on how to carry out their dastardly deeds, and ran things single-handedly (of course with the backing of his KGB masters in the Kremlin!).

Another article, published by the regime mouthpiece *Rapport* before the press conference, claimed that the Soviet ambassador in Lusaka, Vladimir Solodovnikov – "a KGB General" – had been the master planner behind the escape. This piece of "information" came from "Western intelligence sources". Read: Pretoria.

The high-ups in the regime's propaganda factory knew as well as we did that these stories were a pack of lies, but they needed to repeat them as often as possible to stoke white prejudices of communist infiltration, to win support for any actions they took against the ANC and to play on the anti-white sentiments of blacks to create splits and opposition to the ANC and SACP. But such lies also showed that the apartheid rulers fell victim to their own racist propaganda by believing that every time they suffered a blow, there had to be a white person behind it and that black people needed whites to show them how to liberate themselves.

Our departure from Zambia took place on 3 January when we were flown to Dar es Salaam in Tanzania, accompanied by the Umkhonto commander, Joe Modise. On the way the plane stopped unexpectedly in Malawi and all passengers were told to disembark while it was being refuelled. One glimpse out of the window of the plane convinced us that we were not going to move: a short distance across the apron was parked a South African Airways Boeing and a military helicopter of unknown origin. Malawi had – to its shame – strong ties with the apartheid state and colluded with the racists in providing support to mercenaries and counter-revolutionary gangs throughout the region.

At Dar airport Eli Weinberg, the renowned photographer of the ANC and executive member of the South African Congress of Trade Unions (SACTU), met us at the bottom of the gangway. He drove us directly to his home where we were to be lodged. All our entry and documentation matters had previously been sorted out.

The friendship of the Tanzanians was demonstrated in a large way during our brief stay.

Unfortunately, Dar has one of the most unbearably humid climates in the world. During the three weeks that I was there, I did not manage to get a single wink of sleep. An oversized fan blowing full blast on me at night did not help at all. To pass the time the three of us spent most of our days at the beach. Although we had swum in Luanda, it seemed to be more enjoyable now that we were "above ground" and had announced to the world that we were free. On the first occasion that we were taken to the beach at Dar, the three of us could not stop ourselves laughing as we bathed together. The scene of us floating on our backs in the tepid tropical water with tall palms hanging over the beach was suddenly too incongruous for belief. Less than four weeks earlier we had been languishing behind the high walls of captivity, where we could never have contemplated such a scene. Our uncontrollable guffaws made people on the beach look up, but we were not embarrassed by our appreciation of freedom.

On 8 January, the anniversary of the ANC, the three of us were taken to the Solomon Mahlangu Freedom College (SOMAFCO) at Morogoro. SOMAFCO was set up by the ANC, on land donated by the Tanzanian government and through contributions from all over the world, to provide for the educational needs of refugees from South Africa. For a long time, the enemy's propaganda had maintained that Umkhonto freedom fighters were press-ganged into fighting after being lured out of the country by false promises of higher education. The establishment of the college in 1978 put paid to these lies: the ANC could now provide those who had fled apartheid repression and persecution, and who had joined its ranks, with the means to complete their education. The college provided an academic and technical education of a standard and quality far superior to anything any black person could expect in South Africa. The aim of the college was to provide future cadres for the ANC and go some way towards providing for the educational needs of people who would be the future leaders of a liberated South Africa. It was also a laboratory where people were working out the forms of a democratic education system that would be applied in post-apartheid South Africa.

On the following day Alex left for France, having obtained clearance from the French authorities to arrive in Paris without documents. At the airport to give him a rapturous welcome were his wife, Marie-José, whom he had not seen for seven years, his mother, his seven-year-old son Boris and many friends and well-wishers. When Alex appeared out of the arrivals exit there were tears and cries of joy as Marie-José and Alex's mother clung onto him for several minutes with Boris jumping up and down shouting, "Papa! Papa!" Boris had got to know his papa through his twice-yearly visits to Pretoria Prison with Alex's mother. Marie-José, as mentioned previously, was never allowed to visit Alex.

Stephen was the next to leave, arriving in London on Sunday, 13 January. Since our 1974 trip to Europe, he had possessed dual South African/British nationality but shortly after arriving in Pretoria he had renounced his South African citizenship. This made things easier for him when he tried to leave Tanzania: The United Kingdom High Commission swiftly issued him a temporary permit to enter Britain.

As the only one without a claim to some other friendlier passport, I had the most difficulty obtaining papers to enter Britain. As a temporary measure, I was issued with a travel document by the Tanzanian government in terms of the 1951 Geneva Convention, otherwise known as a "United Nations passport". In effect, I was granted Tanzanian asylum.

Robin in London, through the Anti-Apartheid Movement, put pressure on the British immigration authorities from her end while I harassed the high commission in Dar for a visa. The commission could promise nothing and kept advising me to be patient and wait until they had heard from London. Extra telexes produced no results.

Finally, on Friday 18 January, Robin phoned to tell me that I should forget about the visa and just arrive in London: everything had been sorted out and all I had to do was explain my case to the passport control when I arrived and they would let me in. When I informed the high commission of this, they were horrified and said that I would be entering Britain at my own risk and against their best advice.

Ignoring their "best advice" I took the Sunday (20th) flight to

London, my ticket having been booked for some time in anticipation of a hasty departure. The plane arrived at Heathrow in the late evening. After presenting myself at passport control with no visa and a story that permission had been given for me to arrive without one, I was accompanied to a room behind the control. I explained to the immigration officials the circumstances of my arrival and said that the ANC and the Anti-Apartheid Movement were expecting me. The officials, of course, pleaded ignorance and used the opportunity to go through all my belongings. In my briefcase were the plans of the prison as well as the photographs of the three of us dressed as guerrillas and holding AK rifles. The briefcase was carted off in defiance of my protestations and obviously had its contents carefully perused and copied, as it was only returned two hours later. The contents certainly excited their interest and prompted a long session of heavily loaded questions. I felt as if I was back at Caledon Square being interrogated by the apartheid security police.

After detaining me for several hours while they "checked up" on my story, the officials agreed to see if there was anyone waiting for me. True enough there was and they must have known it all along because those waiting had been making frantic enquiries through the enquiries desk from shortly after the plane had arrived, and an MP had even made an intervention on my behalf. Eventually I was allowed to go, on condition that I reported to the immigration authorities at the airport within two days.

Relieved at overcoming that ordeal, I made my way down to the arrivals exit. As I turned the corner, I saw Robin and Stephen hanging over the railing looking as if they were about to give up hope and go home. But as soon as I appeared, their eyes lit up, flashes started popping and people started cheering. There were quite a number of people standing with them, but as I recognised none of them, I did not know at first that they were waiting for me. I hope those good people have forgiven me for not appearing appreciative of their having waited into the early hours of the morning. I was blinded by happiness and relief at finally winning the long struggle to be free.

Chapter Nineteen

Consequences

The escape had profound consequences for many people: for our comrades who stayed behind it meant three years of unhappy confinement in the condemned section of Pretoria Central; for political prisoners in other jails around South Africa it served as an inspiration and a boost to morale; for a prominent member of the ANC it meant an international kidnapping; for Sergeant Vermeulen it meant a five-month-long trial to prove his innocence; for several comrades in South Africa and my brother it meant detention, torture and jail; for our enemy, the apartheid rulers, it meant a terrible embarrassment and defeat; for Alex, Steve and me it meant freedom and the chance to throw ourselves back into the struggle against apartheid.

Our comrades who stayed behind were moved out of Pretoria Prison in March 1980 and transferred to "Beverly Hills", the colloquial name for the ultra-maximum security, condemned section in the Pretoria Central complex. There they remained for nearly three years while Pretoria Prison was refurbished and its security enhanced. They were moved back in November 1982, after more than half a million rand had been spent on upgrading the security arrangements.

The old prison was barely recognisable. What had been the *pos* was turned into the administrative offices and what had been the administrative offices were cells. The yard was completely concreted over and divided into four separate areas. In the middle was a sentry post and running to it were four passages like a giant cross that gave access to the four yards. The cells were fitted out with new furniture and the beds were turned around so that the warders could see the prisoners' heads. The passage windows were covered over with sheet metal, which had a flap through which warders could converse with prisoners if necessary. The outer doors (the number two doors) had a solid glass panel that enabled the warders to see inside. There was no way that a prisoner could use a key crank to open his outer door.

Everywhere electrically operated doors had been installed, and they were controlled from a central console. The passages were equipped with closed circuit television cameras, and metal detectors and X-ray machines were fitted for screening visitors and their belongings. Worst of all, the comrades were divided into groups – new arrivals and old lags – and right-wing "political prisoners" formerly housed at Central were moved into another section of the prison.

Escaping was made much more difficult – but not, I believe, impossible. Expensive security equipment is only as good as those who operate it; and it gives a false sense of security to those who rely on it. Doubtless, the warders who first operated it did so with much enthusiasm, like children with a new toy. As months and years go past, operating equipment becomes routine and a chore; warders get bored looking at the TV monitors, everything operates smoothly and vigilance slips. Meanwhile, the prisoners are – or should be – looking for cracks in the system. Eventually, they learn how it operates, how they can operate it, how they can sabotage it, how they can beat it...

Political prisoners on Robben Island and in other prisons were elated by the news that a group of fellow political prisoners had eluded the enemy and made it to freedom. When the Robben Island prisoners first heard of the escape it was in the form of a rumour. Later, when it was confirmed, the victory was celebrated with toasts all around. Security measures on the island and in other prisons housing political prisoners were stepped up with extra locks and chains placed on the doors. These only served to heighten morale and confirm that the prison authorities were shaken by the fact that they had been outwitted.

On 12 December 1979, the day the escape was discovered, the Director of Internal Propaganda in the ANC's Department of Information and Publicity in Lusaka, Zinjiva Nkondo (Victor Matlou), was kidnapped as he was entering Lesotho. South African police seized him when his scheduled Lesotho Airways flight from Maputo to Maseru was forced to land at Bloemfontein due to engine trouble. He was arrested at the Ladybrand border post while he and the other passengers were being taken to Maseru by bus, and held in Bloemfontein under the Terrorism Act.

The timing of the incident more than suggested that it was a desperate attempt by the regime to show the ANC that if some of its members managed to get away, others would be seized in retaliation. Perhaps they were also thinking that they could exchange him, as an ANC "big-fry", for the three of us "small-fry".

The ANC condemned this act of piracy, and in a statement said: "if Pretoria is allowed to get away with this unprecedented violation of international law, no air traveller in Southern Africa will be safe". The case was taken up with the United Nations and the Organisation of African Unity (OAU) and a Supreme Court action was brought against the Minister of Police by Nkondo's brother, on the grounds that the detention infringed the territorial integrity of Lesotho. The application was dismissed with costs in March 1980 but in May charges were dropped by the state and Nkondo was escorted to the Lesotho border by South African police and released. While in detention he was regularly threatened with violence and subjected to long sessions of interrogation.

Sergeant Vermeulen appeared in court for the first time on 5 May. He pleaded not guilty to the charges of "aiding terrorists" or alternatively, aiding three people to escape from the maximum-security wing of Pretoria Prison.

Vermeulen shocked the court by telling how he was forced to make a statement that he had assisted the three of us to escape. After his arrest, high-ranking security policemen interrogated him at the prison for several hours. He was then taken to Pretoria Central Police Station where he was shut in a room with two policemen. They took off their jackets, loosened their ties and said: "We don't care if you're 57 or 87 we'll beat you up till you talk." Under this and other pressures, Vermeulen agreed to make a "confession" to a magistrate. He said that during his time as a warder he had seen many awaiting-trial prisoners with bloodied faces and been told by them that they had been beaten by the police.

His "confession" was brilliant. Despite having to suck it out of his thumb on the spur of the moment, it was so realistic that it took his defence team five months to prove that it could not have been possible. It seems that he must have been sitting alone at night for 11 years thinking how he would escape if he were a prisoner. Or did he perhaps have some help from the security police?

In short, Vermeulen wrote in his statement that Alex had approached him a number of times to assist in an escape attempt. At first he had refused, but finally agreed when he was offered R200. The conspirators agreed on a place to leave the money for him to collect. On the night of 11 December, a Sergeant Joubert had brought two awaiting-trial prisoners to the prison at 6.10 pm entering through the yard gate as usual and going to the window of Vermeulen's office. He, Vermeulen, was given a bunch of keys to open the key cupboard. He took out the section keys and quickly went up to the first floor to let us out of our cells.

Back on the ground floor, he had made us stand out of view of Sergeant Joubert and the awaiting-trial prisoners while he took them to the top floor where he locked them up. After letting Sergeant Joubert out into the yard, he went back to his office where the three of us were waiting.

Sergeant Vermeulen then opened all the other grilles and doors on the way to the front door. He had opened the electrically operated door by pressing the button in his office. After opening door nine he had said to us that there was one more wooden door ahead that we had to break open ourselves as he was scared that the guard on the *pos* would see him. He then went back to his office, locked the section key in the key cupboard and gave the bunch of keys containing the key to the cupboard back to Sergeant Joubert through his window. Needless to say, he never received the R200!

The prison high-ups must have known all along that this was a fictitious story, but failed to say so and provided Vermeulen's attorney with so little information about the layout of the prison and the security arrangements that it was almost impossible for the defence to prove its case. Clearly, the prison authorities wanted a scapegoat and hoped that Vermeulen would not be able to deny his statement. They certainly weren't going to help him do so.

Many of the warders gave evidence in the trial. Some extraordinary tales came out that showed a severe lack of security and discipline, quite at variance with the image of themselves that they usually tried to put across. A Sergeant Badenhorst, who took over duty from Vermeulen on the night of the escape, explained that he arrived at the prison just before midnight. He noticed that the outside light at the front door was off and went to switch it on. When he did so he noticed that the door was slightly ajar. He opened it and saw that the electrically operated door was also open. Surprised, he went down the passage and shouted to Vermeulen through door six. Vermeulen replied that everything was in order. Badenhorst then checked the visitor's waiting room, the toilet and the captain's office and found nothing amiss.

He went to a Sergeant Joubert in the "non-white" section and told him about the open doors and then made his way into the prison in the usual way through the yard. When Vermeulen opened the door to let him in, Badenhorst asked again if everything was all right and Vermeulen again said yes.

After Vermeulen had gone off duty, Badenhorst, still suspicious, checked all the cells. He saw a "body" in each which satisfied him that everybody was there. The dummies had done their job! He repeated his checks throughout the night, in the normal way. At five thirty in the morning he switched on the lights to wake the prisoners.

At 5.45 am the first of the day staff, a warder named Van der Merwe, came on duty and was given the keys to enter through the front door of the prison. He noticed that the locking plate of the front door was bent back but did not question it. It was only when a Sergeant Pieterse arrived at 6.45 am that questions began to be asked. Van der Merwe said he had assumed that locksmiths had worked on the door the day before and had not finished the job.

After rechecking the door, the warders were able to see that it had been broken open. Suspecting something wrong, the bell was rung for the prisoners to stand to attention in front of their grilles (this was not actually true, as we found out later that the cells were opened at the normal time).

At cell 17, my cell, there was no one standing to attention. Badenhorst opened the grille and saw that what appeared to be me was still sleeping. He pulled back the blankets and found that a dummy had been placed in the bed.

Sergeant Joubert explained to the court why he had not acted on the report that the front door had been found open: he had understood Sergeant Badenhorst to mean by a damaged door not one that had been broken open but one that was faulty. He said that it sometimes happened that workmen did not manage to finish repairs to locks in time each day and left the job incomplete. Sergeant Badenhorst had told him that he had re-closed the electrically operated door and that no people could enter the prison.

The defence attorney, Ike Swartzberg, revealed after this that Joubert had told Badenhorst not to enter the damages to the front door in the night-book but to report them the next day. The open door was also not reported to the street guards. After revealing these and other irregularities, the quality of evidence declined as witness after witness tried to cover up for their slackness and incompetence.

A warder named Beukes told how certain tools were missing from Alex's tool chest after the escape, but that it would have taken ingenuity to smuggle them out as we were searched every day as we left the workshop! This same warder was the one who was on duty when the bottle of spare keys was dug up in the yard. He could not say if Alex had made the keys, as Alex was "not a good carpenter".

Locksmiths testifying could not decide whether the electrically operated grille would remain unlocked after the release button was pressed or only so long as it was being pressed. One claimed that the electrically operated door was damaged after the escape, only to be contradicted by another that it was not. One of these "experts" lied to the court that each of the cell doors was locked with a different key (only half of the cells used two different keys, as explained earlier). It was also claimed that the locks in the prison were 20 years old and worn out. They could consequently easily be "blocked" by stuffing paper in the bolt hole. To prove this claim a (faulty) lock was produced as evidence of how we could have got out. When the defence lawyer was told to hold his finger on the bolt, the key was turned four times and the lock clicked as if it were locking, but the bolt only moved slightly and fell back into the lock. If it was not Vermeulen then it was the fault of the locks. No credit was given to the ingenuity of the escapees.

Halfway through the trial, Stephen received a letter from

Vermeulen's attorney asking him to make a statement on Vermeulen's behalf. The letter was sent to Stephen because he had written to a South African newspaper to explain that Vermeulen was innocent and that the prison authorities were using him as a scapegoat for the failure of the prison's security arrangements. Alex and I were not pleased that Stephen had written the letter and were therefore keen that he should ignore the appeal from the attorney – it would not look good for a former political prisoner to be defending an apartheid jailer. As a compromise, Stephen sent a short sworn declaration stating no more than that Vermeulen was innocent of the alleged offence of helping us escape.

The trial dragged on for five months with Vermeulen eventually being acquitted. Stephen's letter was one of the factors that contributed to this, but it was mainly due to the many inconsistencies between the facts of the escape and the claims in Vermeulen's "confession". Although Vermeulen had claimed that he had not unlocked the front door with his keys because he feared being seen by the *pos*-warder, he could have done so as no one would actually have seen him doing it: he could simply have asked us not to open the door until he was out of sight. The damaged front door with its bolt still protruding proved that he did not unlock the door and that he had just adapted his story to fit this fact. Also, the wooden keys that were found were shown to be perfect replicas of the prison's keys and to be able to open the doors for which they were made. The prisoners would not have gone to all the trouble of making replica keys and removing tools from the workshop if the plan involved Vermeulen doing all the unlocking. Vermeulen's attorney was also able to prove, by timing exactly what Vermeulen claimed he had done in his statement, that it would have been impossible to release us in the short time it was alleged that he did.

The defence accused the chief investigating officer of withholding vital information that could have been used to show that Vermeulen's statement would not have been accepted by the court. It further claimed that the state had not proved its case and that the evidence had been contradictory. Vermeulen had not been told his rights when pressure had been put on him to write his statement and he had done so under duress.

In an interview after the trial, Vermeulen spoke of his "twenty-six days of hell in a prison cell". Before he was granted bail, he spent 26 days in the very same prison he had guarded for 11 years. For the first time in those 11 years he was forced to consider what it was actually like to be on the other side of the doors that he locked and guarded nightly.

"I thought I was going to be in jail for life. I don't know how those men stand it. They are disciplined, strong men. The cells were so small. I thought I was going mad," he confessed. He admitted that he had never wondered how the men he guarded coped with their lives. Now he had come to admire the way they conducted themselves. "They were still so strong and disciplined after all those years. They must lead a hell's life." Vermeulen referred to the political prisoners as "the communists".

"The communists are very clever people. I was surprised when they told me three of them had escaped. I felt as though a bucket of water had been thrown on me. I couldn't work out how they had done it," he said.

His experiences of the previous 10 months, starting on 12 December 1979 when he was awakened at his home and told of the escape, had convinced him that he never wanted to see a prison again. He had decided to retire early.

Vermeulen added that he was grateful for the letter written by Stephen to his attorney confirming that he had not helped in the escape. He then spoke to the interviewer about the three of us: "Moumbaris never used to say good morning or talk to us warders. He was also a tense man. Jenkin and Lee were much nicer. I remember how fit those three were. They used to train every morning for half an hour, running around the courtyard. Maybe they were training for their escape." The nicest prisoner he had guarded in the prison was Bram Fischer, a former central committee member of the South African Communist Party, who died in prison in 1975 while serving a life sentence. "Fischer was very keen on rugby. We used to talk about it a lot. I felt sorry when he died. He was a gentleman. He was the leader of the prisoners. When he died, Denis Goldberg took over as leader. He took over everything. He even spoke to me about rugby like Fischer did. He was a much quieter man, though very polite," he recalled.

Despite having formed a distant relationship with Fischer and Goldberg and despite admiring them for their self-discipline and ability to withstand "a hell's life", he could not be like them: "They are communists who want to destroy South Africa." Relief at being acquitted had wiped out any bitterness he had felt for the police: "I forgive everyone for everything, because I am a free man now."

At the end of 1981, in the wake of a mass upsurge of resistance to apartheid, South Africa was faced with a severe wave of repression and a great number of people were detained. Among those detained was Prema Naidoo, one of the people who had helped Stephen hide and flee from the country after the escape. Prema, a great-grandson of Mahatma Gandhi and a member of the famous Naidoo family – one of the most persecuted families in the history of South Africa – was detained in connection with the part he had played in the successful anti-South African Indian Council campaign. This was to discourage people from voting for the segregated political structure created for South African Indians by the regime. Prema was very badly tortured and given "truth drugs", which unfortunately made him divulge some information regarding his part in assisting Stephen.

As a consequence, six more people were detained between 5 and 8 January 1982 in connection with the escape. These were: Esther Levitan, a member of the Black Sash (a women's anti-apartheid organisation); Shirish Nanabhai, a former political prisoner and friend of Stephen's; my brother Michael; his common-law wife, Cathy Hunter; my former girlfriend, Daphne Smith, again; and Stephen's former boss at the University of the Witwatersrand, Ralph Wortley.

The detentions at first appeared to be connected with the detention of Stephen Kitson, the son of Dave Kitson, who was arrested shortly before for making a sketch of Pretoria Prison after visiting his father. Stephen (Lee) had never revealed who had assisted him in his flight, but as soon as my brother was detained it was obvious what was happening. Michael had only helped Stephen in a small way by providing money and taking him to a hotel that first night. The cops were not to know this, of course, and subjected him to most brutal tortures to find out who else had assisted and what else he knew about the escape (i.e. who had helped Alex and me). He was subjected to electric shocks while blindfolded and handcuffed but when they failed to extract anything more than the little he knew, they gave up.

Shirish was similarly tortured, but the others not. Daphne and

Kathy were released nine days later; Esther was admitted to hospital for a respiratory complaint but released on 4 March together with Ralph.

Michael, Prema and Shirish appeared in court on 5 March and were charged under the Prisons Act with assisting a prisoner to escape. Their appearance under the Prisons Act came as a relief as it had at first appeared that the three were to be tried under the Terrorism Act that had a statutory minimum sentence of five years' imprisonment. They were not asked to plead and only Michael was granted bail – no doubt because his skin was the "correct" colour.

The three were sentenced on 1 April to three years' imprisonment, with two years suspended for three years – an effective one-year sentence – for "harbouring a prisoner after escaping". Prema shouted "Amandla!" on hearing his sentence and there was a scuffle with an orderly who attempted to shove him down the stairs to the cells below. The court found that Michael and Shirish had been moved to assist Stephen because they were close friends, while Prema had assisted because he was a friend of Shirish.

The state had called for long sentences in order to deter others from harbouring or concealing escaped prisoners. The defence had appealed for suspended sentences as Stephen had escaped without the knowledge and assistance of the accused who had found themselves in a unique situation which was never likely to occur again. It was impossible for them to refuse assistance to a friend who just appeared on their doorstep.

Michael served six months and was then granted parole. The other two, in a separate prison of course, served the full period. Doubtless this discriminatory treatment was because they were black, but also because of their previous convictions.

For the apartheid authorities, the escape was an event of utter embarrassment and defeat. This was reflected in the way they responded after the discovery that three prisoners had gone missing. The first thing they did was to surround the prison with a ring of police. What this was meant to achieve after the birds had flown is not certain – more than likely it was a panic response. Very shortly afterwards, our descriptions were broadcast over the radio and our pictures shown on television and published in all the major newspapers. Luckily for us, these were not very detailed or accurate: "All three are about 1.8 metres tall [wrong], clean shaven, and have [relatively] short hair. Lee is strongly built while Moumbaris and Jenkin are thin [only me]. Moumbaris has black hair, Lee's is reddish and Jenkin's light." Best of all, the descriptions said that we were dressed in T-shirts, blue prison shorts and tennis shoes. This obviously put many people off the scent because reports came in from all over the country from people who claimed to have seen us jogging around. Police launched a "large-scale search" for Alex in Cape Town, of all places, after receiving a report that he had been seen parking a car in the city.

It was reported that the escape provoked one of the largest manhunts ever mounted in the country. Roadblocks were set up all over South Africa and all cars crossing borders were searched at border posts. At one stage, the queue of cars on the South African side of the Oshoek border post (into Swaziland) stretched for more than 2 km. Railway stations and airports were watched and helicopters used to observe sections of the border known to be favoured by fugitives.

Speculation, rumours and false alarms were rife. After a few days, "informed sources" reported variously that we had been seen in Swaziland, Botswana, Mozambique, Zambia and Lesotho. These reports were only to be denied by the respective governments of those countries. Other reports "confirmed" that we were still in South Africa waiting for the fuss to die down before crossing the border. There is no doubt that false reports emanating from internal supporters, the ANC office in London and from Marie-José in Paris served to lay a false trail. After a week when the police had more or less given up hope of finding us, they issued an appeal to the public to help them in their bid to net the three convicts still on the loose: the public was requested to report to their local police stations should they see any of us.

Reports appeared about secret "underground pipelines" and "escape networks". Then followed the stories of Joe Slovo's and the KGB's assistance, which in turn were followed by more sober "theories" of how we had done it. Obviously, the question got asked why we did not free all the other prisoners. The Deputy Commissioner of Prisons saw no reason why we could not have opened the cells of the other prisoners in the same section. We could see no reason either.

Freedom for each of us meant much more than just a release from captivity. Within 10 days of my arrival in London, Robin and I were married – "Daughter's marriage to a terrorist came out of the blue", reported one South African newspaper on Robin's father's response. Two years later, Alex became the father of a daughter, Zoë, who was born – believe it or not – on 11 December, the second anniversary of our escape. All three of us were welcomed back into the ranks of the ANC and in our different ways, continued to play a part in the liberation struggle.

By freeing ourselves we drastically reduced our sentences: Alex's by five and a half years; Stephen's by six and a half years; mine by ten and a half years. Best of all, we emancipated ourselves and didn't have to wait for the indignity of being released by our jailers. We did not rely on the apartheid courts; we did not wait for remission and we did not wait for our sentences to run their course. Terminating our sentences was all our own work, which was much more satisfying than our jailers doing it! The time saved meant that we could throw ourselves back into the struggle against apartheid sooner and with more conviction than our captors had hoped.

The escape was also an act of defiance against the apartheid regime and their so-called legal system: a pair of raised fingers to their "laws", their prosecutors and their "judges". We never accepted their judgments and sentences – nor their prisons – and escaping was the best way of telling them so.

In a way, our escape symbolised the plight of black South Africans living under apartheid and their liberation therefrom. They were prisoners in their own country under a monstrously evil system. In the same way that we did not wait to be released by our captors, they did not wait to be "liberated" by the apartheid rulers. They did it themselves and in a way they deemed best. The "reforms" offered by the regime were not the keys to the front door; they were merely enhanced "privileges" – an upgrade from D Group to C Group. The people were not impressed with these reforms because, like all prisoners, they wanted nothing less than complete freedom. They made their own "keys" and got out in their own way.

For the opponents of apartheid, the struggle continued until the doors of all apartheid political prisons were flung open in 1990 and those living in exile returned. In our small way, we proved that the apartheid regime was not invincible. With will and determination, we demonstrated that its supposedly impenetrable security barriers could be breached.

Epilogue

As I worked through earlier manuscripts of this book, bringing it up to date for this new edition, it was difficult to believe that I was one of the characters in the story. It read so much like a novel that I found it hard to believe that it was a true story. I even experienced some of the emotions that many readers had reported to me on reading the book: feeling scared for the prisoners, not believing they would have the temerity to do what they did, wondering how they coped with the fear and tension, and being amazed by their patience, perseverance and attention to detail. I suppose it is the passing years, all the events in between, and where we are now that makes it difficult to believe the things we had to do in those days.

For years after the escape, I had nightmares about being back in prison, a new prison that was impossible to break out of. But now it is all a distant memory and from the perspective of the present day it is almost unbelievable that we were given such harsh sentences for what amounted to not much more than distributing some leaflets. These days anyone can say just about anything they like, and with modern electronic media there is no need to go to extremes to get alternative messages across.

I look back at the years we were active and realise how naïve we were. In fact, it is amazing that we lasted for two and a half years as an underground cell. Afterwards, we spent a lot of time reflecting on our mistakes, but it was time well spent as we were able to pass on our valuable experience to others and advance the body of knowledge relating to underground work in apartheid South Africa.

A lot of water has passed under the bridge since 1980, when the escape adventure ended. But that water swept us with it, and for all three of us our lives today are what they are because of the escape. For all of us the escape meant the start of new lives and coming to terms with our new realities.

But before going on to describe what happened to each of us, I would like to go back to the day after the escape, 12 December 1979. Denis Goldberg wrote in the German edition of my book, *Und Fur Uns Die Freiheit*, published in 2002, the following description of the discovery of the escape and the consequences for the remaining prisoners:

> *The escape was discovered by Sergeant Badenhorst when he unlocked our cells the next morning. Every day the heavy steel doors were opened and we were still locked up behind the second doors, the steel grille in each cell. Badenhorst had come in through the street door with the broken lock but had not noticed anything suspicious.*
>
> *He opened the first door. Tim was still lying in bed. He opened the second door and Stephen Lee was also still in bed. I was third in line and I was at attention, all innocent, standing to attention behind my grille.*
>
> *Badenhorst, turning back, saw that the first two had not got up. Suddenly he realised there were dummies in their beds.*
>
> *I watched him the whole time. He turned chalk white and staggered back against the passage wall. I thought he had fainted or had a heart attack. After a moment he pulled himself upright and called for his superior. From the fright his voice came out as a weak little whisper. "Oom (uncle) Piet. Oom Piet." Now he stumbled to the stairs and I could hear him going down.*
>
> *Prison officer Pieterse, in reality a friendly type who seldom lost his nerve, came up the stairs, saw the damage and then briskly opened all the cells to see if there were others missing. I thought I saw him give me a small smile.*
>
> *Alex, much further down the passage, had also*

escaped.

We were told to "carry on as usual" and even got breakfast before the inquiries began. When I was asked about the escape, I naturally knew nothing. I had played my guitar and I had listened to the nightly concert of recorded music. Helen Suzman MP had got us the equipment for this wonderful entertainment. We were allowed to buy a limited number of records that the night warder played for us according to our choices for about three hours every evening. Then I had called Vermeulen because the lights had gone out. Nothing unusual had happened. I did not think it necessary to add that Alex had passed my cell and waved goodbye, the signal for me to give the three time to hide in the cupboard after they had tripped the light switches, before I called Vermeulen.

The Security Police put David Rabkin and Tony Holiday through the wringer. What they thought they would get from them remains a mystery.

Many high-ranking Security officers came to the prison. Each first made sure that I was indeed still there and seemed to become much calmer when they had seen me.

Perhaps the long-planned and authorised visit of David's father from England had something to do with sparing us the worst responses from the authorities. Because of the unusual circumstances, Rabkin senior – now a British businessman – was able to meet with General le Roux, the second highest officer in the Prison Service. He ended their conversation with the remark, "In business there are gains and losses and you cannot win every time. I hope that the prisoners remaining behind will not be punished for the escape." Probably because the authorities were always on the lookout to protect themselves against international criticism, our treatment and the interrogations were more moderate than we expected.

... In March 1980 we were removed to another prison in the same complex while our prison was rebuilt with

much higher technical security measures.

Our new accommodation was in a prison known ironically to prisoners as Beverly Hills because it was up on a hill. It was the most awful place in the whole complex of prisons that held about eight thousand prisoners. There were large sections for black and for white criminal prisoners. A women's prison, a prison for those held for investigation and a prison for those charged with prison offences and awaiting trial. Beverly Hills was for the most serious offenders in the whole of South Africa. It was a punishment prison for those who committed prison offences. In addition it was the hanging prison for all of South Africa because under apartheid the death sentence was often imposed. Only now has it been done away with. Every week there were hangings with about one hundred and fifty people being executed every year.

Beverly Hills is composed of a number of terraced blocks. Our section was directly below the gallows block. That was a terrible psychological torture.

Our community life was sharply curtailed. Each of us was in a single cell. Above us there was a steel grille over which the guards, armed with loaded rifles, patrolled up and down. One heard every step all night long.

The windows, totally covered with grilles, were our only source of ventilation, but they were opened only when the warders wanted to look down into our cells to observe us. In the winter, freezing cold air would pour down into our already cold concrete boxes. In summer time the cells were hot with no fresh air and it was even more uncomfortable as the sweat poured off your body even when you were sitting dressed only in your underpants. We were there for two years and eight months until November 1982.

... In Beverly Hills, after the escape, there was no possibility of sports activity. We had a daily exercise period in the small courtyard on a cement surface. My health suffered. To that was added the psychological

stress of being right next to, almost under, the gallows that we heard during the testing and then again when prisoners were executed. We heard when the bodies were removed and the cleaning gang moved in to scrub the floors.

That was a trauma that stays with me to this day, but usually it wakes me in the small hours of the morning. It is an experience that one never forgets.

... When we returned to our prison after nearly three years it had been greatly altered. Our courtyard was concreted from wall to wall. There was no earth in which we might have planted a garden. Tim's spare keys had been found in the garden after the escape, but only after it had been dug up three times over. They had taken away any possibility of burying things in the earth. Our carpentry workshop had been removed. When I protested about this to Brigadier Gericke he asked without hostility, "What do you need a workshop for? Do you want to make more keys?" Work for our group of political prisoners had come to an end.

The windows from our cells onto the passage had been sealed closed with solid steel shutters that could not be opened. But the windows to the outside with their multiple openings less than the size of one's head were still there. I would stand there for hours to feel the wind and to breathe the fresh air. When it rained I would put my hand out to catch the raindrops and rub them over my face. I hadn't felt the rain or even seen much of it for nearly three years.

The time in Beverly Hills had taken its toll on our health. I was quite strongly built but now my body was weakened. My muscles were soft and my skin was slack. Not only had my back given me constant pain but my feet and legs too. My injured knee became swollen again. In the small, hard courtyard there was no real possibility for exercise. To run a kilometre took between 12 and 14 rounds, so small had they made it. The previously open space had been divided into four with a guard post in the middle. Now they could divide us into even smaller groups, each with its own courtyard.

The window was the only pleasure. I laid wet paper on the window sill and spread apple pips on it. Warders gave me uncooked maize kernels and I sowed them too. Sometimes I got some dried beans. I had my little green island about ten centimetres by ten centimetres. But of course every little plant grew until the few pairs of leaves used up all the nutrition in the seed and then died.

I read this many years later and it affected the way I had felt about our fellow prisoners who stayed behind. We caused them a lot of suffering by being responsible for their three-year stint in Beverly Hills, and for bringing about the destruction of everything they had worked so hard to create at the original Pretoria Prison.

We came to hear of their plight much earlier, from released prisoners who passed through London. For many years I felt nothing, arguing that they had been given a chance to get out of the prison but had decided to stay, and therefore whatever befell them was the result of their own wrong decision-making.

When we got out of prison, we were angry, very angry, not only with the apartheid state for criminalising our activities and caging us like wild animals, but with our comrades for failing to accept the challenge. We realised after getting away that we could easily have cleared out the entire prison. The escape wouldn't have been so clean but it would have made an impact of immense proportions. Just imagine what the headlines would have said the next day: "Pretoria Prison Cleared Out", "All White Political Prisoners on the Run", "Nationwide Manhunt for Ten White Political Prisoners".

As the years went by, and especially after I read Denis's account of their time at Beverly Hills, I began to feel sympathy for what our comrades went through – though none of them ever expressed any anger towards us for causing them so much suffering. I think, in a way, they all realised that what we achieved was a major victory over the apartheid regime and they could not condemn that because of their personal choices and suffering.

As I mentioned in the last chapter of this book, Robin and I were married within a week of my arrival in London in January 1980. This marriage never worked out and, looking back, I have never counted it as a proper marriage. The problems started the moment I arrived in the UK. I was given just two weeks to sort out my papers, and as the papers could not be sorted out from inside the country, I had to leave and apply for refugee status from abroad. The ANC sent me on an extended speaking tour of Canada, where I travelled the length and breadth of the country explaining how we managed to escape and defeat the apartheid security apparatus. I made countless radio and television appearances and talked to anti-apartheid groups all over the country. I was amazed at how much sympathy there was for the anti-apartheid struggle and at how much people knew about what was going on in South Africa.

My papers were sorted out after about three months and I returned to the UK, where I was met by Robin who had understandably gone cold.

Almost immediately, the ANC decided to send Steve and me off to Angola for military training. We arrived in Luanda and were dumped in a hotel for several weeks while arrangements were made for us to travel to one of the ANC training camps up north. The conditions in Luanda were terrible as the country was in a state of devastation due to the war being waged by Jonas Savimbi's Unita and its South African backers.

The hotel dining room had no menu, as the only food they had to serve was rice and sardines. There were no vegetables or fresh fruit. In fact, there was not even fresh water to drink at mealtimes. Instead, they offered us beer. Before that, I could not stand the taste of the beverage but after a few weeks in Luanda I became quite partial towards the local *Cuca* beer. To this day, I find it hard to understand how there was water for the brewery but none for the people to drink!

The months in the ANC training camp were among the toughest I had ever experienced. The conditions were absolutely appalling and it is no wonder that there were mutinies in some of the camps around that time. We slept in underground bunkers that had fewer beds than people. This was deliberate, as some people had to be on guard duty while the others slept. When your stint was over, you had to wake the next batch in order to find yourself a bed. It was a bit like musical chairs.

The nature of the training left us feeling rather disturbed, as it was training for rural guerrilla warfare. As we well knew, ours was not a rural guerrilla struggle. It was not even an urban guerrilla struggle. It required people being trained in underground work so that they could operate secretly in an urban environment. The training we were given was completely off the mark, we felt, though it certainly did toughen us up and provided us with knowledge of how militaries work and what our fellow comrades were going through.

After our time in the bush, the comrades – including Stephen – were sent off to East Germany (GDR) for further training in military combat work. I requested to be sent back to London as my nerves were feeling somewhat frayed after the experiences of the previous months.

I got back to London and found that Robin didn't really want to know me anymore. I felt as if the bottom had fallen out of my world and spent a few months in a tranquilised daze. Repeated visits to drug-pushing doctors did me no good and I succumbed to the most debilitating depression. Within months Robin and I were divorced. It was a marriage that never happened.

Towards the end of 1980 I started working for the International Defence and Aid Fund in north London. The job was in the research department and my work consisted of categorising newspaper articles relating to the political situation unfolding in South Africa. I was also required to write for a monthly publication, and later engaged in research for various books that were being produced by IDAF. If it were not for the tasks given to me by the ANC, I would surely have become depoliticised, for the work became so routine I felt as if I could have been working in a bank.

During the mid-80s, I trained many activists in the methods and tasks of underground work. These were people who had left South Africa, as Stephen and I had done in the 1970s, in order to "do something for the struggle". Most of them were white South Africans who wanted to get seriously involved in the struggle against apartheid. Like us, they had come to the conclusion that to do anything meaningful it had to be done in the name of the ANC.

In 1987 I left IDAF and began to work full time for the ANC. It was lonely and poorly paid work, but once again I was doing something that was meaningful. Activists were leaving South Africa in droves as the political situation heated up. Many came to London to make contact with the ANC, and my job was to train them in underground work and set up and maintain communication channels.

My own underground experiences in the 1970s served me well. Over several years, the few of us doing this training in London developed a very thorough course for trainees. This went way beyond anything that Stephen and I had received during our training in 1974. I am proud to say that none of my students got arrested. So if nothing else, getting arrested and passing through the apartheid "justice" and "penal" systems was a valuable experience that helped me advise others how to avoid detection and evade capture by the apartheid security forces.

In 1988 I was drawn into Operation Vula, a project to secretly infiltrate leadership figures back into South Africa in order to build up the underground structures. This project, directly under the president of the ANC, was the most prestigious, spectacular and successful underground operation ever carried out by the ANC. Instead of going into detail here, I will ask you to read my article titled "Talking to Vula", available from the O'Malley Archives at https://omalley.nelsonmandela.org/omalley/ and other places. There is also a documentary about the project called *The Vula Connection* that is currently available on YouTube.

In 1991 I was granted indemnity for escaping from prison, by the then State President FW de Klerk. This was published in *Government Gazette* No. 13379 of 26 June 1991. This included "a remission of sentence in respect of the unserved portion of [my] sentence of 12 years' imprisonment". That opened the way for my return to South Africa in August of that year, where I took up the job of chief communications officer in the new ANC headquarters in Johannesburg.

I returned to South Africa with my partner of eight years, Sarah, who was carrying our first child, Jamie. He was created in London, in celebration of the tumultuous events of those times, and born in Johannesburg.

I worked at ANC HQ in Johannesburg from September 1991 until the end of 1994, and in that time managed to bring the organisation to the forefront of the electronic communications revolution that was beginning to unfold. Using regular dial-up modems and bulletin board software, I connected electronically most of the ANC local offices to ANC HQ in Johannesburg, long before the World Wide Web came alive. The network was used to distribute a daily news briefing, and prior to the 1994 election it was used to distribute daily briefings to party election campaigners.

After the ANC victory in the first democratic elections in 1994, I was sent to Cape Town to set up a research and electronic information unit at the ANC's new sub-headquarters building. This was meant to service the needs of the new ANC members in parliament. In 1995 we launched the ANC website, which was one of the very first websites in South Africa and certainly the first political site in the country. The site grew into an enormous resource of documents relating to the struggle against apartheid and was hailed as one of the best political party websites anywhere.

In 1996 my second son, Aran, was born – curiously on 2 March, the anniversary of Stephen's and my arrest in 1978. Prior to the birth of my sons I had not the slightest interest in children or the institution of the family. Now, I feel that having children is the greatest thing I ever did. I may still be in for a shock as they move deeper into adulthood, but the joy they brought surpasses anything else that happened in my life, including emerging unassisted from the front door of a prison!

In 1997 the ANC decided to close down its sub-headquarters in Cape Town because it never got used and was costing a lot to maintain. Members of Parliament never used the offices assigned to them in the building because they had perfectly good ones in Parliament just down the road. The entire office block turned out to be a white elephant.

The ANC offered us retrenchment packages but the three of us who were in charge there decided instead to form our own company, take over the equipment and continue providing the very same services to the ANC. The ANC agreed to this and we carried on as if there had been no change. The experience we had gained in developing the ANC website proved to be valuable, as we were able to offer our services to Parliament and a number of government departments, which at that time had no electronic media departments. All three of us, coming from political backgrounds, had not the slightest idea how to run a business, but from a shaky beginning we managed to develop Unwembi Communications into a relatively successful company, employing on average 15 people in the field of electronic media. In 2013 I sold my half-share in the company, and resigned the following year after passing on my knowledge about the workings of the company.

I stopped being politically active during this time, in the sense of doing things for the ANC or any other political organisations. I wasn't made for conventional politics. The underground struggle was one thing, but the moment they said we had to come out from hiding it was all up for me. I am a doer, not a meetings person. Conventional politics seemed to be all about meetings and talking, and getting others to carry out your decisions. That was not for me.

Not being politically active does not mean that I stopped being concerned about the things that had always concerned me. In a sense I became more active, but not in the pointless activity of promoting one political organisation over others. Politics, as I now perceive it, is a form of entertainment, a reality show that serves to distract our attention from what is really going on, and a means to keep us all divided and hating one another so that our anger and frustrations are misplaced and dispersed.

I am often asked to tell the story of how I managed to escape from prison, and after giving my exposition one of the questions people regularly ask is: "How do you feel about the ANC today?" During the Zuma-era it was difficult to say anything good about the organisation – now political party – but my normal answer is that the ANC of the liberation struggle was a different entity to the party that bears its name today. The good name of the ANC was hijacked by a gang of thieves, and the current entity that calls itself ANC has little to do with the ANC that I was once proud of serving. I go on to say that I am proud of playing a part in the liberation struggle, for escaping from prison and for devoting many years of my life to the struggle against apartheid. Being involved in the anti-apartheid struggle was a noble act, and that can't be negated by present-day outcomes.

People often ask if I would get involved in underground work again if I found myself in a similar situation. The answer is obviously "yes", though the next time I will make sure that I don't get caught! I still feel strongly about things and remain the kind of person who believes you need to DO something about the things you believe in, not just TALK about them. The prison experience did not mellow me in this respect at all. If anything, it hardened me. There is no need to be afraid of prison if your cause is just and your motives pure. Most people fear prison for the label that it pins on them, but being in prison for unselfish motives and where there are no victims does not do that.

The most valuable personal consequence of the prison experience and escape is that it provided me with a valuable philosophy of life. I have applied this philosophy to the many projects and complex challenges that I have faced since then – including life's challenges – and it has served me well.

It goes something like this: if you are faced with a complex project or challenge, you can't simply sit down at the start and work out the complete solution in your head or by looking inwards. Your starting point is to define your goal, not to work out a detailed plan of how to get there. The plan for reaching your goal evolves along with your practical efforts of attempting to reach it – after you have done a lot of research, testing and practical work to become familiar with your terrain. In other words, solving a complex problem is as much a practical as a theoretical task. A plan is a dynamic, evolving set of guidelines to inform your actions, not something set up at the start and followed blindly.

Trying out your ideas provides experience and feedback that you can then think about and apply to your next round of probing and testing. It is always important to take small steps, and each step should have contingencies that make it reversible if it fails. After each "door" is opened, the new situation needs to be assessed to see what opportunities it provides and how the overall plan needs to be adapted to tackle the next "door". It is only from the perspective of the far side of each "door" that the next step can be planned.

Overcoming obstacles along the way actually changes the situation that existed when you started out. Eventually, as you develop a better understanding of your situation, you can begin to control it. This helps your plan evolve exponentially in scope. The plan must never be rigid, as you will have to adapt it as you learn more and the circumstances change. You must be prepared to improvise in the face of unpredictability, abort if your plan really is not working and adopt another if you have the perseverance. Eventually, you will become so familiar with your terrain that the solutions will present themselves and you will realise that you could never have thought of them at the beginning.

This might all seem obvious, but too often ambitious goals are not pursued or even considered because the way to reach them cannot be seen from the start. In such cases, lesser goals tend to be pursued. If the goal is believed to be achievable, insisting on a fully worked out plan before the start is a serious mistake, and rigidly following such a plan is a recipe for failure. Our experience taught us that you can never know if you can reach your goal without trying, and you cannot arrive at a final solution until you are well on the way there. Reaching your goal is a process, not the result of blindly following a blueprint. Of course, you need initiative, determination, conviction, resourcefulness, perseverance, precision, understanding, patience, attention to detail and faith in yourself. Without these ingredients you are unlikely to get there. Finding the solution to complex problems is a combination of trial and error and strong motivation.

Another lesson learned from the escape experience is that it is always better to take a non-confrontational route. As far as possible, seek ways around obstacles rather than tackling them head on. If you opt to use force it means that you have not understood your obstacles correctly, your planning is defective, you have not worked out satisfactory contingencies or you are seeking shortcuts. Likewise, don't openly announce your goals if they are likely to be challenged by counter forces. Quietly get on with your preparations, keeping below the radar and outside the box. Opponents will only see what they are expecting to see and will not take seriously activities that do not appear to openly challenge the status quo.

The escape has served as a metaphor for all the major projects that I have been involved in since the event. I have applied the lessons learned in reaching the physical front door of our prison to the metaphorical "front doors" of these projects. Opening the front door is not necessarily the most difficult step, because by the time it is reached the plan should be fully developed and the experience of getting there will have provided all the knowledge and skills required to emerge from it. Using force or opting for a non-planned action at the final stage is a big risk, but if at the moment it appears viable then it can be employed. Force should never be part of the main plan. It should be a contingency in case something goes wrong or nothing else works. If force needs to be applied, it should be minimal and not something that causes harm or loss to others. The main thing is never to give up or lose faith in yourself when facing the final obstacle.

The escape has also served as a metaphor for life in general. As we go through life, we somehow get trapped in various "prisons" that we have to work our way out of. Each of life's prisons is like an onion with a number of nested layers. Starting from the inside (your "cell"), you have to penetrate each layer ("the doors") until you reach the outer skin (the "front door"), which has to be peeled off before you can release yourself from that particular prison. Like the onion, the final layer is weak and brittle and removing it can result in some damage, but once through it you are free.

What happened – or rather, didn't happen – in the years following the ANC's 1994 election victory, set off a powerful chain reaction of new thinking that completely overturned my previous world view.

From the moment I became politically aware in the early 1970s, and all the way up to the late 1990s, I, and all those I was associated with in the liberation struggle, believed that what we were fighting for was a new political dispensation. This meant that our struggle was about replacing the apartheid regime with a democratic government. Then, with a people's party in power, we would be able to overcome the legacy of apartheid and create the non-racial utopia that we had all dreamed about for so long.

This was a naïve dream because it focused almost entirely on the political. I believed, like all my compatriots, that the pinnacle of power was the political power. Once you are in charge of the political realm, all else flows from that: you can define economic and social policies and impose them on society. If some don't like what you are doing, that's too bad because their time is up. It's now time for a new, democratic dispensation where everyone is equal.

It was an arrogant point of view as well. Where did we get the right to impose our version of authority – or any authority at all – on South Africans? It couldn't have been given to us by those in whose name we were struggling, as they didn't have it to give. And if they didn't accept it, were we going to force it down their throats? Is all authority ultimately based on violence?

We all believed that "government" was one of the essential components of a civilised society and that there couldn't be a country/nation/society without one. If there was a "bad" government, it had to be replaced with a "good" one. So, like every "government-in-waiting", we would appoint ourselves as its functionaries and then get the masses to endorse us in a "democratic" election.

As the years marched on and I saw no signs of utopia appearing, I realised that our long struggle had been off target. The ANC had gained political power but it did not seem to be in control of where South Africa was heading. It sold out to the IMF and adopted neoliberal economic policies in order to "attract investment". Were these the policies we had fought so long and hard for? Were these really ANC policies or were they imposed on the ANC by hidden powers higher than the political power?

It didn't take long to realise that the real power resided with the economic and financial institutions that actually ruled South Africa all along. These were the giant mining, industrial, agricultural and financial houses that had always ruled South Africa, and they were integrated with the forces of global capitalism that dwarfed our little, dependent government. It came as a shock to realise that, far from being at the top of the power pyramid, political power was a stratum several levels down. The ANC had been tricked into believing that it was really in power, whereas it was actually just relegated the role of enforcing policies decided by those who were still in control of the real power, the money power.

This realisation made me wonder what could be done about it. If our government was subordinate to higher powers that had no territorial base, how could we ever hope to create a better South Africa, let alone a better world? Political apartheid could be stripped off, but economic apartheid would remain in place. Everything seemed hopeless. Government itself was an integral part of this hierarchical power structure and had no incentive to challenge it. It was therefore part of the problem, not the solution. The monster that we should have been taking on was not the pathetic apartheid regime, but the entire edifice called global capitalism. That was a moving, intangible target too big to contemplate, having a moving "front door" too difficult to locate!

The ideological belief system to which I had subscribed during the years of struggle had revolution as its highest goal: a revolution would be staged, using both peaceful and violent methods, and the apartheid regime would be overthrown and replaced with a revolutionary government, guided by a revolutionary party that would act in the name of the oppressed masses. But as I began to understand the hierarchy of power, I saw that a revolution in one country was not going to change much. The monster would bite back and quickly swallow up our shallow, localised "revolution". Apart from that, our prison experience had taught us that to successfully transition from one state of existence to another, the "big bang" approach is one that is very unlikely to succeed. That would be like blasting a hole in our prison wall, alerting the counter forces and inviting them to fight back.

Liberation from the concentration camp staffed by the apartheid regime made it clear that it was just a release from a minor prison located inside a larger one – much like Pretoria Prison was inside the larger Pretoria Central Prison complex. The container prison had more formidable fortifications to prevent anyone escaping from it. In fact, it was difficult to see what freedom would look like on the outside of this prison, or even if it had a front door. Perhaps we were all trapped inside one giant prison with infinite layers of prisons within prisons? Instead of wasting our time trying to escape from one prison only to discover that it was inside another, shouldn't we rather be making our current prison as habitable and comfortable as possible while serving our "life sentences"? Were our prison comrades correct when they suggested that we should rather concentrate on our immediate predicament than on some abstract, elusive "freedom" that is probably just an illusion?

While living in Johannesburg from 1991 to 1994, I discovered an alternative way of doing what money is supposed to do (facilitate exchange). A group calling itself the Yeoville Local Exchange Trading System (LETS) was set up, and I joined out of curiosity. The newly signed-up members compiled a directory of the goods and services they could offer each other. The directory was duplicated so that everyone knew what they could expect from the others. While I sometimes battled to find anything I wanted, I helped a number of people solve their computer problems. When I did something for someone else, instead of the recipient of my services giving me money, they wrote out a cheque in the amount that I would have charged them in rand. I took the cheque down to the local health store where the owner, who was also a member of the LETS, entered the amount into a spreadsheet. At the end of the month he compiled "statements" for the members and posted them to us. Your statement showed all the trades you had been involved in during the month: what you had provided and what you had received. When you had received something, it was recorded as a negative amount and when you had provided something it was recorded as a positive amount. The sum of all the negative and positive amounts was your "balance". A positive balance meant that you had provided more than you had received, while a negative balance meant that had received more than you had given. The object, over the long term, was to keep your balance as close to zero as possible. This meant you were receiving as much as you were giving. This was true "balance", something that rarely happened with money.

I found this to be a truly amazing innovation. The idea that people could trade with each other without using money seemed to have far-reaching implications. I had been taught in the economics class at university that the option was binary: barter or money. Before money, people must have bartered. That was inconvenient so people invented money. If the money system collapses people will resort to barter again. LETS showed this to be arrant nonsense. The more that I looked into it the more obvious it became that there are many ways to facilitate exchange, and that money was just one of them – and not a very good one at that. Using LETS, we had traded with each other in a manner that was actually more efficient and elegant than using money. There was no need for a money supply, which meant that no one had to create it, issue it and manage the quantity of it. I knew pretty well that those who created and controlled the money supply were hugely advantaged over those who were obliged to use it. With LETS, the creation, issuance and ownership angles were eliminated altogether. We were trading with a "virtual money" that had no existence and therefore no quantity. All it did was measure the value of the goods and services provided and received. Imagine that: "money" that did not have to be lent into existence. That meant no money lenders, loans, lending rates, interest, usury, monetary debt, manipulation, control or slavery!

If people could trade with each other without having to earn money first, then surely this was a way of making irrelevant the notions of inequality and poverty. People could do and provide things for each other where there was little or no money. "Unemployment" would be rendered meaningless. People could, in effect, create their own local, parallel "economies" simply by keeping records of who did or gave what to whom. This would build local support networks, and when neighbours got to know each other better they would start doing things for each other without having to keep records.

Scaling up this whole idea, I could not see why the whole world could not work with this new way of facilitating exchange. A parallel, no-money "economy" could grow alongside the conventional one and, who knows, maybe one day supplant it. I had always believed that the way the world worked was because of the way our economies worked. Now I started to take this a step further by holding that the way our economies work is because of the way our exchange systems work. The exchange system we have inherited (the money or financial system), despite its modern electronic trappings, is an historical relic that was designed for the industrial revolution. It is totally inappropriate for the modern world and responsible for the destructive growth imperative that drives our economies. It is what forces us to believe in infinite growth in a finite world and is what is driving humanity headlong towards the destruction of its life support system: Planet Earth.

In 2002 a group of money activists got together to create a new LETS in Cape Town. I had been developing some trading software that allowed traders to record their own trades and advertise their "offerings" and "wants" on the internet. I showed it to the committee and they immediately decided to use it, instead of running the group according to traditional, manual LETS practices as described earlier. This proved to be a huge innovation because it spread the load amongst the members: everyone could manage their own accounts and it relieved the administrator of most of the burdens. It was a truly democratic "money system" without owners, controllers, manipulators and exploiters.

In February 2003 our experimental exchange system was launched in Cape Town. It was called the Cape Town Talent Exchange, a play on the name of our "currency" that was called Talents. The rand was used as our reference for pricing in Talents, but the Talents were purely a unit of measure or account, like litres or kilograms. There was no need for a circulating medium of exchange: the goods or service was provided first, then the value (in Talents) of whatever was provided was recorded afterwards.

Within a few years the idea had caught on all over South Africa, and then spread to the rest of the world. A network was created, allowing the separate groups or communities to inter-trade. We called this network the Community Exchange System (CES). By 2020 over a thousand exchange groups in over 100 countries had joined or been created on CES. Admittedly, many of these never managed to get off the ground but it has been a grand experiment and tens of thousands of people have discovered a new way of "doing money".

At first glance, this might seem like a cute little online "barter club", allowing people to do a bit of trading in their communities without using money. But simply because money is not used does not make it a bartering system. In fact, using money is more akin to barter than trading on CES, because each monetary transaction is a one-to-one affair where goods and services are "bartered" for money. After the transaction has taken place, the recipient (buyer) feels no sense of obligation to the provider (seller) or to the community at large. It is a done deal.

In CES, a "transaction" is more like an "action", a one-way affair, where something is provided but nothing is required from the recipient in return – apart from a promise to provide something of value to other members of the community at a later time. All that happens is that a record is made of the action, which credits (increases) the provider's (seller's) balance and debits (decreases) the recipient's (buyer's). A positive balance represents a claim against the community, while a negative balance represents an obligation to provide something to other members of the community. Balances operate in a band between a maximum credit ceiling and a minimum debit floor, with the aim being to keep one's mean balance close to half way between the two, which is zero.

Keeping records like this is just one way of facilitating exchange, but there are many others. Organised bartering, swapping, time banking, time trading, gifting, sharing, and "paying it forward" are some other methods. When people help each other and provide for each other, there is no need to keep records of everything they do and then call that "the economy". The money system attempts to do that by denying other exchange methods and monetising everything it can. If something cannot be monetised then it is said to be an "externality" outside "the economy", and any form of exchange not involving money

– and therefore not measurable and taxable – is demonised as being part of the "dark", "black", "parallel", "shadow", "underground" or "informal" economy.

As CES evolved and hundreds of thousands of transactions were taking place all over the world, and between different communities, I couldn't help wondering why the entire financial system didn't work like this. There didn't seem to be any reason, apart from the financial elite not wanting it to work this way because they would then not have anyone to lend money to, and would subsequently be out of business. No money, no money lenders, no controllers and, flowing from that, no governments to enforce and benefit from this corrupt system of robbery, exploitation and servitude. That was a pretty earth-shattering realisation!

It became increasingly apparent to me that the money system (the currently predominant exchange system) is the prison that has held much of humanity in servitude for millennia. We had emerged from a physical prison imagining that we had achieved freedom, only to discover that the world we live in is one giant prison that has enclosed upon practically all of humanity.

I started to wonder if it was possible to make a "key" for the "front door" of this prison, and if there was true freedom on the outside of it? How do we make this key, or do we have to use force? Can we get everyone out, or will some stay behind because they fear freedom? And how do we evade the guards (creditors, appropriators, expropriators and their state coercive agents) once we're out? Money won't do it. Best to keep that up the body orifice as it is what keeps us trapped in this penal institution in the first place.

At the pinnacle of the power pyramid sits an elite that has ultimate control over the means of exchange. They decide how the distribution or allocation system works and hence who gets what or anything at all. Since the beginning of "civilisation", those who have controlled the distribution of the means of life (by controlling the means of exchange) have wielded ultimate power. They have always decided where the society (tribe, nation, country, empire) is going, where it focuses its energies, who benefits from all the activity, who is rich and who is poor, who lives and who dies. If control of the means of exchange is dispersed and democratised – where everyone is in control (for the first time in history) and not a self-serving elite – then surely, we will have a society free of controllers, manipulators, exploiters and parasites (i.e. a society free of "masters"). A society that manages its own means of exchange operates outside the walls of subservience and therefore must experience true freedom.

In the same way as our prison had its myths about how secure it was and that if you did manage to get out it would be a futile action as you would soon be dragged back inside, there are money myths that serve the same purpose. Money is portrayed as one of the constants of the universe, like energy and matter. It is presented as a top-level concept like God, a subset of nothing. It is an all-encompassing orb with an impenetrable outer skin. There is nothing beyond it, and therefore no point in seeking a way out. But if this myth is seen for what it is, then we can see that money is actually a concept subsumed under the higher-level concept of exchange and that there are many ways of facilitating exchange. Exchange is subsumed under life itself, for exchange is a property of life and probably of the universe as well. Beyond the "money wall" is true freedom, not another restraining wall. True freedom means freedom from slavery *and* freedom from masters; not freedom to make money without restraint. So long as we use the masters' exchange system (their money system) we will continue to be their slaves and at the same time enhance their power over us.

Once we realise that money as we know it is a fake fence containing us in an illusory concentration camp, the barbed wires around the periphery turn to paper streamers. The "guards" are hardly necessary, as the slaves keep themselves in voluntary servitude by believing that they cannot survive outside of it; they have "bills to pay", after all. The "guards" are themselves prisoners, granted small privileges by their masters for keeping the slaves hard at work inside. The "money prison" is an illusion based on the false belief that we need a medium of exchange (money), created and managed by "them" for us to survive.

Our prison experience serves as the perfect analogy for the condition that we all find ourselves in. Humanity has been trapped for aeons inside this "money prison". To escape from it requires the same determination and desire for freedom as was required to escape from our hard penitentiary in Pretoria. The plan of escape needs to follow the logic that flows from accepting that in the internet era there is no longer a need for an issued, circulating medium of exchange for organised exchange to take place, that "money" only needs to be a unit of measure/account like a kilometre or a kilogram. This takes us directly to the front door instead of wasting our time aimlessly and endlessly pacing up and down the prison yard like demoralised captives who have accepted their fate. The consequences of following this logic are so utterly profound that even those of us who have gone some way down the corridor in the administrative section on the way to the front door, find it hard to come to terms with the mindshift required. All the economic concepts that we take for granted, such as jobs, employment, unemployment, wealth, inequality, poverty, demand, supply, borrowing, lending, debt, interest, inflation, profit and even the economy itself, either fall away or take on completely new meanings. If the economy is the place where businesses and people make money, then what do you have when money (as a medium of exchange) is no longer required for exchange to take place? That would surely dissolve the boundary between "economic activity" (making money) and other social activities. What would the world look like if making money ceased to be the prime motivating force of human behaviour? Can there be a society that has mutual assistance and sharing in the production of its means of existence as its primary motivation instead of making money? Can we even talk about an economy where people produce and exchange their means of life without using money? Can there be a moneyless economy; economics without money?

Most of the assumptions that we make about human behaviour suddenly come into question when it is realised that such behaviours are for the most part undergirded by a certain conception of money and are not manifestations of human nature as such. When it is accepted that exchange can take place other than through the medium of money, whole new possibilities for solving the major problems facing humanity suddenly unfold. There is no reason to believe that the way CES works could not be applied to the whole realm of social production and exchange. This realm would look very different to what we call "the economy" today, which is what you get when the sole aim of its participants is to generate the maximum amount of money for themselves instead of sufficiency, co-operation, happiness, health, wellbeing and care for all life and the planet that supports it.

The logic of money is expansion, because everyone who touches it needs and wants more. Ultimately it will lead to a single, centralised, monopolised currency empowering a single global elite, managing a single global economy with a single globalised polity under its control. When communities implement their own exchange mechanisms, they can turn this expansionary trajectory around. Instead of multinational corporations, giant industrial complexes and a global financial system free-floating above humanity and consuming our finite earth at an exponential rate, there will be localised, human-scale, productive exchange and organisational units that serve instead of dominate.

Every day articles appear about how capitalism is destroying the world and how we need a "new economic system" to save our planet. All of these take money as a given, and then try to devise a system with fairer rules or where the issuance of money is taken away from self-serving banks and devolved to local financial authorities. All of these schemes are non-starters if money is taken as a given, because as long as exchange is mediated by money – in whatever form – there will still be an economy, where all participants have the single aim of increasing the amount of money coming their way. The single product of every economy is money, and can't be otherwise.

To call for reform of the financial system or the replacement of capitalism with a more benign economic system (such as socialism), is a call for more of the same. Every economic system is a product of the exchange system that it uses; any economic system based on the logic of money is the same economic system, no matter what it is labelled. So long as money is seen as one of the foundations of reality, the masters will still be the turnkeys and the slaves will continue chipping rocks in their compound without realising that there is a way out.

A different economic system might ease the slaves' burden, but the improvement in conditions is just a move to a higher classification category granted by the masters, who remain firmly in control through their management of the distribution system. The continued use of a monopolised exchange medium (money) implies that the masters are still in control. Masters themselves are the product of an exchange system that permits and promotes claims on social wealth greater than what the claimants have provided to society. Slaves cannot be free while they remain dependent on the masters' allocation system – the tool that has always kept them in their place.

Freedom is also not achieved by changing the prison guards. That still keeps everyone inside, even if the new guards seem to provide a little more freedom than the previous ones. Some slaves will prefer the old guards and will fight with the other slaves to ensure that their favourite guards stand over them. Most of the slaves have been blinded by the bright lights of the masters' work camp or are so busy working in the vain hope of one day joining the masters at the dinner table, that they don't even realise they are in bondage. Those slaves who realise that they are subjects and are prepared to make an investment in freedom, need to quietly get on with creating their own set of "keys" to slowly and methodically, "door by door", find their way out. The guards will not notice the freedom experimentation if it does not appear to undermine the security of their masters' servitude system. Those in bonds can begin to practice freedom inside the prison walls when they have most of the "keys" they need. They can even simulate a full escape, all the way up to the "front door". "Escape day" comes when they have their full complement of "escape tools" to break free and evade the guards. The masters don't like it when any of their slaves escape. They will tighten security afterwards and punish the remaining slaves, and offer a bounty for the runaways.

I truly believe that it is possible to escape from the masters' prison, and that it can be achieved by creating our own "set of keys". This does not require high technology; we can make our own "wooden keys" using whatever tools and materials we find at hand. This involves using and creating a polyculture of exchange methods instead of the monoculture that has been imposed on humanity over the millennia (i.e. the masters' system of money). The masters remain masters through their monopolisation of the means of exchange (the "master key"). They will fight back if and when anything challenges their monopoly. We see this with the crypto-currencies now invading their space. The masters' response is to co-opt them or create their own, which reveals that the cryptos are not the key for releasing ourselves from the "money prison" but something that will only prolong our incarceration. Crypto-currencies are still "money" in the sense that they are "issued" media of exchange that can end up in fewer and fewer hands, creating new masters to dominate us.

True freedom comes from an exchange system that prevents the formation of masters. Where there are no masters there are no slaves.

Such an exchange system is possible, as has been adequately shown by the hundreds of communities around the world that use a variety of alternative exchange methods instead of the masters' system of currencies conjured by them out of fresh air. In the pre-internet era, it was not possible to keep records as easily and efficiently as it is today, so the scope for a "people's exchange system" was limited. With exchange options such as those provided by CES, no one can "get rich" other than by providing real values to others. Speculation, usury, theft and the multitude of other devious ways of "getting rich" without delivering anything of value – as is possible and encouraged under the current monetary system – are simply not possible. When all these options for appropriating others' wealth are eliminated by a truly democratic exchange system (one that no one owns or controls), the chances of creating a more sustainable, happier, healthier and more caring world are greatly increased.

In the same way that we did not ask our jailers for permission or assistance to escape from Pretoria Prison, the slaves do not need to engage their masters in order to escape from their "money prison". To release themselves, the slaves need to quietly craft their own "wooden keys" in order to be able to exchange what they have and can do without having to pay tribute to the masters for using their exchange system ("chains system"!). In this way they can slowly unlock the fetters of dependency and create an ever-expanding zone of freedom inside their prison, until they reach the "front door" and break free completely into the master-free realm.

* * *

People often ask if I am still in touch with my fellow escapees. The answer is yes. Every year on the anniversary of our escape, 11 December, the three of us exchange congratulations in one way or another. Usually, it is by email but a few times in the past we have had a "Skype party", where we popped bottles of champagne and toasted good health in front of our webcams. Stephen and I exchange e-mails fairly regularly and I have visited him several times at his home in Crouch End, a suburb of London.

Soon after arriving in Britain in 1980, Stephen had to make a choice of career between taking a job as a journalist at the *Morning*

Star newspaper, or a job as an electrician's mate at the London *Daily Mail* newspaper. He chose the latter because it allowed him more time to continue working for the South African Congress of Trade Unions (SACTU) and do other ANC work. So he took a City and Guilds Electrical Installation course and qualified three years later. He worked as an electrician for the *Daily Mail* for many years. He met Siobhan Geraghty at a fundraising event for the *Morning Star* in 1981 and they have been happily together since then. He has three sons: Ciaran born in 1986, Brendan born in 1987 and Sean born in 1994. It could now be said that Stephen has retired from being a wage slave, but not from the political views he has always held.

After seven and a half years in prison, Alex found life on the outside a somewhat strenuous experience. It took him about eighteen months to find his bearings and overcome phobias such as entering government offices and filling in official forms. For Alex, his arrival in Paris did not signal the end, but merely an interval in the struggle. He understood that the struggle would have to take a different form and that he would have to go back to ordinary everyday life. After a round of speeches and public meetings to which he was invited by various organisations, it became clear that it was necessary to set up an ANC office in Paris. After several months of discussion, he succeeded in obtaining finance for the rent. This was covered by the French Communist Party, while other organisations helped in other ways. In this same period, he succeeded in bringing the main anti-apartheid organisations together to demonstrate in support of James Mange, an ANC activist who had been sentenced to death. Two thousand demonstrators converged on the South African embassy, which at that time was a great success.

Godfrey Motsepe was appointed as the first ANC chief representative. Alex started working in the office but could not come out on 1,500 francs the ANC offered him, and had to go out and find full-time employment. He continued participating in anti-apartheid activities within the limits of the time available to him. For about ten years he organised the South African Communist Party's stand at the *Fête de l'Humanité*, producing translated leaflets, badges and so on.

The chief representatives came and went: Godfrey Motsepe, was replaced by Neo Mnumzama, and he in turn by Dulcie September who was assassinated at the front door of the ANC office in March

1988. After her came Solly Smith, who died later in South Africa under suspicious circumstances. He in turn was replaced by Michael Msizi, the last chief representative. After him there was an ambassador.

In 1996 Alex and Marie-José, who had also been active both in MK and in France after her release, and Chloë their daughter, born in 1982, were officially invited to South Africa by the ANC, on the initiative of the then Deputy Minister of Defence, Ronnie Kasrils (Alex's commanding officer). In 1994 Alex started a political monthly magazine in French, and this kept him busy for many years. Alex still lives in France and it would be correct to say that he is also now 'retired'.

As for our fellow prisoners, I have kept in touch with some of them; others I bump into occasionally; several have died and others seem to have slipped off the radar screen.

David Rabkin was released in 1983 and went to Maputo where he worked as a journalist. He was due to move to Lusaka but before doing so he went to Angola for military training with Umkhonto we Sizwe. Unfortunately, he was killed on 22 November 1985 in an accident during his training.

Jeremy Cronin was also released in 1983. He left South Africa during the state of emergency in 1987 and worked in London and Lusaka. He came back to South Africa in the early 1990s and was involved in setting up the South African Communist Party after it was unbanned. In May 2019, he retired from parliament and government office. He is at present a member of both the ANC's National Executive Committee and the Central Committee of the South African Communist Party.

Dave Kitson was released from prison in 1984, seven months short of serving his 20 years. After his release he remarried his former wife, Norma. Norma founded the City of London Anti-Apartheid Group, which was set up in opposition to the original Anti-Apartheid Movement. The ANC demanded that Dave denounce his wife for this, as the Group did not have its blessing. When Dave refused, he and Norma were suspended from the ANC. Years later, at the behest of Walter Sisulu and Nelson Mandela, the couple were reinstated by the ANC and honoured as "veterans of the struggle". Ian David Kitson died on 9 November 2010 at the age of 91.

John Matthews was released in December 1979 on his due date a few days after our escape. After his release he assisted many underground cadres with their practical needs. John Edward Matthews died in 1998 at the age of 85.

Raymond Suttner was also released in 1983. After his release he became involved with the United Democratic Front and was arrested and detained in 1986. He spent a further 27 months in detention. He was released in 1988 and placed under house arrest, which he defied when he left the country in 1989. He returned to South Africa the next year, after the unbanning of the ANC. He has been on the NEC of the ANC and a member of the Central Committee of the SACP. For several years he was the South African ambassador to Sweden. He took up the position of visiting professor and strategic advisor to the Dean of Humanities at University of Johannesburg in 2018 and is emeritus professor at the University of South Africa.

Tony Holiday was released in 1982. He returned to journalism and taught philosophy at the University of the Western Cape's School of Government. Charles Anthony David Holiday died on 10 July 2006 at the age of 65.

Denis was released in 1985, after 22 years in prison. After his release, he went to London where his wife Esmé was living. He worked for the ANC for a number of years, managing their stores and mail order department. After the 1994 elections, Denis founded the development organisation Community HEART in London to help improve the living standards of black South Africans. Denis returned to South Africa in 2002 and was appointed Special Adviser to Ronnie Kasrils, the then Minister of Water Affairs and Forestry. In 2010 he published his autobiography, *The Mission: A Life for Freedom in South Africa*. Denis Theodore Goldberg died on 29 April 2020.